# HEALING
## FOR
# EVERYONE

*Medicine of
the Whole Person*

EVARTS G. LOOMIS, M.D.
and
J. SIG PAULSON

DeVorss & Company, Publisher
P.O. Box 550
Marina del Rey, California 90291

Printed in the United States of America
by Book Graphics, Inc., Marina del Rey, California

"Honour a physician with the honour due unto him for the uses which ye may have of him: for the Lord hath created him. For of the most High cometh healing, and he shall receive honour of the king. The skill of the physician shall lift up his head: and in the sight of great men he shall be in admiration. The Lord hath created medicines out of the earth; and he that is wise will not abhor them. Was not the water made sweet with wood, that the virtue thereof might be known? And he hath given men skill, that he might be honoured in his marvellous works. With such doth he heal (men) and taketh away their pains. Of such doth the apothecary make a confection; and of his works there is no end; and from him is peace over all the earth.

"My son, in thy sickness be not negligent: but pray unto the Lord, and he will make thee whole. Leave off from sin, and order thine hands aright, and cleanse thy heart from all wickedness. Give a sweet savour, and a memorial of fine flour; and make a fat offering, as not being. Then give place to the physician, for the Lord hath created him: let him not go from thee, for thou hast need of him. There is a time when in their hands there is good success. For they shall also pray unto the Lord, that he would prosper that, which they give for ease and remedy to prolong life. He that sinneth before his Maker, let him fall into the hand of the physician."

From Chapter 38 of Ecclesiasticus,
The Apocrypha

THE COVER DESIGN: The threefold symbol is particularly appropriate for this book on healing. It is of Japanese origin and represents elements of the whole person — spirit, mind, and body — as well as the Divine Source of Being and Wholeness — Father, Son, and Holy Spirit. The comma-like figure is identical to the tenth letter of the Hebrew alphabet — YOD, meaning God, symbolic of "In the beginning God." The circle (serpent holding its tail) symbolizes wholeness, completeness, universality. Light has long been visualized as the source of LIFE. Fundamental in its refraction are the primary colors — red, yellow, and blue, symbolizing the power of the emotions, the light of the intellect, and the peace of the spirit.

# CONTENTS

# ACKNOWLEDGMENTS

Thousands of unnamed persons have contributed to this book. We think of the many and of some particular few whom we have known in pastoral counseling circumstances and in doctor-patient relationships. We hope we were helpful to them; they do not know how much or in what ways they helped us. We thank them all, both the many and the few.

There are some whom we must single out for special mention: Dr. Anthony Pescetti for his assistance in matters dealing with nutrition; Dr. William Jackson for his review of the homeopathic material; Professor Margery Potter for her critique of the chapter on exercise; Myron L. Boardman for his counsel and inspiration; and Charles N. Heckelmann of Hawthorn Books for his enthusiastic sharing of professional insights and advice. In the production of the manuscript: Catherine Roberts and Joann Landreth for the preliminary editing and typing; Mary Lou Butchart for the second typing; Katherine Erickson for the third and final typing.

Professor John Day came along at our time of need. We express special feelings of appreciation to him for relieving us of the responsibility of final editing and for carrying the project through to completion.

Quotation from *Breakthrough to Creativity* by Shafica Karagulla, Copyright 1967 by Shafica Karagulla and Viola P. Neal, reprinted by permission of De Vorss and Co., Inc.

Quotation from *Talks with Great Composers* by Arthur M. Abell, Copyright 1955 by Philosophical Library, 15 East 40th St., New York City, N.Y. Reprinted by permission.

Excerpt from *Physical Fitness and Dynamic Health* by Thomas K.

Cureton, Jr., Copyright 1965 by Thomas K. Cureton, Jr., reprinted by permission of the publisher, The Dial Press.

Quotation from *The Symphony of Life* by Donald Hatch Andrews, Copyright 1966 by Donald Hatch Andrews, reprinted by permission.

Quotation from "The Ancient Sage" by Alfred Lord Tennyson, in *The Poetic and Dramatic Works of Alfred Lord Tennyson,* Copyright 1899 by Houghton, Mifflin & Co., reprinted by permission.

Quotation from *Hymn of the Universe* by Pierre Teilhard de Chardin, Copyright 1961 by Editions du Seuil. Copyright 1965 in the English translation by William Collins Sons & Co., London, and Harper and Row, Inc., New York. Reprinted by permission of Harper and Row.

Quotation from *The Phenomenon of Man* by Pierre Teilhard de Chardin, Copyright 1955 by Editions du Seuil. Copyright 1959 in English translation by William Collins Sons & Co., London, and Harper and Row, Inc., New York. Reprinted by permission of Harper and Row.

Quotation from *The Language of Silence* by Allen Boone, Copyright 1970, Harper and Row Publishers, Inc. Reprinted by permission of the publisher.

Quotation from *Son of the Wilderness: The Life of John Muir*, by Linnie Marsh Wolfe, Copyright 1945 by Alfred A. Knopf, Inc. Reprinted by permission of the publisher.

Quotation from *The Plant between Earth and Sun*, by George Adams and Olive Whicher, Copyright 1952 by George Adams and Olive Whicher, reprinted by permission of the Goethean Science Foundation.

Quotation from *Hara* by Karlfried Dürckheim, reprinted by permission of the author.

Quotation from *Nutrition and Physical Degeneration* by Weston A. Price, D.D.S., published by and courtesy of Price-Pottenger Nutrition Foundation, 2901 Wilshire Blvd., Ste. 345, Santa Monica, Cal. 90403.

Quotation from *The Art Spirit* by Robert Henri, Copyright 1923 by J. B. Lippincott Company, copyright renewed 1951 by

Violet Organ, reprinted by permission of J. B. Lippincott Company.

"The Three D's of Health" by J. Sig Paulson, Copyright 1973 by the International New Thought Alliance, reprinted by permission of the publisher.

"Life Treatment" by J. Sig Paulson, Copyright 1970 by Unity School of Christianity, reprinted by permission of the publisher.

Quotation from *Psychosynthesis: A Manual of Principles* by Roberto Assagioli, M.D. Copyright 1965 by Psychosynthesis Research Foundation. Reprinted by permission of Hobbs, Dorman, and Company, Inc.

Quotation from "Moon Talk" by Edson J. Andrews, M.D., *Florida Medical Journal*, vol. XLVI, no. 11, p. 1362. Reprinted by permission of the Florida Medical Association, Inc.

# PUBLISHER'S NOTE

This book is the story of a lifetime of work in the healing arts carried on by two remarkable men, Evarts G. Loomis and J. Sig Paulson. Dr. Loomis comes to healing as a leading exponent of the Medicine of the Whole Person and carries out his dream at Meadowlark, near Hemet, California. J. Sig Paulson is minister of the Unity Village Chapel of the Unity School of Christianity, located at Unity Village, Missouri.

Their personal acquaintance goes back to 1965, when Sig Paulson, along with other Unity ministers, visited Ev Loomis at Meadowlork to find out more about the Whole Person doctor and his program.

Sensing a real community of interest in the out-of-doors, they have adopted an interesting practice in recent years of getting away for two weeks in the summer for a complete change of scenery, experiencing nature as directly as possible in order to obtain the refreshment and renewal that they need to carry on their intensive lives of service to mankind.

In 1970 they backpacked in the White Mountains of New Hampshire. In the summers of 1971 and 1972 they canoed in the wilderness of Canada's Ontario Province.

Though the seeds of this book had been planted unconsciously and were taking root early in their respective careers, it was during the 1970 trip that they decided to collaborate. On subsequent trips the seeds were watered, and the plant really started to grow and take form.

Ev and Sig made one concession to modernity on their wilderness treks. They took a tape recorder so they could talk to each other and have a record of what they said. The transcription of some of these conversations seemed to be a good way of "getting the reader into the book." Imagine, then, a Canadian wilderness lake, two fast friends in an eighteen-foot canoe, and a tape recorder to capture conversations about the subject nearest and dearest to their hearts: Healing and Wholeness.

When the authors started their most recent nine-day canoe trip, they left their watches behind. They traversed the wilderness with compass and map because they believed this was a way to better discover their own rhythms. After all, in healing, the individual can do much more toward bringing about his own body-healing than can the physician. They discovered it is a delightful experience to forget about time. Their rhythms being very similar, they were usually up before sunrise, had their fire built, breakfast done, and were ready to enjoy the morning hours exploring some lake or river.

We invite you now to join these two dedicated individuals, and we expect and hope you will obtain new insights about the miracle of healing, so you, also, can experience the wonder of wholeness.

Hawthorn Books, Inc., 1975

# AUTHORS' NOTE

To the Reader:

You are important to us—as a person, as a human being, as a vital part of the wonderful world we share. Your health—physical, psychological, spiritual—is also important to us, and this book is designed to open the way for a greater expression of this most precious of all gifts. If you are ill, unhappy, or depressed, we think you will obtain hope, help, and healing in the courses of action shared in these pages. If you are already healthy, happy, and optimistic, we believe that some of the ideas you find will inspire you to be an even more radiant person and perhaps enable you to help someone else more effectively.

This book is our contribution to your health, your enjoyment of the incredible experience of life, and your success as a human being. It comes from our hearts, out of years of experience in trying to help people to the best of our abilities in two different and yet uniquely related fields—medicine and the ministry.

We do not pretend to know all the answers, or even all the questions, for that matter. Like you, we are often confronted with seemingly unanswerable problems and insurmountable obstacles. Nevertheless, we both feel that every situation, dark or even hopeless as it may seem, contains a ray of light, a way to move, a source of help.

Over the years we have gained a healthy respect, and, we hope, a real love for that most remarkable creature—the human person. We have watched men and women, boys and girls, meet adversity, illness, shock, and even death itself—and our admiration for people and their potentialities is virtually unbounded. We are convinced that in every individual, regardless of outer appearances, there are vast, untapped and largely unemployed reserves of health, life, love, and joy. Our desire is to inspire you to tap and use these often unsuspected reserves of healing energy.

Frankly, we believe in miracles. Every healing has elements of the miraculous in it. We have seen miracles take place when people turn from doubt to faith, from despair to hope, from resignation to action, from condemnation to forgiveness, so that the healing power always present can find an opportunity to act. We know that every doctor, minister, psychiatrist, and worker in the healing service can testify to such miracles.

To our colleagues in the many fields of the healing arts, we extend our best wishes, our appreciation, our desire to be of service. We respect your dedication, your integrity, your willingness to discover and implement new approaches to health and vital living. We hope you will join with us in deepening and expanding efforts to discover and share ways to call forth the elements of health in those wonderful members of the human family we are all dedicated to serve.

Perhaps the day is near at hand when every hospital, doctor's office, clinic, church, synagogue, cathedral, and sanitarium will be a radiant center where those who come will be taught and inspired to follow the ways of health, wholeness, and creative living. This seems a reasonable and highly desirable goal.

Whoever you are, we welcome you into the healing community that serves humanity. You are as much a part of it as anyone else. All humanity needs healing in some area, and in a deep sense each person is doctor, minister, psychiatrist, and counselor as well as patient. Thank you for joining us in the creative process of healthy living.

# HEALING
## FOR
# EVERYONE

# 1

---

## CONVERSATIONS BETWEEN
## A DOCTOR AND
## A MINISTER

SIG: Ev, since we are collaborating on a book, I think it would be of interest to our readers to know why we felt we should write the book. I have no desire to write a book just to be writing a book. But I feel there's a real need for a book that brings together the wholeness factors of the individual for the sake, not only of so-called patients who need healing, but for ministers and psychiatrists and doctors and anyone involved in any way in the healing arts.

Perhaps, as we move into this book, we'll discover that the healing arts embrace a great deal more than we ordinarily think. I can see from my own viewpoint as a minister that there is a tremendous need for something of this nature. I feel that so often, as ministers, we use some pretty pat little phrases and often express glib ideas even about the healing power of God. We're probably agreed that there is only one healing power in the universe, but I find that it is easy to get lopsided and off-base unless we're in tune with what the rest of the world, and in this instance what the healing world, is doing.

Ev: I guess my real excuse is to share with others a deep

I

feeling that the healing of the patient has to start within the patient or it will get nowhere. The doctor actually doesn't have much to do with the healing of the patient. He is something of a guide. He can help remove certain areas of resistance, such as surgically removing a diseased organ, which is only an end result of a process going on in that body.

It's been very aptly said by an Indian medicine man that there are four essentials in the healing process. First of all, the patient must want to be healed—he has to have a reason to get well. Second, the patient must have faith that he can be made well. Third, he must ask forgiveness of anyone in his life whom he has injured. And fourth, he must change his way of life and no longer follow just the material way.

This is equally true for us. I think we can learn a great deal by looking at some of the long-established traditions of healing, such as that of our American Indian. We have sent out little health stations and hospitals to all the reservations, but a large number of the Indians have not gone to these hospitals because they knew they had something we did not have.

We have undoubtedly helped them to control infectious diseases and a number of things of this nature. Now it's time for us to look and see what they have to give to us: It's this feeling of oneness with the totality of life, a feeling of the rhythms of life. It's the timing, the breathing in and exhaling of the life forces and the life energies and letting them become one with us. It's an identification with the growing seasons, an identification with the sun and the moon and the planets, an understanding that we have a cycle interrelated to their cycles.

This tremendous beat of the universe—the rhythm of the universe—seems to be deeply inculcated in their souls. I learned much of this from a wise Indian medicine man who visited us at Meadowlark and talked to us about his life as a healer.

SIG: I suppose part of the purpose in writing this book is to share with the patients and our coworkers in the healing profession the great truth that health or wholeness is a vital part of the universe—that the whole universe in a very real sense is interested in seeing that its creatures are whole and strong. As you mentioned through your experience and contact with the Indian medicine man, these are people who are very close to nature, and they have discovered and are utilizing elements in their natural environment—both the visible and invisible part of that environment—to heal.

Part of our purpose and intention, then, is to share with those in need of healing, regardless of who they may happen to be, that the desire for healing is a very natural part of their own make-up. It's part of the universe, and the elements for healing are also part of their own make-up and part of the universe.

We realize we are not miracle workers, but we do point to the miracle of healing, and the miracle potential of healing is a vital part of the whole person. Sometimes, when a person is ill or hurting it's difficult for him to realize this. Perhaps through the medium of this book, and the ideas and experience we can share in it, we can bring to the attention of the readers the fact that healing is a very natural element in our lives.

## Health: The Natural State

Ev: Healing is such a very natural thing, yet in our system of medicine today we have made it unnecessarily complex. We associate it somehow with X-rays and laboratory tests. This must be very frustrating to the patient, and I think his healing is frequently put out of perspective. Back in medical school, a good many years ago, we were told that 65 percent of learning about the patient's illness is obtained from his history, about 25 percent from our examination, and about 10 percent from the laboratory. So often we see this reversed in practice because of the rush of patients through a doctor's office today.

Many patients who have come to Meadowlark, where I'm

able to take a little more time to listen than I can at the office, are so relieved to talk about themselves. Things have been bottled up and they can give clues that they can't possibly provide in a fast ten-minute history. They begin to see in perspective some of the forces and energies that have taken them away from a sense of wholeness or a sense of health. I'm sure, Sig, that you find people coming to you who, perhaps, have regularly attended church but are still very much at odds with themselves about some crucial thing in life.

SIG: Yes. That's certainly true, Ev, and I suppose that one of the greatest healing elements is permitting a person to express himself, to tell about himself—about not only his hang-ups and his misdeeds and the things he's done wrong or the things he feels he's failed to accomplish, but also his dreams, some of the things that make him uniquely a human being. So often when people are in difficulty they are trying to find someone who will listen—who will accept them as they are, and who will hear them out.

I know it's true in my work. We are all so pressed for time that frequently we come up with a pat answer, an immediate answer that gets the patient or the individual "off our necks." Not that we do this in any negative sense, but we are forced to it because of the pressure of business. We feel we are on an escalator of some kind and must keep things going at a certain pace.

EV: I think we in the United States have a great tendency, certainly as outsiders see us, to get very fanatical on certain things. For five or ten years something seems to be *the* thing, and everybody goes out after it. I think this is true, too, as far as healing is concerned. Groups of people feel compelled to go off to a certain center for a weekend where they hope to find something that's going to change their lives; or they have to eat a certain food that is supposed to do wonders for them; or they are supposed to take a brand-new miracle drug they've seen advertised. These various things seem to capture the popular imagination. So often people have sought after these various modalities, only to be very much disappointed.

SIG: I can recall a time when it was very popular to remove the tonsils and adenoids and the appendix. In fact, I heard doctors say it would be well if, every time a child was born, they just automatically removed the tonsils and the adenoids. I think the same principle applies in our so-called religious structure in trying to help people. We get all hung up on certain sins and we conclude that a person is in difficulty because he's done thus and so.

A certain sin seems to be popular for a time, and then, fortunately, humanity outgrows it. Perhaps that's the way it's handled. I'd like to have the people who read this book—the lay people and the professional people—realize that ministers and doctors aren't gods. We don't have all the answers; in fact, I'm not sure we have many of the answers to anything. The answer more likely lies within the individual himself.

Somehow we must bring out the idea that the minister and the doctor are part of a healing team. We're part of a group of human beings, each one with his own limitations. Perhaps by pooling our understanding, our know-how, our enthusiasm, our faith, our love, our skill, we can make healing more effective. I'm convinced that health is a natural state. It's a natural state of the body, a natural state of the mind. In a sense it is never absent from us; it's just obscured by some of the attitudes or some of the activities, or perhaps by some of the processes that take place in the mind and the body of the individual concerned.

EV: So it would seem that to find health all we're trying to do is rediscover the natural harmony that should be ours and has been ours but from which we have departed for an interval. Rather than a book concerned with diseased states of body, mind, and spirit, we're really looking at the person in health and trying to discover how he can stay that way. How does he maintain this harmony that is associated with wholeness, and health? Hopefully, as a result of this process, the disease or the dark state of mind will disappear.

SIG: In this connection, it might be helpful to think about what health or wholeness really is. Perhaps if we spent as much time in the medical and religious professions in studying health and wholeness as we do in studying disease and sin and evil, we'd have a completely different result. We do discover that the elements or factors to which we devote our concentrated attention tend to reveal themselves to us. Accordingly, it might be very helpful to take a look at the positive side. From a medical viewpoint how would you define health, Ev? What sort of state is it?

Ev: First, I'd like to comment on what you say to back up this point. I have noticed that doctors who enter a certain specialty frequently die of a disease in that specialty, because, as you say, they have spent their lives concentrating their mind on a particular area. I recall a famous surgeon who did a great deal of research on lung cancer and who died of lung cancer. I know of two doctors specializing in diseases connected with the rectum who died of cancer of the rectum. We regularly see this phenomenon. That which the mind dwells on seems to be that which the individual becomes. "As a man thinketh in his heart, so is he," as it is stated in the Bible.

Frequently health has been thought to be the absence of disease. Somehow I can't be satisfied with that concept because I know a number of people who are outwardly not diseased. To all appearances they're in excellent health, yet I would say they are far from whole. So I think rather than the absence of a negative state, that health must be a tremendously powerful state of potent ongoing awareness and growth.

Sig: I like that. It would probably be true from my viewpoint, too, that health is a state of wholeness or holiness (they both come from the same root) in which the individual is dynamically and vitally in tune with his Creator, with his fellow man, and with his environment. It seems to me that that would be a good all-around definition of health. When the person departs from that position, he is sick.

He may depart from it on a rather passive basis. As you pointed out, just the absence of disease or, theologically, just the absence of sin, isn't enough in itself. That doesn't really mean anything. Health is not a neutral state. Health is an

active, dynamic, vital state in which the individual partici-
pates in the life of the universe, in his own life, and in his own
activities in a constructive, vital, healthy, and whole-hearted
way where he senses his importance as an individual as part of
the creative plan.

Ev: If I'm correct, Jesus spent about sixty percent of his
recorded ministry in healing, and it seems to me that frequently instead of saying "be made well" of a certain disease
he said, "be thou made whole." Would you like to comment
on what you think he meant by this statement?

SIG: What the words mean to me is that you must be restored to the natural state. In other words, if somehow you
have stepped out of attunement, now you need to get back in
tune with things as they are. Jesus always seems to me to
possess that sense of wholeness. He could see through a disease, whether it was the man with the withered hand or the
man who had been blind from birth or the woman taken in
adultery. He seems to have had the capacity to look right
through what the seeming difficulty was to that which tended
to warp or blunt the state of wholeness. He had the faith, the
conviction, and the power, to speak the word, or to think the
thought, or to share the feeling that restored that person to a
state of wholeness. Healing could take place instantaneously.

This would seem to me to be precisely the area of a doctor's
ministrations. He's trying to restore a state of wholeness. Certainly it's what the minister is doing. He's striving to bring the
person back to a realization of his oneness in the Love that
created him—his oneness in the universe and with his fellow
man. Perhaps all healing is a restoration or return to the natural state that has always existed.

Another purpose for this book is to impersonalize the disease or the illness that the patient is experiencing by enabling
him to realize that it isn't completely his problem. In other
words, he must be made to understand that he also is part of
the healing team and, to some degree at least, the illness is a
problem that the doctor or the minister or the psychiatrist also
has. If the professional who is involved in the case is healed—

that is, if he can see the wholeness that shines through the appearance of illness—a great stride is taken toward the healing.

The patient himself so often comes in with the feeling "What have I done wrong?" or "Has my thinking been off base?" or "Have I been doing something else that has got me into this state?" or sometimes with just his bewildered cry, "Why does this happen to me?" Somehow we must try to get him to feel that he is part of an activity that is working to solve a problem, to bring about a solution, a return to a state of wholeness, but that he's only part of it. The whole burden is not really on his shoulders. If the physician or the clergyman or the psychiatrist can't see beyond the disease, he is almost as much a victim of the disease as the person who carries it in his body and his mind!

I'd like to quote a case history at this point from a patient of some years ago who had had a cancer that had spread into the bones some twenty-five years after the original cancer. She went to a specialist and recorded what he had said to her. I'd like to give you an excerpt:

> DOCTOR: How are you feeling this morning?
> PATIENT: Oh, fine. In fact, right now, doctor, I'm sitting on top of the world. Isn't it wonderful that I feel so completely well!
> DOCTOR: You'd better enjoy that feeling while you have it. Surely you know it's only transitory. I think I'd better inform you now so you can make suitable arrangements, that three months from now you'll be growing steadily worse, weaker, and more uncomfortable. In another three months you'll be quite helpless, paralyzed from the waist down. After that, well maybe six months at the most.

This is the kind of approach that really isolates a patient, hems him in, and traps him in a verdict of impossibility. Undoubtedly the doctor was sincere and perhaps even felt he was being kind and realistic in his statement, but we can imagine what effect this could have on the patient, her family, and friends, who are also a part of that healing team we have been describing. Do you concur?

Ev: Decidedly so, because that doctor really had no idea how long she was going to live; he was just impelled by a need to exhibit his superior knowledge. In fact, many a doctor who has made such a statement has died long before the patient to whom he gave the verdict. I think we physicians and ministers need to instill in our patients a confidence in life, not a confidence in death. Death is going to come when it's going to come, but we don't have to live in a state of constant anticipation of it. Every moment can be a tremendous experience.

Sig: I have a feeling that some ministers probably reach hell before the people they threaten with hell-fire and damnation. One of the quotations from the Bible that interests me (and I think it has application in the medical world as well as in ours) states that "any man who thinks his brother is a lost soul is himself headed straight for the fire of destruction." I believe that when we pass verdicts on someone else, regardless of the evidence on which we base that verdict, we set up a state of consciousness in our own mind that's bound to have some kind of effect.

### The Healing Team

Sig: Well, we've done a great deal of talking about the healing team and I don't know exactly where to start, Ev, except just to get right into it. A healing team can consist partially of all the professional help that's available and might include a medical doctor, a psychiatrist, a psychologist, a minister, other counselors, and, if it is a hospital case, the nurses and the staff. I think that more and more doctors and ministers realize they are part of a healing team, that no one individual or no one profession has all the answers, that as we work together we can be a very potent combination.

We ministers would like to have the patient understand that he, too, is part of the healing team. He is not just an object of probing and research and analysis and laboratory techniques. He is part of a group working to bring about a solution to a problem.

Ev: I'd like to talk a little bit about our experience at Meadowlark with the healing team, which brings out some of these points you've raised. Our general approach has been, first of all, to examine the patient medically with the idea of finding out how we can help him physically. We are realizing increasingly that health of the body and the brain is very much dependent on proper conditioning and proper biochemical balance, which implies proper nutrition. If the patient is not eating adequately, he cannot have a brain that is functioning adequately. The person who uses too many stimulants as a regular part of his daily life will soon begin to fail in mental capacity and, I would think, in his spiritual life. So we start out with a careful survey to see what we can do physically.

Our general tendency is to take people off tranquilizers and drugs as rapidly as we can, using them only for crutches, and stressing that tranquilizers and drugs are, for the most part, just crutches. They really don't have much to do with the healing process. They usually just mask symptoms. We're not interested in masking symptoms; we're interested in seeing people healed.

Food intake is extremely important. After all, food nourishes the body instrument, and if our mind and soul are to function in this body form, we'd better have a good instrument with which to work. It means a return to natural foods. We will go into many more particulars in our chapter on nutrition.

We also find that the glands of internal secretion, or the endocrine glands, are very critical in adapting the body to life stresses and situations. A smoothly functioning endocrine system is extremely important. So we look to the patient's hormone needs.

Then we feel that the body is given limbs to exercise and lungs with which to breathe in air containing the oxygen that is so necessary in the utilization and conversion of food into energy. An adequate exercise program is a very strong part of the daily schedule. Relaxation techniques and relaxation itself are another extremely important thing. We emphasize creative exercise for relaxing muscle tissue because many of us have extremely tight muscles that are working, although performing no useful function at the time. We find that with free body movement in the arts (including dancing, working with pastels, colors, clay) we can begin to get an inner feeling of freedom; a chance to express ourselves on paper or in some other concrete form as a manifestation of the functioning of our own creative center, which, due to various stresses in life, has become atrophied. Next we believe that a psychological survey is important. We usually conduct a simple psychological test that will point out things in the personality that need further development or are perhaps overdeveloped, thus producing a sense of imbalance. This test is done with the help of a professional psychologist.

In addition, we feel that the role of the minister in looking at our spiritual life is tremendously important. Very often this area carries over things from childhood that are unhealthy, need stimulation or a kind of new birth. Sig, I'm sure you can comment specifically in this area.

SIG: When you're dealing with nutrition, the mental aspect of a diet is as important as the physical. I'm sure you agree with me on that point. It is essential to give the person a new mental and emotional diet, a new way of looking at himself, a new self-image, and a new sense of his relationship to the Creator and to life itself. This borders on the spiritual and is a part of it.

Also from the spiritual viewpoint, the person must have faith in something greater than himself, greater than his own personal desires, his own personal work, his own personal hangups and pain and misery; he must realize that he's part of something greater than himself. Then, as he lifts his vision, or even begins to think about it, he must also realize that there might be changes that make all the other things more effective.

The diet and the medical treatment and the relaxation are ways to a destination which is the return of the individual to the source of wholeness. To put it in orthodox religious terms, we would call it a return to God. The name we give to it is not too important so long as we understand that it is basically a return to the source of wholeness, which involves many factors.

The most significant element is that of forgiveness. Quite often an individual who is ill for one reason or another has entered a state of unforgiveness. In some way, he's unwilling to forgive himself or forgive someone else. He's unwilling to accept himself not only as a spiritual being, but as a human being. He probably looks back on things he has done with remorse, regret, or resentment. Somehow we must try to help the individual to find a greater sense of his own worth and potential, of his own capacity for living and forgiving and for making a new start.

So often, in states of so-called incurable disease or mental conditions, the person has reached an end to life, a milestone of finality in his experience. There seems to be no real purpose in going on. At least, there's not any discerned purpose that will call up the elements within his own being and enable him to rise out of the particular experience, or disease, and instill in him a firm will to live. We really need a purpose that goes beyond personal desire if we're going to engender a will to live strong enough to utilize effectively the professional skill and techniques and medicines and diets that are available. We must gain the patient's cooperation in searching for a purpose in living. This, of course, isn't something that is performed by magic.

Quite often I find, and I'm sure you do, too, that in times of trial an individual is more receptive to spiritual concepts or spiritual approaches than he would ordinarily be. Perhaps he feels he's come to the end of the other ropes available to him. Many times people will indicate they are open to a spiritual experience. That is, they're open to questioning the "why" of the disease or perhaps the significance of it. They're willing to listen to a suggestion that there may be something that goes beyond the physical or medical or even psychological dimensions of the problem confronting them, with the possibility of looking at it in terms of its relationship to their whole existence. It may indicate a change in life that's been resisted, or a change that should have taken place. There are all kinds of elements here from a spiritual viewpoint, and it seems to me that they are all a part of the treatment of the whole person.

### Love and Fear

SIG: It seems to me that the final healing, or the great healing, is something that has to take place in individual consciousness with the realization that God the Creator, the Source of all, is Love. As I see it from a spiritual viewpoint, the cause of all disease and the cause of death is fear. Fear and all of its elements lead to procrastination, indecision, unwillingness to give ourselves completely to life. Fear disrupts the basic rhythms of the universe and the rhythms of wholeness or health. As long as we retain fear in any of its many degrees in our consciousness, we are going to have disease and death.

In reading the scriptures of the world, one finds that every great leader and every great savior ultimately winds up with this conclusion: that Love is the final answer. Love of God, love of self, love of neighbor, love of life—these are the only permanent solution. And it seems to me that even some of the saviors themselves—the great spiritual leaders and lights of the world—are brought to this conclusion almost reluctantly.

Even in the case of Jesus, we know that he gave a lot of different instructions and approaches, but when he was finally pushed into a corner—if one can look at it that way—and was asked "What is the greatest law, what is the greatest commandment?" He quoted from the Old Testament and said: "Love the Lord your God with all your heart and soul and mind and strength, and love your neighbor as yourself, and on these two laws hang all the law and the prophets." I'm sure that in your work as a doctor, as in my work as a minister, when we get down to the basic difficulty in dealing with anyone we always encounter a form of fear. I have never counseled anyone on a problem of any nature that I didn't find that fear was, in one way or another, at the root.

I have a feeling that religion and medicine and many of the other so-called service agencies of humanity have a partial responsibility for instilling this fear. Certainly in many of our basic religious approaches there is fear, and the threat of punishment, which is supposed to herd people into some kind of heaven. Perhaps even from a medical viewpoint we threaten people with the expected dire results of diseases.

Since we're discovering that we live in such a responsive universe whose rhythms are so subtle and so pervasive, I'm inclined to believe that the thoughts and feelings of humanity are somehow imprinted upon us. As long as there is fear of any kind in human consciousness, there will always be some little bug or microbe or some element in the universe that is going to have to respond to that fear. Even the atoms and cells and organs of our bodies ultimately have to bear the penalty. I don't want to instill any more fear by fearful thinking.

In my opinion, the basic sin in the world is fear. If God is love—and even intellectually we can reason out that the Creator of all must be Love—then to be afraid of Him is a sin. This somehow is transmitted into everything we think and feel, probably even into the food we eat and the activities in which we engage.

Somehow the final healing, the final freedom of man, must come through the realization of Love. Our good friend, Donald Hatch Andrews, professor emeritus of chemistry of Johns Hopkins University and author of the book *The Symphony of Life*, defines love as freedom; he feels that love and freedom are synonymous, that we live in a free universe, a universe in which even the atoms have independent streaks, and somehow the only way we can work together in freedom is to work together in love.

Ev: I find the same things with my patients that you find with your counselees—that fear is the basic problem in all life and all diseases. The person who comes to you ill is a fearful person. This is the basic thing we should be treating. Anything else is ancillary and secondary. A doctor from India, trained in the West, has said he feels that empathy is probably responsible for sixty-five percent of healing. Without that love-empathy, there really is no healing.

I think you've touched upon another important point, Sig, and that is the basic need for this love in the physician and the minister. We don't pass anything on to another person that isn't evident in us and that we're not broadcasting into the space all around us. The doctor who is fearful or stands in awe of a disease, and has made it something of a god, is not going to be much help to that patient.

It is absolutely imperative that we, as physicians, become much more conscious of this basic interrelation between fear and illness. We must not pass on our own dread of disease processes to our patients, by giving them bad prognoses and instilling more apprehension in them. We put a limitation on their very life's breath by engendering feelings of fear in them because of our own personal, unresolved mastery of life.

The old adage "Physician, heal thyself" is the number-one commandment for physicians to obey. We must spend enough time in our own daily discipline so that we conquer fear and replace it with joy and love, which are essential parts of our own being, seen not only through our words but in our every act and in everything that we emanate. The patient is going to catch this emanation, and when we carry this presence with us the patient can't help but benefit.

Sig: In this connection, "Physician, heal thyself" could be paraphrased as "Physician, love thyself." This might be a project for ministers and doctors to get under way, because as the commandment points out, "You shall love your neighbor as yourself." Our attitudes toward ourselves are automatically transmitted and projected onto our neighbors. An apprehensive minister or doctor can't help but radiate that emotional reaction to the individual who consults him. As a matter of fact, we become so conscious of the deeper levels and rhythms of communication that often the lip-to-ear communication is at a relatively superficial level. We communicate more directly at subconscious or deeper levels of consciousness regardless of what we are saying or of the outer appearance.

Until, and unless, a minister, doctor, or psychiatrist who is working with an individual in need of healing really has an inner conviction of this love—the reality of it, and the potency and the power of it—he can't transmit it to his patient. If he has it, he can't help but transmit it. It flows automatically. As you pointed out, the sick person is a fearful person, and when he comes for help he is, in essence, coming to obtain love. The medication, or the meditation treatment, or any other therapeutic action we take is just a means or an avenue through which we channel the love; but the love is what he is really seeking.

In this connection, the greatest formula for healing is in this simple statement from the Bible, "God is Love." Of course, the expansion of that statement is that those who love God live in God and God lives in them. This is what ultimately every healing center and every church is going to become. It will be a center of love, a center of healing, and a center of life.

Many times people don't realize that fear is their real problem, and as a result of it they become afraid of the concept of fear. One of our great presidents, Franklin Delano Roosevelt, said, "The only thing we have to fear is fear itself." Sometimes we become more afraid of fear than anything else. If we are willing to take a look at it and face up to it, we can begin to overcome it. The realization that God is Love, and therefore the nature of the universe is Love, means that there is nothing in the universe to fear regardless of what we have done, what we have been, what we have thought, what we have felt. The antidote of Love is never punishment or condemnation; it is always forgiveness and growth. When we understand this, we have the key to helping people, no matter what the outer situation in which they find themselves.

We live in a world conditioned by fear. I recall that as a freshman in college I was a member of a group that subscribed to "hellfire and brimstone" religion. It finally came to the point where something in me rebelled so strongly that I couldn't contain myself. I went up to the minister after a service and said that if he was right then I would rather do business with the devil than with the God he was preaching. I could trust the devil: He was a stinker all the time, but the God who was going to put most of humanity into hell for eternity just couldn't fit into my way of thinking.

Naturally I was told that I'd committed an unforgivable sin against the Holy Spirit. I suppose this made some kind of impression on me, but I'd gone beyond the point of no return. I said I didn't care. If that was God's nature, then I'd just have to go to hell for eternity.

The interesting thing is that this stand on my part revealed something in my own consciousness, because for the next six months every time I walked around the corner I was sure the heavens were going to open and that God was going to strike me dead with a bolt of lightning. I had been so deeply conditioned into this fear concept—and I think in many ways much of humanity has been—that even though I rejected it consciously, I still had these old elements of fear in me.

As I let it boil up from within me so I could examine it, there was still something in me that was so certain this couldn't be God's way of working with his creatures that I said that no matter what, I had taken my position and was going to stand firm in it. Eventually I began to see some of the ridiculous aspects of the fears and the old images of God that I had picked up through association and through my religious training.

I won't say that I'm anywhere near being free from fear, because I think anybody who is honest realizes there are many elements of fear within him. From a psychological viewpoint and from a medical and spiritual viewpoint, these apprehensions are always active even if they are submerged in our subconscious mind. I definitely feel that they are the cause of our diseases and illnesses. If we truly attempt to overcome the fears that constantly plague us, the key energy we can arouse to carry on the fight rests in the understanding that God is Love.

Ev: It might be appropriate at this point to give an example of what we're talking about in terms of an actual patient. The person I'll be describing is a thirty-year-old woman, a mother, who came to Meadowlark with a history of two- or three-day headaches that recurred about every two weeks; other symptoms included swelling of her tongue and face, loss of vision in her right eye, and drooping of her right eyelid. All of these symptoms were accompanied by intense salivation. The whole thing was a very frightening experience to her.

She had undergone heart surgery ten years previously. Going back further into her history, we found that she had matured at the early age of nine. She was the child of a very strict and domineering father, often frightening in his strong disciplinary actions and in his perfectionist tendencies. She was never allowed to cry.

As a child she studied piano and had taken lessons for twelve years. She had studied voice, but she had not been able to sing or play the piano for the previous three years. Her arms had become so tense that she could scarcely write a letter. She was seen by a number of doctors, most recently an allergist, who had taken her off most foods and contactants; she had built up a great sense of fear and anxiety. She was put on fasts but experienced only temporary improvement. She was told that she was allergic to a great number of foods, to many contactants, and even to the gas used in heating her home.

We set up periods of meditation during the attacks described above, and she was soon able to release tears for the first time. The blocked creativity that was so strong in her began to find release. The salivation had taken over her tear function. Her headaches were also expressions of this suppressed creative energy.

Gradually as she began to feel the love of a group of people around her and the freedom to express herself and came to realize that it was her life force and her life energies that had to find expression for her to live, she began to improve. With this improvement she started to play the piano and to sing and soon found new creative interests. And the healing process began to manifest itself.

One of the first things that fear produces in patients is a sense of isolation. The sicker the person, the more isolated is that person, because fear and isolation go together. Love and a joining together similarly are associated closely. Whether the patient is mentally, physically, or emotionally ill, this same isolation is evident. With it there is a turned-inwardness as though the signals broadcast from the antennae, instead of reaching out to the world, had been curved around going back into the self. Such a person can think only of himself and seems to have lost contact with friends and everything else around him. Very often at this point the first treatment has to be love and acceptance.

The group working with me at Meadowlark waits on these guests, loves them, and assures them that nothing is asked of them. I believe that healing has to start in this great dimension of love. Gradually, as some of this love seeps into their cells, the cells begin to respond with healing. Isolation is less apparent, and the guest who previously was unable to come to meals and insisted on eating meals in his own room gradually and rather fearfully comes to the table to share a meal. Slowly he begins to open up, to talk, to establish a relationship with other people. So it is that many things seem to start with this great activity of love. Without this activity there can be no healing in a true sense.

SIG: What you said, Ev, reminds me of one of my strangest experiences in counseling. A woman came in who was very fearful about a number of things. It seemed to me that I detected a beam of light flowing through her. I'm not given to seeing visions, but to me it was a very real thing.

As we discussed something of the nature of God as Love, and the goodness of life and the potentiality of healing and freedom, this light would straighten out and shine directly. Then she would go back and start enumerating her fears and I could see that light beam distort. Sometimes it almost disappeared completely.

It was a very startling thing to me to realize that in each one of us there is a beam of light. Of course Jesus said, "You are the light of the world," and some of our top scientists now state that this is a literal scientific truth as well as a spiritual truth. But this was one of those rare occasions in my mind's eye, or in whatever area of the consciousness one perceives such things. I could see so clearly that when she was relaxed and was beginning to think of God as Love, and life as love and joy, that the beam would straighten out and shine directly with no distortion. But the moment she began to turn to her fears and talk about them and to give in to those negative feelings, the light itself was completely distorted and sometimes turned off.

Perhaps one definition of health could be the flow of light without disruption through all our systems of self-expression. Love, of course, is Life, and Life is Light, so they're all connected.

Sometimes people say, "How can I love my enemies, they're so distasteful?" or "How can I love a condition that's so distasteful?" We're not talking about generating a state of affection as much as we are about releasing a beam of energy, of light, of spiritual power into the situation.

We learn to love by loving. Even though we might not know very much about the power or nature of love, a conscious effort to direct a beam of love as our friend did does produce results. We learn to think by thinking, we learn to fear by fearing, we learn to complain by complaining, and we learn to love by loving.

Ev: I think another very important thing, Sig, to bring up

at this point is the problem of the person who has never received love, because we can't realistically ask this person to love. We have to give him the opportunity to receive love before he can put it out. We've had a number of people come as guests to Meadowlark who have never experienced love. Perhaps the mother died in childbirth, or the father was an alcoholic. They have come to us with various types of illnesses. It is of tremendous importance to let them receive love, not one time but, as Jesus said, "Until seventy times seven." We have to keep repeating this, because those of us who have been brought up with love in our childhood take it for granted and we know something about returning love. But the person who has never had this exposure must go through stages of loving.

Perhaps it's appropriate to talk about the evolution of love. Love is a growth experience. It starts with a little baby being cast out into the world very much by itself, after having been held and cuddled within the mother's womb. The tremendous importance of the mother's breast-feeding is often deemphasized these days. The child needs to be held, needs to feel the closeness of the mother, needs to feel the warmth of the mother's breast, needs to be cuddled and sung to and talked to. Many experiments have proven the importance of this. Multiple instances show that children raised in nurseries where they are scarcely touched by human beings and fed bottles without being held by any person will not do as well as the child who is close to the mother from the beginning.

SIG: Love is the ideal atmosphere in which children should be reared from their early childhood to adolescence. Unfortunately this doesn't happen too often. Love is not so much a matter of permissiveness or strict discipline as it is a resiliency of spirit that expects the greatest good, the greatest potential from the child, without attempting to force him or her into a particular pattern. Love takes time, it takes interest, it takes attention. All too often in this busy age, parents are just too occupied running a home, making a living, and conducting a business to give the proper time and attention to the children.

It is easier sometimes to be overly strict or overly permissive as a substitute for love.

Love itself is always on the job and it seeks not itself, not its own, but the unfolding and growth of the child's potential. Love recognizes the individuality, the uniqueness—or if we put it in terms of rhythm, the different rhythm of each individual—and encourages him to stand in his own rhythm, and to live his own self into expression always realizing that there is a responsibility to selfhood. If the parent has the feeling of love, then he becomes a source of strength for the child.

There seems little doubt that in our childhood experiences we accept and establish patterns of thought and feeling, and ways of looking at life, that accompany us through our entire lifetime. I know a very successful Sunday school superintendent who exerts considerable discipline in a wonderful way. She says that she loves the children too much not to expect the best from them and to let them know that she expects it.

We speak a great deal of nutrition, both mental and physical. Probably one of the most painful lacks in life is love starvation. Love is an atmosphere in the home or the school or other educational center in which each individual is recognized as being a unique self-expression of life and encouraged to bring that uniqueness into greater unfoldment. Quite often it is easier to be overly permissive or overly strict than to encourage the uniqueness of life within each individual. But undoubtedly we are coming to that point in human unfoldment where, if we will take the time and the energy and provide the teachers, we can establish this kind of atmosphere.

## Conclusion

Ev: Sig, I feel that the most distant stars, the sun, the moon and the planets, the surrounding atmosphere, the earth that grows our food, all are in relation to the temple of the body. The creatures of the sea, the world of insects, the birds and animals all have their place in one delicately balanced system. I wish I knew them better.

Most significant of all, the human beings who surround me every day, those whom I know by name and those whom I may never see, somehow all live in relation to me. Walt Whitman, in his "Song of Myself," saw why you, my friend Sig, and I go away each year and rediscover ourselves in a truer perspective:

> In all people I see myself, none more and not one a
>     barleycorn less,
> And the good or bad I say of myself I say of them.
>
> I know I am solid and sound,
> To me the converging objects of the universe perpetually flow,
> All are written to me, and I must get what the writing means.
>
> I know I am deathless,
> I know this orbit of mine cannot be swept by a carpenter's
>     compass,
> I know I shall not pass like a child's carlacue cut with a burnt
>     stick at night.
>
> I know I am august,
> I do not trouble my spirit to vindicate itself or be understood,
> I see that the elementary laws never apologize,
> (I reckon I behave no prouder than the level I plant my
>     house by, after all).
>
> I exist as I am, that is enough,
> If no other in the world be aware I sit content,
> And if each and all be aware I sit content.[1]

# 2

## THE WONDER OF MAN

And God said,
"Let us make man in our image,
After our likeness."

Genesis 1:26

It is a wonder-filled experience to deliver a baby. At first there is a limp, seemingly lifeless form. Then, with the first breath, comes animation! What happens in that moment? What is the nature of this sudden change? From where did this life energy come? Our human minds are quite incapable of comprehending the source of life or life as a whole. Of necessity we look at its various dimensions from different perspectives, depending very much upon our background and training.

According to Albert Einstein, every energy system in the universe is a localized condensation of energy of specific form, linked to every other by the psi factor in a unified field.

Publisher's Note: Chapters 2 through 7 have been written by Dr. Loomis.

Even a human being is made up of an extremely complex series of interrelating energies. This is indeed an energy universe. As we establish a living, daily relationship with it, it becomes a constant source for renewing our own energies. It has been estimated that there are approximately five octillion atoms in the human body and approximately a quadrillion cells. These figures boggle the imagination. To make them a little more comprehensible, imagine each atom to be the size of a pea. Five octillion peas would stand four feet deep over the entire face of the earth, and over 1,250,000 other planets of equal size.[1] A calculation shows that if the cells in one body also were the size of peas, they would fill all the buildings in the city of Philadelphia from cellar to roof.

There are certain things we must take on faith if we truly want to progress along the path of life. The most important of these things cannot be written; they can only be experienced. I know that a perfect sunset drives deeply into my soul, but anything I might say about it cannot possibly convey completely to anyone what I feel.

I have never composed a piece of music in my life, but my life is richer for my exposure to the inspiration of such musicians as Bach, Beethoven, and Brahms. I know I have gathered a certain strength after listening and entering into the musical experience of Bach's Toccata and Fugue in D Minor or Beethoven's Ninth Symphony.

Many psychiatrists are of the opinion that they must be quite uninvolved with the consciousness of their patient. The effectiveness of this approach is open to question.

A retired musician came into my office quite irate that on the top of the medical history questionnaire, he had been asked to specify his religious faith. He informed my secretary that it was none of my business, that his chief complaint was insomnia—and what did that have to do with religion? He told me that as soon as his head hit the pillow at night he would be wide awake.

It seemed very possible to me that, unconsciously, he identified sleep with death. Now retired, and with no real outlets, he was frightened. I asked him if, in his career as a violinist, he had any favorite composers. "Most assuredly," he said. "Mozart and Brahms have a special meaning to me." "Isn't that something of a religion to you?" I asked. "Oh, yes," was the reply. With this as an opening we had meaningful discussions about ways to get back into his creative life. He clearly had great need to reestablish his roots in the universe, and it is doubtful that the prescription of a sleeping pill would have done the same thing for him.

When we limit ourselves to the outer shell of life and its processes, we miss the very center where these processes originate. There is much evidence that science now is attempting to penetrate these depths, and let us hope that medicine will follow.

Man is a product of the evolutionary process. It is an interesting fact that the growth of every embryo mirrors each stage of the evolutionary development of man.

Pierre Teilhard de Chardin, the great Jesuit priest-paleontologist, posits the presence of two distinctive types of energy involved in the process of evolution.

> We shall assume that, essentially, all energy is physical in nature but add that in each particular element this fundamental energy is divided into two distinct components: a *tangential energy* which links the element with all others of the same order (that is to say of the same complexity and the same centricity) as itself in the universe; and a *radial energy* which draws it towards ever-greater complexity and centricity—in other words forwards.[2]

Radial energies relate to consciousness and very possibly, in the subtler forms, they may well relate to the various levels of "love energy." The late Harvard sociologist Pitrim Sorokin referred to this powerful energy in the following way:

Everywhere in the organic, inorganic, and psychosocial worlds the integrating and uniting role of love functions incessantly. Untiringly, it counteracts the dividing and separating forces of chaos and strife. Without the operation of love energy, the physical, the biological, and sociocultural cosmos would have falleₙ apart. No harmony, unity or order would have been possible. Universal disorder and enmity would have reigned supreme. As a creative energy, love unites what is separated, elevates what is base, purifies what is impure, ennobles what is ignoble, creates harmony in the world of enmity and peace in war. Love raises man as a biological organism to the level of divinity.[3]

Through the centuries the great philosophers, seers, prophets, and poets have caught glimpses of this man who is created in the divine image. Before Christ, Pythagoras was conscious of the harmony of the universe and described its inherent music. The seventeenth-century poet John Dryden writes, "From harmony, from heavenly harmony this universal form began. . . ."[4]

## Energy Fields

Several years ago I stood in front of Tintoretto's *Madonna*[5] amazed at the master's understanding of the inner light that shines out of the human soul. Tintoretto must have been conscious of Mary's supporting light and perceived the heavenly host that accompanied her.

The Light was again present about the Christ in Tintoretto's *Deposition*.[6] This "light" was not the stylized aura of an earlier period of painting, but a scintillating light, portraying a power and strength that supported and surrounded the figures as only he could have observed it. This seems to me to be the actual "force field" that supports the human body.

Neurologist Shafica Karagulla has made a study of energy fields as observed by "sensitives" and comes to the conclusion that there are three or more such fields. When observed, they reveal different color patterns depending on the individual's consciousness and state of physical, emotional, and mental health. She says,

> Many of the more intelligent and integrated sensitives with whom I have worked describe interpenetrating fields of energy around the human being. One of these is the *vital field* or *energy body* closely related to the physical. Much of my experimental work so far has dealt with this field in its relationship to physical conditions. The emotional field, extending a foot to eighteen inches beyond the body, and the mental field, extending an average of two feet or more beyond the periphery of the body, are a part of the unified field surrounding the human body.[7]

Dr. Kargulla goes on to describe the nature and characteristics of these auras, showing that their intensity and color vary with the intensity and nature of the emotions and thoughts as well as with the general state of physical health. Enthusiasm brightens and intensifies the aural color, while depression shows up as a muddy color.

I have never personally experienced these colors or auras, yet I have met many who have and would not wish to deny their experiences. My understanding of life processes is more complete because I have shared with others—and thus have made more valid for myself—certain related phenomena that I have come upon in the course of my studies.

### The Aim of Yoga

The body is the reflecting mirror of the whole cosmic process. This fact has long been known in India, where meditation has been an essential part of life through the centuries. Much benefit can be derived from a sharing of insights derived from the Western study of endocrinology and the science of yoga, since the aim of both is integration of the individual. The former approaches integration from the physical and emotional perspective; the latter from the spiritual perspective.

Yoga has been defined as the mystic reunion of man's spirit with the one Eternal Soul of the universe. The yogi is the practitioner of yoga. There are many diverse systems of yoga. The form most commonly practiced in the United States is *hatha yoga*, which concentrates on attuning the body through physical postures and breathing. *Raja yoga* is the yoga of right action; *jnana yoga* takes the intellectual pathway. And *bhakti yoga* moves to God through love and devotion.

The aim of all forms of yoga is to make man the master of his body rather than its servant and to arouse recognition of his true spiritual nature. Its study is very demanding and necessitates great discipline and the guidance of an experienced guru (teacher). The disciplines include such practices as the following: the avoidance of all stimulants, a largely vegetarian diet, moderation of sex life, expecting much from oneself but little from others, truthfulness, noninjury to others, and simplicity of living on a small and often shared income.

The various systems of yoga are staged to unfold step by step the basic sources of man's energy—physical, mental, and spiritual.

Today the great majority of people are quite unaware of their potentials and live life in a rather routine and unimaginative way. The student of yoga sees himself in relationship to great reservoirs of energy that are all about him. If he is to avail himself of these energies, he must tune his body instrument. This means developing the control of certain energy valves, referred to as chakras (see figure). Seven of these are of major importance, and it is to these alone we refer. These vortices of energy selectively suck in cosmic energy and relate it directly to one of the endocrine glands. These latter, which are guardians of health, exert a strong regulatory control, through hormones and the involuntary nervous system, on the body organs.

There is a latent source of power, figuratively pictured as a

## Correspondence Between the Chakras and the Endocrine Glands

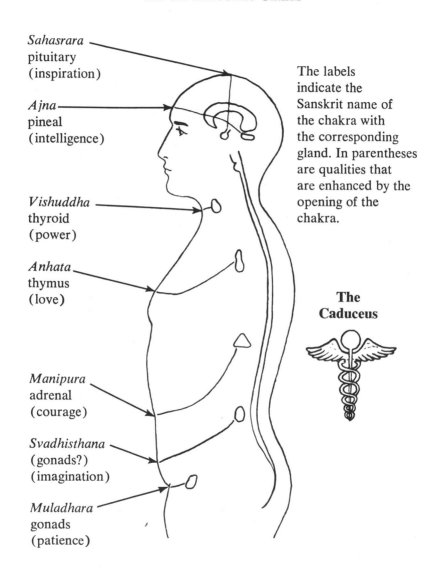

*Sahasrara*
pituitary
(inspiration)

*Ajna*
pineal
(intelligence)

*Vishuddha*
thyroid
(power)

*Anhata*
thymus
(love)

*Manipura*
adrenal
(courage)

*Svadhisthana*
(gonads?)
(imagination)

*Muladhara*
gonads
(patience)

The labels
indicate the
Sanskrit name of
the chakra with
the corresponding
gland. In parentheses
are qualities that
are enhanced by the
opening of the
chakra.

**The
Caduceus**

coiled serpent, located at the base of the spine, which is referred to as the kundalini. When the kundalini is fully awakened, the power ascends and activates, one after another, the chakras and thus brings about progressive enlightenment. If the centers are opened before the student is prepared, the energy release may be so great as to cause a psychotic break with reality. Through the practice of yoga the sleeping serpent is aroused and starts the ascent toward the thorax and brain as visualized in the caduceus.[8]

The serpents in this symbol are seen to cross at five points, which are the five chakras of the abdomen and the chest. In their center is the spine and at the upper end are a pair of wings, symbolizing the ascent of the forces: the male (positive) referred to as Pingala, and the female (negative) termed Ida. In yoga these forces are aroused by breathing through the left and right nostril with a deep concentration on the power of the inflowing breath.

Speaking in the terminology of psychosynthesis, the arousing of the lower centers is the personal synthesis that must precede the spiritual synthesis. This is accomplished through self-discovery, through recognizing our ego and accepting ourselves just as we are. Having recognized our sensual life and given it expression, there follows a period of raising the consciousness through character-building, clean living, and controlled emotional life so that we become masters of our emotions rather than servants. The solar plexus, with its close connection to the adrenals, is the master center in this area of building and purification as it is a center of strength. The adrenal hormones are our primary source of body defense.

As this stage of life nears completion, personal desires are raised to the heart chakra in the chest area, and, through sublimation, they are transmuted into a higher form of love energy directed away from personal concerns and toward humanity in general. Meditation then becomes a vital part of everyday life, and one's life takes on an organized purpose. Through further meditation, the forces rise eventually to the highest head center of the pituitary and pineals. At this point one no longer lives for himself but finds his life is lived through grace. Saint Paul describes this state as:

> I (the ego) am crucified with Christ: nevertheless I live, yet not I, but Christ liveth in me. . . .[9]

N.L. relates the story of her own kundalini experience:

> After a two-year bout with increasing depression, I surrendered myself totally to God, not knowing or believing consciously in God—like casting oneself into an abyss of unknown. For six months following this surrender I simply lived without concern and worry or particular desire for anything, but awareness of my duties in caring for our children and other family activities.
>
> At the end of the six months, my husband became quite ill and was hospitalized so that the demand on my energies was much greater than normal, yet there was no feeling at all of stress, rather more like a stimulant to keep all things running as smoothly and the children well cared for as possible.
>
> One afternoon between two and three P.M. the house and surroundings were very quiet and sunny. I sat alone reading Peter Marshall's sermons, when one particular phrase mentioning the *Pearl* of Great Price took hold of a higher emotion. I felt it in the heart *center* like a white bird taking wing and flying upward through the head *center*. Somehow, I went completely with this feeling, and there was a rush of energy from the base of the spine flowing up through the center of the body and out the top of the head. It was like golden-white liquid light fire that does not burn.
>
> It took no more than three seconds for this rush of light to envelop the body and "take" everything with it. It flowed out the top of the head and down over the whole body. I thought briefly "this is 'my cup runneth over' " before *all*—house, landscape, world, and universe—became this same light everywhere. No forms at all and no separation of being. All this oneness was God, without words.
>
> I do not know how long it lasted, perhaps only five or ten minutes before a filtering-back-down process slowly proceeded, taking another few minutes. The first thing I was

aware of was the phrase "All in One," and then the rest of the usual scenery and place was apparent again. I felt great joy, peacefulness and marvel at understanding through experiencing the basic divinity and unity of the entire creation, a blessing which by its nature desires to be shared and known by everyone.

The effect of lightness and transformation stayed on in diminishing degrees for several months, and the basic "contact" with God has never left. Not long after the experience (within the hour) I again felt such joy I said, "Soul, come forth," and a lovely rush of joy and lightness flowed up from the heart center to the head, making all the landscape look bright and shimmering (I was then driving a car and had to keep from losing that awareness, too).

I had never read or heard of this experience before, but later read of similar ones in many books, largely Eastern philosophical ones.

## Light in the Spirit

There is nothing new about this idea of music and light flooding all the interstices of the universe. Three thousand years B.C., we find this statement from the Bhaghavad Gita: "The glory and amazing splendor of this mighty being may be likened to the sun rising at once into the heavens with a thousand times more than usual brightness. . . ."[10]

According to Pythagoras, "There is One Universal Soul, diffused through all things, eternal, invisible, unchangeable; in essence like truth, in substance resembling light."

For a moment on the Mount of Transfiguration, three of Jesus' disciples were permitted to see the light energy that is the true building material of man:

And after six days, Jesus taketh with him, Peter, James, and John, and leadeth them up into the high mountain apart by themselves; and he was transfigured before them. And his raiment became shining, exceeding white as snow; so no fuller on earth can white them. . . .[11]

Looking at these radiation phenomena from the vantage point of today's research, Dr. Donald Andrews informs us

> . . . the light streams into the person from all the organs and also from the universe and the different planets. It is also radiated outwards. The essence of the stars is in this room. The music is broadcast out in different wave lengths. Every heart beat and thought goes out as a wave into the universe. We are in contact with the Eternal, embraced by it and in it.[12]

Ervin Seale, in a recent lecture to New Thought students, gave definitions of Body, Mind, and Spirit.[13] He envisaged the world as a realm of unity, proclaimed by all the great world religions. Out of this he saw a stepping-down of energies to the level of Mind, where for the first time, duality makes its appearance, in that we are dealing with both the universal and the individual minds. As these energies are stepped down still further, there is the appearance of the physical body.

In further unraveling these divine harmonies as they apply in the plant world, George Adams and Olive Whicher have done a masterful piece of work described in their book *The Plant Between Sun and Earth*. With the acknowledged help of leads provided by Goethe, they have discerned something of the great symmetry underlying plant structure and illustrated in geometric forms involved in the plant's growth patterns. Once again in this book we are conscious of the interplay of two worlds of energy: one, physical and "tangential," and the other, spiritual and "radial."

> What is the magical secret which is spoken silently yet eloquently from the heart of every flower? Hidden in the undergrowth or flaunted high upon the hedgerow, a message is forever being sounded if we could but hear it—a thousand modulations of a mighty theme. . . . through the centuries, Nature—above all Plant Nature—has spoken to the heart of man. In the glory of color and individuality of form the plants

speak. In the past, man listened to Nature as though in a dream; in recent centuries he has determined to become more consciously aware of her secrets.[14]

Following this thread from the plant life into the animal world, the research work done at Yale Medical School by Dr. H. S. Burr is particularly outstanding. He has made a study of energy fields of the animal world, noting that electromagnetic fields regularly determine the pattern of organization in biological systems. This being the case, certain parts of animals (including man) must carry a positive charge, whereas other parts must be negatively charged.

Dr. Burr proved this to be the case. Studying frog eggs, he found there was always one point on the egg where a higher potential difference could be registered. Keeping with this mark, it always turned out to be the point where the head was to appear. Thus he established the relation of the electrical field and the form and always found the field preceding the form.

Dr. Burr further discovered that in 90 percent of the cases, the right side of man's body carried a net positive charge, and the left a negative charge. The reverse was true in 10 percent of the cases. This, incidentally, was not correlated to right- or left-handedness.

The loss of our natural relationship to Nature has been a gradual result of the so-called progress of civilization. It seems to be the penalty of an overdevelopment of the personal ego that sees itself as existing by itself alone, in competition with Nature at large.

## In Tune with Nature

Through the ages there appear to be cycles of man living in very close contact with his environment, and then in times of isolation, each man fending for himself. This past century has been one of the latter periods. The physician and the priest have now long been separated. It has generally been forgotten that the father of medicine, Hippocrates, was a priest. While not suggesting that priests start practicing medicine or that physicians take on ecclesiastical orders, each needs to be something of the other. The priest needs to realize the needs of the physical man, and the physician needs to be aware of the sanctity of a human being. Scientific advances in this century have exceeded the wildest stretches of imagination—radio, television, radar, computers, and all the rest. But what a price we are paying in terms of the dulling of our own inborn sensitivities!

The physicians of the past century had much more acute clinical acumen. Their fingers, ears, and eyes had to take the place of X-rays, electrocardiograms, blood chemistry profiles, and radioactive scans. The young medical student and resident physician of today never hear the sounds audible to the ears of their predecessors nor feel the slight skin temperature changes nor see the peculiarities of the tongue that were so important in the diagnoses of former times.

Medical physicist Francis Woidich, a profound student of latent human energies, refers to man as "the cosmic resonator" and declares that the human being is capable of conscious response to any type of energy. Griffith Evans, M.D., believed that we human beings resonate on a harmonic system of vibrations tending to give a basis for our establishing rapport with another individual by tuning in his field of consciousness.

The research of G. W. de la Warr in his Oxford laboratory illustrated the power of thought on cellular growth and on photographic emulsion. He has also designed a number of diagnostic and therapeutic instruments that have aided him and his physician wife in diagnosing and treating patients at a great distance through a drop of the patient's blood to which they mentally tune in.

The rapidly growing field of parapsychology is piling up evidence of this type. In this connection I recall an example told me by the well-known student of psychic research Harold Sherman, who described his daily logged mental communications with an arctic explorer. One day Sherman awakened with a severe headache that he was at a loss to explain, inasmuch as he was not subject to headaches. Comparing diary notes on the explorer's return, they discovered that the timing of the headache coincided perfectly with a severe bump on the head his friend had suffered.

There is basically nothing new about these ideas, which we are rediscovering, since they are practiced unconsciously by all forms of life. An amateur naturalist for most of my life, I have been deeply impressed by the cosmic resonance theory as I have listened by the hour to the rhythmic chanting of frogs or the friendly whispering of crickets or watched the instantaneous departure of every member of a flock of cedar waxwings as they received some signal quite imperceptible to me. Many are the stories of this relationship of man to Nature, as told by the Kahunas or the American Indians.

Recently, J. Allen Boone, author of *Kinship with All Life* and *The Language of Silence*, described an experience of his that took place in Africa when he was traveling with a group of game hunters. He had heard of a place in the interior where a large band of monkeys frequently congregated and indulged in amazing acrobatic performances for which they had become famous. He set out for the place with the intention to arrive well ahead of his party. Picking a quiet spot under the shade of a tree, he sat down, identified himself with his surroundings, and waited.

After a reasonable lapse of time, monkeys seemed to arrive from everywhere. The out-of-doors became a great stage. They were climbing, swinging, chattering in a performance more remarkable than any zoo or circus could possibly provide. In the midst of this rare spectacle, all motion suddenly ceased, and there was a silence so profound it was practically audible. In another moment every monkey had disappeared.

Boone glanced at his watch, for he wished to test a theory that had suggested itself. When the hunting party arrived some hours later, he queried them as to the exact time they had left camp. It was the same time that the monkeys disappeared![15]

Captain Hounsell, the skipper of one of the Newfoundland coastal steamers, was well known to me during my time of medical service with the International Grenfell Hospital at St. Anthony, Newfoundland. Icebergs and heavy fogs were everyday hazards to these skippers in the days before radar. My wife tells of a trip with the captain to St. John's from our home port of St. Anthony. They were plying their way through White Bay in a dense fog one morning. Mrs. Loomis asked the mate how the captain knew where they were going. The mate replied that he had no idea but knew that the captain had another sense that most of us don't know how to use. Shortly the boat's whistle blew, and the anchor was dropped at Seal Cove. Nothing could be seen but fog and water. Then the motorboats from the shore began to arrive at the ship's side. The trip was completed as if there had been no fog, but how?

A close friend who has spent much time on the Arizona Indian reservations tells of a personal experience he had while attending an intertribal council meeting. He and the Indian chief walked silently together to the meeting place at a distant secluded area. They sat down in a circle while the other chiefs gradually assembled. After an hour of silence, my friend inquired of his host when the meeting would start. The reply was that it had started an hour before. As time went on, the pipe was passed around in ceremonial fashion. Then, of one accord, all got up and walked off in their various directions.

"What did this accomplish?" my friend asked in wonder.

"All has been decided," was the reply. Nearing the home village, an Indian ran out to meet the chief, exclaiming how happy he was with the success of the meeting!

In conclusion I am reminded of a few simple lines of the great English poet William Wordsworth, who had the sense of awe and wonder:

The world is too much with us; late and soon,
Getting and spending, we lay waste our powers,
Little we see in Nature that is ours;
We have given our hearts away, a sordid boon!
The sea that bears her bosom to the moon;
The winds that will be howling at all hours,
And that are up-gathered now like sleeping flowers;
For this, for everything we are out of tune;
It moves us not. —Great God! I'd rather be
A Pagan suckled in a creed outworn;
So might I, standing on this pleasant lea,
Have glimpses that would make me less forlorn;
Have sight of Proteus rising from the sea;
Or hear old Triton blow his wreathed horn.[16]

# 3

## ON BETTER NUTRITION

Thy food shall be thy remedy.
Hippocrates

The doctor of the future will give no medicine but
will interest his patients in the care of the human
frame in diet and in cause and prevention of disease.
Thomas A. Edison

Whatever I take into me should become a part of me,
whether it be the words I hear, the sunlight that warms me,
the air I breathe, or the food that nourishes my body. The
choice is mine. Intelligent and wise choice brings me to the
threshold of a more abundant life; the wrong decision is the
path to disease and premature death.

### The Human Ecosystem

The planet Earth is part of an ongoing process. It is constantly being bombarded by radiations from its father sun. It receives its water from the clouds, while the plants that dot its surface drink in the light energy, transform it into material plant form, which eventually becomes humus and identifies itself with the earth. Its secret of life is stored in the seed that again will rise out of the earth, grow, blossom, and give back the essence of its perfume to the surrounding atmosphere. In the words of Goethe, "Heavenly forces ascend and descend, passing golden chalices from hand to hand." Classical ecology has long recognized the relation of bacteria to plant and animal life in the nitrogen cycle. Dead animal matter decomposes with the aid of bacteria, liberating ammonia, which is an essential part of protein structure. Many examples of animal and plant dependency on each other are to be seen throughout nature. Certain hawks feed on snakes and rodents, which, in turn, feed on plants. These plants feed on the soil, which contains the minerals so vital to their existence.

The soil, in turn, looks to the decaying life of the animal and plant world for its fertility and completion. If hawks are killed indiscriminately because one particular hawk has killed a few chickens, the farmer may pay through the overrunning of his farm and destruction of its crops by rodents, which the hawks naturally control. If a bounty is put on coyotes, rabbits may become a similar nuisance.

Natural farming practices need once more to be reexamined. In the process of improving soils, it must be remembered that plants have first made the soil, not soil the plants! Nature intended man to put back into the soil what he has removed from it. The rotation of crops follows this principle. Protein is a very essential part of food, and nitrogen is the important constituent that distinguishes proteins from carbohydrates. However, for some of the reasons already mentioned, nitrogen should be returned to the soil from recently living nature forms, plant and animal, rather than from petroleum distillation products, which are many thousands of years removed from the living energy systems and quickly deplete the soil. In addition to adding manure, nitrogen-rich plants such as vetch and alfalfa can be rotated, turned back into the soil, thus keeping it alive and productive of superior vegetables. Anyone who has been eating such organically grown, nonsprayed vegetables can easily distinguish between the two types both by appearance and taste. A further point of interest is that the pesticide industry has grown in almost exact proportion to the growth of the chemical fertilizer business. In other words, healthy plants are not attacked to the same extent by insect or viral pests as are artificial culture plants removed from their normal habitat. So, too, human beings in health have their natural immunity to bacteria and viruses. In both instances the bacteria and viruses are nature's scavengers and look for unhealthy and dying cells.

## Nutritional Deficiency

Nutrition has been sadly neglected in medical instruction beyond the teaching of the recognition and diagnosis of the advanced states of disease resulting from nutritional deficiency such as xerophthamia (an eye disease), beri-beri, and pellagra, scurvy, and rickets. These are certainly not the major nutritional problems to be encountered in our country today. Most medical students probably have never seen any of these diseases.

The symptoms and signs of nutritional deficiency are so general and all-inclusive that nutrition should be one of the first items considered in all cases of chronic illness where energy is below par or the person is not functioning as he or she should be.

The physical examination may reveal nothing to the physician, and extensive blood and urine examinations may be reported as normal in the early stages. But the patient may still realize that all is not well and must not be lulled into a false sense of security by the assurance of a physician who is not nutritionally oriented. The body has a tremendous ability to adapt itself to stressful situations of life and diet and still keep its constituent parts operating within the limits usually considered normal. But external conditions sometimes can become too severe.

I had an early indoctrination into this subject, working for five years as a house officer in the International Grenfell Hospital at St. Anthony, Newfoundland. During that time I saw well over a hundred cases of beri-beri, one or two cases of scurvy, and an occasional child with rickets, in addition to 200 or more cases of tuberculosis, where malnutrition had played a causative role.

One of my most dramatic encounters with malnutrition occurred during a dog-team medical trip in Newfoundland that included a stop at the little fishing village of Boat Harbor on the Straits of Belle Isle. On our arrival one cold February morning, we discovered that not one man in the village of thirty families could stand on his feet. All were ill with beri-beri.

The usual first sign is the feeling of something like a tight band being drawn across the abdomen followed by increasing numbness and weakness of the legs. On further inquiry, we found that the people's diet consisted exclusively of white bread and tea. That was all—not even fish! The only store in the area was operated by the Hudson Bay Company, and it would not stock brown flour because it spoiled too quickly. The people couldn't afford other foods. As the result of this and other similar experiences where there was no competition between various stores, and the people were really in abject poverty, the Grenfell Mission instigated the cooperative movement, which, in the course of a few years, markedly changed this state of affairs.

But, as we all know, such extreme deprivation is not the prevailing problem in America today. What we need to look at is the subclinical nutritional state, which is very common and is perhaps not due to undernutrition but rather to malnutrition. Too often we, as physicians, have had a tendency, when questioned by patients about their diet, to put them off and tell them to just eat good, well-balanced meals and that all would be well—as if they knew what that meant. In fact, we have little knowledge of its meaning ourselves.

Most of what I learned about nutrition in medical school concerned the diet for diabetes and consisted in figuring out how many grams of protein, fat, and carbohydrate a given patient should have. This treatment today is temporarily controlling, though not solving, the problems of diabetes and the associated arteriosclerosis that is probably the more serious aspect of that disease.

It may be helpful to think of the body as the instrument that we are daily building and remodeling. If one wishes to build a house, he must first select a good architect who can assist him to visualize his dream house and who can lay out the plans. Second, he must have a good idea of the materials the architect will use to bring out the effects that he wishes. Certainly he would not want a house built of termite-infested wood, with rusty pipes and paint that was going to peel in the first year or two.

There is a direct analogy here to the food that we feed our bodies. Should we not as physicians and human architects give similar consideration to the nutritional building blocks that we prescribe for our patients, whose building is infinitely more delicate than the house made of wood or bricks?

Possibly we do tell the underweight, hard-working man that he should make an effort to eat at least 2,500 calories a day to maintain his weight and health, and that his daily diet should include a liberal amount of protein in the form of meat.

Is that sufficient advice? Are there no qualitative differences in the foods available to him? Is the energy quota of all foods to be measured only by their calories? Is their heat energy all that we need consider? Is it not possible that there are living foods and dead foods, and that the effects of these foods on our energy systems—physical, mental, and spiritual—might not be the same?

## Biologically Active Foods

Living foods might more accurately be characterized as biologically active foods, containing types of potential energy not present in substances that have been synthetically prepared through a heat process. These latter substances still may reveal their chemical presence, as in the case of a vitamin, but it has become something of a lifeless skeleton.

For those who wish further evidence of this biological activity present in natural foods and vitamins and relatively absent in those processed with heat or cold, Kirlian photography and chromatograms reveal designs in the former that are not present in the latter. Also the polygraph records energy fields present in the former but absent in the latter.

If we see man as a component of a great energy system that includes all living things, an important matter is the quality of the food he ingests. Is it living food that has resonances with his body, or is it relatively dead? Dr. Bircher-Benner, treating thousands of patients from many parts of the world in his world famous Swiss Clinic and Sanitarium, has recognized that the whole marvelous chemical structure of the living substances that make up the vegetable kingdom is a great storehouse of sunlight. That which nourishes both animal and plant life is the sun's energy stored in the food we eat. We are nourished, as it were, by light quanta.

We have long been aware of the fact irradiation by the ultraviolet light from the sun augments one's supply of vitamin D. We are also becoming increasingly aware of the solar relationship of vitamin C that is so abundant in the leaves of plants. Dr. Linus Pauling in his research has well described the great importance of this vitamin in the maintenance of health, particularly as regards protection against colds.

If you find it hard to make such distinctions between "living and dead" foods, pick an apple off a tree and eat it, and then eat one that has been in the kitchen for two or three weeks, and see if you can notice any difference in the taste of the two.

Are we supposed to assume that there are not differences in food value? We know from vitamin research that the vitamin content of fresh foods drops rapidly in the first day after they are picked. Dr. Bircher-Benner reports from his analyses that the vitamin C content in leafy vegetables such as spinach drops by one fifth after several days' storage in a warm place; the content in potatoes drops one-half after storage in a cellar for two months.[1] In most instances 25 percent of the vitamin C content is destroyed in the cooking water and is thus lost.

The important point is that the chemical presence of a substance such as a vitamin *does not assure its biological activity.* Dr. Anthony Pescetti finds from his experiments that foods cooked for any length of time above 130 degrees F. rapidly lose their biological activity. In these instances it is as though the life-bestowing component had departed and only the chemical skeleton remained.

The long-continued use of devitalized foods is all too evident as one walks through some of our present-day "convalescent hospitals" and sees some of the human forms propped up in their wheelchairs. Inadequate use of the building blocks of nutrition—the proteins, carbohydrates, and fats, with vitamins and minerals providing an essential role in their utilization in the body—consigns these people to a slow and uncertain recovery of their health.

Let us now consider these building blocks in greater detail.

## Proteins

Proteins are all important in the actual cell structure, in the formation of hormones, and as repositories for genetic information. They also can be converted into glucose as an extra source of energy. Good sources of protein include milk, eggs, nuts, soybeans, lentils, and leafy vegetables such as spinach and beet tops.

Protein digestion is initiated in the stomach through the

action of hydrochloric acid and the enzyme pepsin. It is then further carried on through the powerful action of the enzyme trypsin, secreted by the pancreas, in the small intestine. Further breakdown through the medium of enzymes secreted from the wall of the small intestine carries the process through to amino acids, which are absorbed into the blood stream through the intestinal wall.

Amino acids are many and varied in composition and are the building blocks of the many proteins that make up the body's cellular structure. They are referred to as essential and nonessential amino acids; the former must be provided in the diet; the body is able to synthesize the latter if not present in sufficient amounts in the diet.

There has been much discussion in recent years about the value of high protein diets in general, especially in control of obesity, or the toxemias of pregnancy and also in hypoglycemia (low blood sugar). It has been my observation in treating a large group of children with so-called "brain damage"—who in many instances were felt to be hypoglycemic—that a fair number already on a high protein diet were not doing well. When they were changed to a lower protein diet and all refined carbohydrates were eliminated, they did much better. Dr. Bircher-Benner has pointed out the fact that a 40 to 60 gram protein diet was superior to the 100 gram diet, but he also stressed the fact that vegetable sources of protein—a good proportion of which should be in the raw state—were superior to animal sources.[2]

There would seem to be several reasons for this. In the first place, meat is the highest food in the evolutionary scale and consequently is composed of the most complex molecules, which necessitate the longest enzyme chains for their utilization. Any weak point in this chain could cause the production of toxins and put an added load on the liver. Second, meat tends to be cooked at high temperatures and, therefore, much of the food value is destroyed. Vegetable sources, freshly prepared, are much closer to the life process and so might be considered a more "live" form of protein, making gram-for-gram comparison with meat protein rather meaningless.

All the essential amino acids are not to be found in ample amounts in any single vegetable, but, regularly using a variety of green and yellow vegetables in the diet, they will be taken care of.

Eggs are one of the most complete foods available for human consumption. To prevent nutritional loss through heat, eat them soft boiled. Milk, while frequently advertised as a food for all ages, is really not a good choice for older people due to the loss of the important enzyme lactase with aging. The enzyme is lacking in 5 to 10 percent of Caucasion adults, in many Orientals and in about 70 percent of Black adults. This enzyme is needed to digest milk with its high content of lactose. Because of this lack, they may develop diarrhea and abdominal cramps and therefore should avoid milk. This obstacle, however, can frequently be surmounted by using cultured buttermilk or natural yogurt, both of which contain very little lactose. (Many commercial yogurts do contain added lactose). Another satisfactory substitute is soybean milk made from soybean powder.

### Carbohydrates

Carbohydrates are the body's and brain's chief source of energy and comprise the starches and sugars. Vegetables and fruits are their most important sources. Their digestion starts in the mouth through the action of the enzyme ptyalin, which is present in the saliva. Far more important, however, is the enzyme, amylase, secreted by the pancreas, and enzymes present in the intestines, which carry the process to completion, forming glucose, fructose, and maltose, depending on the primary source. Glucose is then absorbed into the blood stream and finally reaches the liver or muscle as the storage product glycogen, or eventually becomes fat.

In the United States between 1889 and 1961, there was a marked shift in the consumption pattern of carbohydrates, with 54 percent reduction in complex carbohydrates and a 50 percent increase in simple sugars. During this time the sale of sugars and syrups more than doubled. In recent studies of heart disease, there is found to be a direct correlation between this trend in diet and an increase in heart disease. This excessive use of simple sugars in the diet is reflected in the elevation of blood triglyceride levels, which are frequently measured during physical examinations as an indication of proneness to coronary heart disease.

The "sweet tooth" is not a natural phenomenon any more than a proneness to alcohol consumption is. With proper diet both of these propensities will disappear. Dr. Weston Price dramatically illustrates the causal effect of refined carbohydrates on dental caries, dental malocclusion, pyorrhea, arthritis, tuberculosis, mental retardation, and the criminal temperament.

He relates his experiences in visiting and studying primitive peoples around the world and their health in relation to dietary habits. In those peoples who were still following the diet that had been in use through the centuries past, he found less than one percent dental caries with an increase to 30 or 40 percent when the group made contact with civilization and adopted refined foods—white sugar in particular. A typical example of this was the until recently isolated Loetschental Valley of Switzerland:

> The people of the Loetschental Valley make up a community of two thousand who have been a world unto themselves. They have neither physician nor dentist because they have so little need for them. They have neither policeman nor jail, because they have no need for them . . . . The valley has produced not only everything that is needed for clothing, but practically everything that is needed for food. It has been the achievement of the valley to build some of the finest physiques of all Europe. This is attested by the fact that many of the famous Swiss guards of the Vatican in Rome, who are the admiration of the world and are the pride of Switzerland, have been selected from this and other Alpine valleys.

The people live largely in a series of villages dotting the valley floor along the river bank. The land that is tilled, chiefly for producing hay for feeding cattle in the winter and rye for feeding the people, extends from the river and often rises steeply toward the mountains. . . . No trucks nor even horses and wagons, let alone tractors, are available to bear the burdens up and down the mountain sides. This is all done by human backs for which the hearts of the people have been made especially strong.

We are primarily concerned here with the quality of the teeth and the development of the faces that are associated with such splendid hearts and unusual physiques. I made studies of both adults and growing boys and girls, during the summer of 1931, and arranged to have samples of food, particularly dairy products, sent to me about twice a month, summer and winter. These products have been tested for mineral and vitamin contents, particularly the far-soluble activators. The samples were found to be high in vitamins and much higher than the average samples of commercial dairy products in America and Europe, and in the lower areas of Switzerland.

From Dr. Siegen, I learned much about the life and customs of these people. He told me that they recognized the presence of Divinity in the life-giving qualities of the butter made in June when the cows have arrived for pasturage near the glaciers. He gathers the people together to thank the kind Father for the evidence of His being in the life-giving qualities of the butter and cheese made when the cows eat the grass near the snow line. . . . The natives of the valley are able to recognize the superior quality of their June butter, and without knowing exactly why, pay it due homage.[3]

## Sugar-to Energy Conversion

In the conversion, through a long enzymatic process, from glucose or its liver storage product, glycogen, to a more available energy form, vitamins and minerals are necessary and must be present in adequate amounts for the individual to be able to function physically and mentally.

Major medical problems may arise if every vitamin and mineral is not adequately supplied in a form that is readily absorbable. This last factor has, in the past, been given insufficient study, with the result that a product such as iron in the form of ferrous sulfate has been a main source of supplemental iron. Experiments show that frequently not more than 4 percent of this iron is actually available and the other 96 percent is excreted through the bowel, or may be deposited in the liver or the gums, causing recession of the gums. This form of iron medication also destroys vitamin E and interferes with the utilization of the female hormone, estrogen, so the two should not be taken at the same time. Preferably they should be spaced twelve hours apart.

## The Hypoglycemic State

Stress and anxiety are common complaints among men and women of our contemporary society. These symptoms can be brought about from a wide variety of causes—the pressure of work, emotional problems in the home or in the marriage relationship. These emotional stresses when added to nutritional stress that results from the overuse of refined carbohydrates and such stimulants as coffee, tea, alcohol, soft drinks, and tobacco are increasingly responsible for many of the symptoms listed below. However, these symptoms do respond to a revised type of diet, in which supplementation of digestive enzymes is also, in some cases, needed.

I purposely do not like to refer to hypoglycemia as a disease since it can be merely a part of the exhaustion reaction that could happen to anyone under stress for any length of time, particularly when there is a history of diabetes in the family.

Dr. Hans Selye, in his very original delineation of the path from stress to overt disease, maps out the roles of stress, adaptation, and exhaustion. The gray area that we are dealing with here lies in the stage between adaptation and exhaustion. Other authorities who have studied this stress-adaptation syndrome include E. M. Abrahamson, M.D., Seale Harris, M.D., and John Tintera, M.D. Closely related to the subject now under discussion is the recent emergence of the new field of medical ecology, spearheaded by Theron Randolph M.D. It offers much evidence that such symptoms as those of allergy, arthritis, migraine, multiple sclerosis, relative hypoglycemia, diabetes and many other conditions are reactions to specific foods, including proteins and fats as well as carbohydrates. According to frequency of their occurrence, milk, wheat, corn and coffee lead the list. To a large extent the offending foods are those most frequently consumed. The symptoms thus produced are related to the fact that they are being consumed in quantities exceeding the supply of vitamins, enzymes and minerals needed in their metabolism.

The so-called state of hypoglycemia has been a subject of much controversy between orthodox medicine and a group of possibly overenthusiastic users of the term. I will try to take a middle road in dealing with this area. The former group possibly might revise their diagnostic criteria and the latter might adopt a new term to describe that individual who knows he feels sick but who is repeatedly told by doctors that they can find nothing wrong with him.

What we shall be talking about is a disorder of metabolism that may be associated with various symptoms, particularly those listed on the table below made from a tabulation of some seventy patients whom I have treated.

This disorder has been referred to variously as hypoglycemia, hypoadrenalcorticism, subclinical Addison's disease, Tintera's syndrome and the maladaptive response or allergic response to certain foods or environmental chemicals. If untreated, it may go on to a prediabetic state, clinical diabetes or possibly in rare instances to Addison's disease.

The symptoms are so variable that, as already indicated, I do not feel they fit into a disease category but might much better be considered manifestations of the general adaptation-exhaustion hypothesis of Hans Selye. As is already observed,

| | Number of Patients | Percentage |
|---|---|---|
| Fatigue-exhaustion | 69 | 98 |
| Difficult concentration | 59 | 84 |
| Depression | 52 | 74 |
| Restlessness | 49 | 70 |
| Irritability | 46 | 66 |
| Bloating-indigestion | 42 | 60 |
| Mental confusion | 41 | 58 |
| Blurred vision | 40 | 57 |
| Insomnia | 39 | 56 |
| Muscular twitching | 33 | 47 |
| Numbness | 32 | 46 |
| Dizziness | 31 | 44 |
| Headaches | 29 | 41 |
| Crying spells | 26 | 37 |
| Sweats | 22 | 32 |
| Fainting | 20 | 28 |
| Loss of appetite | 13 | 18 |
| Tachycardia (rapid heartbeat) | 10 | 14 |
| Convulsions | 1 | 1 |

metabolic difficulties occur early in this clinical picture, and to make the diagnosis of this adaptation-exhaustion state that will respond to the suggested treatment, the five or six-hour glucose tolerance test should be done. The all-too-often-used three-hour test will frequently miss hypoglycemic drops in blood sugar, though it may detect diabetes. Better still, the five-sample two hourly blood sugar tests suggested by Dr. E. Cheraskin need more extensive trial, as it is much more compatible with the individual's own life pattern.[4]

It is quite unnatural for most people (except for the rare person who goes on an extreme candy-eating binge) to eat a quarter-pound of sugar in ten to fifteen minutes, as the standard glucose tolerance test requires. It seems much more logical to take the two-hour tests during the course of the patient's typical day, as he eats, works, plays, and perhaps smokes, drinks, and argues with boss or spouse. Such tests should be conducted, in other words, on the basis of the individual's normal food and drink intake—not on the basis of the ingestion of abnormal quantities of glucose. Notes of the patient's indulgences should then be carefully made and later related to fluctuations in blood sugar.

Dr. Cheraskin has made significant studies on several hundred doctors and dentists and their wives and has reported them in his research. On dietary change, particularly, the removal of refined sugar from the diet has brought about a great improvement in the general health of people in these groups, resulting in less fluctuation in their daily blood sugar curves. It would seem that this test should be further studied in relation to the different exhaustion states already mentioned. Possibly the glucose tolerance test could be replaced, because it can leave a patient feeling quite exhausted for several days.

The graph below illustrates a normal glucose tolerance test and variations that occur in several disorders of carbohydrate metabolism.

As you may have gathered from the above discussion, the adaptation-exhaustion syndrome is a very complex subject, and practically every symptom that man is heir to may at some time fall into this basket. Much credit must be given to endocrinologist John Tintera, M.D., who really brought this vastly important subject into focus and described a rational and very successful plan of treatment that has helped thousands of patients of his own as well as of a growing group of doctors who have been closely following his work—and in this category I include myself, although I have found myself making modifications in his plan of therapy, especially in the field of nutrition.

You may rightly ask why this condition is so common. I should be inclined to answer that it probably relates to man's departure from the study of Nature and her methods. William Harvey, the discoverer of the human circulatory system, advises that Nature herself is to be addressed and the paths she shows us we must follow.[5]

## The Five- and Six-hour Glucose Tolerance Tests

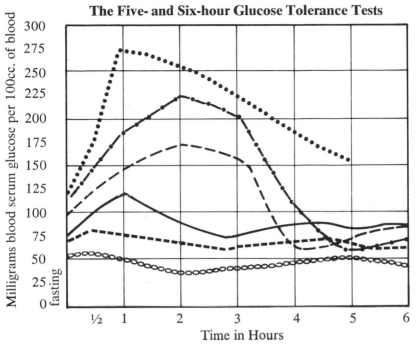

Milligrams blood serum glucose per 100cc. of blood

300 275 250 225 200 175 150 125 100 75 50 25 0

fasting

Time in Hours

½ 1 2 3 4 5 6

———————— Normal curve—starting between 75 and 85 and rising to a
point approximately half greater than the original fasting
value within the first hour.

•••••••• Diabetic curve—the typical feature is the high blood sugar
values with a failure to return to norms until after the
third hour.

— — — — — Hypoglycemic curves—there is much variation. The main
considerations are the rapid high early rises, the precipi-
tous drops any time in the six hours, and the low levels
below 50 or more than 15 to 20 below the fasting level
especially if accompanied by hypoglycemic symptoms.

ooooooo Pancreatic tumor curves—this is by far the rarest and by itself is not diagnostic.

▬▬▬▬▬▬▬ Exhaustion curve—this so-called flat curve is frequently
seen in hyperkinetic children, people who have been using
drugs and other exhaustion states. The response to the
above treatment is slower, as there is a greater extent of
adrenal cortical exhaustion present. Frequently malabsorption states are present, and there may be other glandular, vitamin and mineral deficiencies.

•—•—•—• Diabetogenic hypoglycemia curve—this is one of the most
important to detect, is a prediabetic type of state, and
may be missed with the three hour test. It responds well
to the outlined treatment. This curve is also associated
with maladaptation to certain foods. It is generally present
in multiple sclerosis.

Our processed food is an extreme departure from the substances that man was provided through nature, as will be
discussed further in greater detail. It is consequently a real
source of stress for the body to have to deal with it. This
applies particularly to sugar, which has found its way into a
tremendous variety of prepared foods and which puts a load
on the adrenal cortex, the pancreas, and the liver and which
paves the way for the exhaustion phase of our metabolic
syndrome.

Also, as briefly mentioned earlier, we must implicate the
overuse of stimulants such as alcohol, tobacco, coffee, cola
drinks, tea and drugs—all of which deplete the adrenal cortex and intensify the symptoms with which we are dealing.
Nature has not provided a metabolic pathway for many of
these substances, with the result that they set up "roadblocks"
on the pathway to energy production and frequently destroy
vitamins and enzymes or block their use by the body.

In addition to foods, we must also consider mental nutrition and the role of the mind in these psychosomatic diseases
that concern us so much in this field. Habitual states of resentment, anger, frustration, and jealousy all have a profound effect on the endocrine system through the mediation
of the hypothalamus (a central portion of the brain) with its
intimate relation to the pituitary. These stresses and the
common state of mental depression cause great depletion of
the adrenal cortex.

Another important consideration in this symptom complex
is the problem of malabsorption. This may be due to a number of causes—most frequently lack of hydrochloric acid in
the stomach, lack of digestive enzymes in the small intestine,
deficiency of bile secretion from the liver, and more rarely a
genetic inability of the body to form a certain enzyme.

Lack of hydrochloric acid in the stomach will also mean
that the small bowel is unable to absorb vitamin B12. If you
have had surgical removal of a considerable part of your
stomach, remember that B12 injections may have an important part to play in your health. Such deficiencies should be

considered in the patient who fails to gain weight in spite of a high caloric diet or who chews his food well and still passes undigested food regularly in his stools. Consistently passed clay-colored stools or very bulky ones that float or appear greasy should also be suspected in this relationship. This last-mentioned condition is associated with celiac disease in children and nontropical sprue in adults, a condition due to lack of an enzyme needed for the utilization of gluten (the proteins gained from wheat and other cereals after the starch has been washed out). This condition responds favorably to a gluten-free diet with folic acid supplementation. One may also suspect malabsorption problems when there is much bloating immediately after eating. If appropriate tests reveal the acid to be present, then one should consider pancreatic enzymes and/or bile tablets taken with meals. If many anti-biotics are being used, consideration should be given to the use of acidophilus culture or plain yogurt to restore the natural bacterial flora of the large bowel, the absence of which can cause distention and discomfort and interfere with the synthesis of certain vitamins.

In our Meadowlark experience, we are becoming increasingly aware that assimilation of food is an index of an individual's openness to life: one's capacity to express love, and to accept a responsible role. A 54 year old married woman, M.A., came to Meadowlark who had been practically a bed patient for over ten years. There were extremely few foods that she could eat. Much distension immediately followed meals, she frequently had diarrhea and severe headaches. She had been receiving vitamin and adrenal cortex injections daily for a long time. Hydrochloric acid tablets and pancreatic enzymes especially prepared by a biochemist for her so as to be as readily absorbable as possible, were passed in her stools perfectly whole. Her life attitude was one of isolation from people, even her husband, who in spite of all, dearly loved her, waiting on her hand and foot. She would not allow herself to be brought to the dining room table for meals to eat with the other Meadowlark guests. What is this saying?

Is it not possible that the attitude is conveying this message of isolation to the cells thus causing them to reject food?

Two case histories demonstrate the efficacious use of a carefully adjusted dietary regime in coping with widely divergent physical symptoms connected with the adaptation-exhaustion syndrome. A.K., an eighteen-year-old schoolgirl, complained of lack of energy, abdominal cramps, and headaches. Her diet was largely meat, milk, bread, and sweets. She ate practically no vegetables or fruits. A five-hour glucose tolerance test revealed 102 fasting blood sugar, 155, 133, 112, 77, and 87 in the succeeding hours. The 25-point drop below the fasting level in the fourth hour thus was consistent with the adaptation-exhaustion syndrome. Subsequently she was placed on a changed dietary regime with adequate proteins, vegetables, and fruits and no refined carbohydrates. Supplemental vitamins were also included. Six months later, there was a distinct improvement in her energy, and she suffered no more headaches.

K.S., a ten-year-old schoolgirl, had shown normal development following birth until eighteen months, when she had a severe fright. Her speech did not develop and coordination was poor until she was placed on the Doman-Delcado neurological development program of patterning. Her hyperactivity also subsided under this regime, but her attention span remained poor. A neurosurgeon had made a brain biopsy and labeled the child as having organic brain damage. Her five-hour glucose tolerance test had revealed a prediabetic type of curve, and she was put on a high protein diet at this time.

Further studies made in my office revealed a hypothyroid condition and malabsorption. She was taken off meat proteins and put on a moderate lactovegetarian diet with adrenal cortex and pancreatic enzyme pills plus vitamin supplements.

In five months she was much calmer, her attention span and her muscular coordination improved. In a year her reading was much better, and her talking was improved. In eighteen months, she was able to handle arithmetic for the first time. Within two years, her parents reported that she was "going great guns."

This type of program, the basis of which is patterned after the eighty years of experience of the Bircher-Benner Clinic of Zurich, which I have visited on several occasions, and our own fifteen years of clinical nutritional research in long-standing chronic illness patterns. The patient is frequently started on a water or juice fast, thus putting the gastroenterological system at rest and giving Nature's healing forces an unencumbered freedom to turn their full energy in the direction of the restoration of health. The next addition to the diet would be fresh vegetables and fruits, largely in the raw state. For some this might also be a starting point. As the patient improves, the diet increases to include nuts, yogurt, unprocessed cheeses and grains if no intolerance has been found to these last mentioned foods. Meat is the last addition, if it is to be included at all. The latter was considered in some detail under the previous section on Proteins.

Adrenal cortex extract is a very valuable adjunct in treatment. In the past it has been far too often neglected.[6] Adrenal cortex extract is by no means always necessary in the handling of the adaptation-exhaustion syndrome. Its use, in my opinion, depends on the energy reserve of the patient but is frequently indicated for those who cannot function in their normal life roles because of their low energy. The frequency of injection depends on the severity of the exhaustion. In extreme cases one would start with daily injections, though much more commonly once a week will do. With improvement, the frequency is tapered off until it is finally discontinued or just given only in times of particularly difficult stress or intercurrent illness, such as pneumonia or a heart attack. In these instances, it is extremely helpful and greatly speeds up recovery.[7]

Addison's disease, or extreme adrenal failure, has long been known, but the lesser deficiencies have been largely overlooked, or treated with cortisone. This latter medication has many undesirable late effects, such as moon face, recurrence of an old peptic ulcer, or the lighting up of diabetes or tuberculosis.

Fortunately, with the use of adrenal cortex whole extract, none of these side effects occurs, since it is a balanced, glandular secretion as made by Nature. If Nature chose to combine 8 or more steroid hormones in one glandular secretion, I am inclined to feel they are there for a reason, even though science is still largely uninformed about a number of these steroid hormones.

I have been using it for twenty-five years and have never seen any undesirable side effects in well over a thousand patients on whom I have used it as a temporary measure to help them through particularly stressful times in their lives. Concern for giving this whole gland its rightful place in the therapeutic regime was largely responsible for the formation of the International Academy of Metabology. The length of time that it must be employed depends largely on the patient's readiness for self-examination and growth into a deeper awareness of the lesson inherent in his illness. This new state of consciousness is attended by an activation of the adrenals glandular function.

The adaptation-exhaustion syndrome is frequently associated with the hyperkinetic state of retarded children, delinquency problems, and even crime. An interesting case study is that of H.D., aged ten, first seen because of hyperactivity. His history showed an unusual craving for sweets, plus school discipline and reading problems. Physical examination showed nothing.

However, a five-hour glucose tolerance test read 112 on fasting—which is distinctly high, particularly at this young age, 212 in half an hour, 213 in one hour, 136 in two hours, 89 in three hours, 100 in four hours, and 112 at five hours.

The rapid climb in the first half hour would be indicative of a delayed pickup of glucose from the bloodstream by the liver. The drop of 23 points between the fasting level of 112 and the lowest reading of 89 is indicative of an altered metabolic state, as is any drop of 20 points or more, particularly when accompanied by symptoms for which the patient is seeking explanation. Stool examinations indicated incomplete digestion of proteins and carbohydrates. The urine revealed a lack of vitamin C. He was accordingly put on a regime of adrenal cortex tablets, digestant pills, supplemental calcium and magnesium, and high protein, eliminating refined carbohydrates and stimulants.

Three months after the beginning of this regime, definitely less hyperactivity was reported, reading and math improved, and he was sharing much better with his schoolmates. He had learned the multiplication tables by five months. He was also reading at his grade level, having come up two grades in this short time. By nine months, his school report was very good, and he was to be integrated into classes at his regular school level.

A second case study involved that of E.B., a thirty-three-year-old male. He was an air conditioning repair man, who two years previously had had a near nervous breakdown. At the time of the examination he had been out of work for three months. There was much anxiety and depression present. His energy had been below par for the previous ten years. He complained of numbness in his feet and cramps. He was subject to severe headaches if he missed a meal. Periods of mental confusion seriously interfered with his performance at work. He noted that he would "set thermometers and go back to find that they were incorrectly set." He also noted that during the previous two years he had begun to dissociate from his friends and church and now felt there was practically no one he could trust.

Seven years previously he had been given a three-hour glucose tolerance test, and its report showed a fasting glucose level of 145. At thirty minutes 246, one hour 210, two hours 120, and three hours 130. There was no sugar in the urine at any time, but he was diagnosed as diabetic and put on a diet. The patient admitted on questioning that his diet was quite high in refined starches and low in protein. Five years before, a single blood sugar was taken two hours after a meal and was found to be only 40, but apparently little was done about it. In the hospital a full six-hour glucose test was attempted, but following forced carbohydrate feedings prior to his test and the glucose meal, the patient became very agitated, thought everyone was plotting against him, and became quite violent, requiring medication and psychiatric consultation. The test had to be abandoned. It was felt that the patient had a severe reactive hypoglycemia with schizoid accompanying symptoms and protein deficiency. He was accordingly put on a high-protein, no-refined-carbohydrate, frequent-feedings diet with daily injections of adrenal cortex extract and vitamins. In view of the more recent advent of medical ecology, I would be inclined to think that this severe reaction might have been due to corn, which is the basis of the glucose used for the test, or possibly the artificial color or flavoring used with the glucose solution.

He was discharged eight days following admission, completely rational, with energy improved and with less numbness in his feet. When heard from years later, his energy was normal, his mind perfectly clear and he had no further psychotic breaks. None of the usual drugs for schizophrenia were necessary, but the patient found that he had to stay strictly on his diet or his performance would deteriorate.

As discussed earlier in this chapter under the heading of PROTEINS we have referred to the fact that we no longer employ the high protein diet for reasons already stated. A moderate protein, high unrefined carbohydrate, low fat diet in the long run is more satisfactory.

### The Diabetic Situation

This raises the whole question of treating the diabetic patient. There seems to be much disagreement as to what the ideal diabetic diet should be. This is particularly true in the case of the brittle diabetic, whose blood sugar shows tremendous variations in the course of a day. Perhaps we may succeed in controlling, to a supposedly satisfactory level, the blood and urine sugars and in maintaining a satisfactory weight—all of which are important—but we may still be a long way from high-level health in that patient.

If the diabetic's day is spent weighing his food for all meals, counting grams of protein, fats, and carbohydrates, and checking his urine four times a day, this is not "really living" and is incompatible with what we think of as the ideal life.

Maybe much more attention needs to be directed toward the quality of his nutrition, the ability of his body to absorb the nutrients, and even toward what is going on at the intracellular level that is making the insulin unavailable at the cellular level.

Recent research reveals that an important clue in some diabetic problems is the failure of zinc, copper, and chromium to penetrate the cell membrane. These are all needed for the body's production of insulin. Dr. Anthony Pescetti has compounded an experimental product of chelated zinc, copper, and chromium that has shown interesting results in bringing down blood sugars in certain diabetics. Before its use blood zinc levels in these patients were abnormally high, and following a month of administration of the compound, values tended to return toward normal.**

Diabetic control today does definitely improve the patient's feeling of well-being, but in a certain percentage the frequently associated arteriosclerotic process goes right on and produces the degenerative changes in the eyes, the debilitating diseases of the coronary arteries of the heart, and the loss of circulation in the legs that results in so much debility.

Arteriosclerosis is increasingly being recognized as closely related to carbohydrate metabolism. Three blood determinations are valuable in assessing the risk of the complications associated with arteriosclerosis. They are the cholesterol, the

HDL (high density lipoprotein fraction of cholesterol) and the triglyceride level; the first two with respect to saturated fats, lack of exercise, lack of adequate vitamin E and lecithin and the latter is influenced by the overconsumption of refined carbohydrates.

Thus it is becoming increasingly evident that hypoglycemia, diabetes and multiple sclerosis in that order are progressively increasing signs of maladaptation of the body to certain specific foods resulting in disordered metabolism.

The role of fats is possibly much more significant than one might ordinarily realize, particularly if there is a slight problem of overweight and much concern about its elimination. Fat is a valuable source of energy storage, an important insulating material, an important cushion for holding certain vital organs, and a very essential part of beautiful skin. It exerts an important role in conjunction with proteins in the formation of nerve tissues. It also plays a vital role in the formation of the delicate cell membranes that must supervise the movement of substances into and out of the cells. Fatty acids are obtained from the breakdown of the complex fats that we ingest. Some of our best sources are the vegetable fats in their (unsaturated) oil form found in, for example, olive, sunflower, and sesame oils.

There are several important points that need discussion relative to the body's securing the fatty acids that are needed by its metabolic processes. First, is the fat saturated or unsaturated? There has been much discussion of this point in current literature in conjunction with the reduction of blood cholesterol values. If the fat is unsaturated, there are points in its structure where it can combine with other nutrients within the cell and thus nourish the cell. If it is saturated, it is chemically inert and will be deposited by the body as so much excess blubber.

The simple method of determining this is by noting whether the fat is liquid or solid. Unsaturated fats will tend to be largely liquid, whereas saturated fats are for the most part solid. Thus you will do well largely to eliminate animal fats, lard, margarine, and butter, especially if you have a high cholesterol count or are overweight. You might also note on the label of your product whether there is the word "hydrogenation" present, as this process makes a naturally unsaturated fat saturated. Most peanut butter today has been hydrogenated. This is done possibly for two reasons: It will last longer, and the smooth texture is more salable to housewives who are ignorant of nutritional value.

Also, has the oil been chemically extracted and heat-processed so that, again, its food value is reduced? Today practically all vegetable oils, except a few locally produced brands in the United States market, have been refined. In Spain, Italy, and Greece, while all the olive oil used for export is refined, that used by the natives is for the most part freshly pressed and unrefined to retain its flavor.

The fact that the label of a health food store oil reads, "cold pressed" is very deceptive since it may bear this label and still have been heated as high as 475 decrees F. and undergone other types of processing.

Foods fried in deep fat, such as doughnuts, french fries, and potato chips will be saturated with an altered fat that is implicated in the genesis of the arteriosclerotic process and the elevation of blood cholesterol. The best oils are those from the first extraction and cold pressed in the true sense of the word.

Recently a very important study of nutrition in relation to disease, written by Nathan Pritikin, has come to my attention and is receiving close scrutiny by a group of physician members of our International Academy of Metabology. The information given here is based on Pritikin's experience as well as a review of some 83 references from medical literature, covering many thousands of confirmatory case studies.

Highlights from Pritikin's study include the following: The average American diet contains approximately 40 percent fat; there is a definite relationship between the fat content, irrespective of whether the fat be saturated or unsaturated, and the blood cholesterol level; there is a definite predictable relationship between the degree of atherosclerosis in the coronary arteries (those supplying the heart wall) and the cholesterol and triglyceride levels in the blood. However, the norms for cholesterol and triglycerides in the blood have been established on the basis of American diets, which are too high in fat and therefore are very misleading. Instead of an acceptable normal of 150 to 250 or 300 in the former instance and 125 to 150 in the latter, he would feel that a much more realistic normal should be 150 or less in the first case and 75 or less in the latter. This is based on values in native populations where the fat content of the diet is not over 10 to 15 percent and there is a relative or complete absence of arteriosclerotic conditions. It is also interesting to note in these population groups that there is a notable absence of other metabolic and degenerative diseases such as cancer, arthritis, gout, gall bladder disease, and diabetes, where the fat content is very low and there is no use of refined carbohydrates. This regime, as he points out, can also greatly help the person who already has arteriosclerosis with senile changes in the brain, eyes and ears, thus improving memory in this group as well as vision and hearing.

Pritikin feels, as we have also stressed, that the high protein diet that has so generally been advocated for hypoglycemia and related conditions is far from the ideal. Much to be preferred is a diet high in unrefined carbohydrates and relatively low in protein. His important contribution to what we have said is to be found in the additional control of hypoglycemic states through decreasing the fat content of the diet.

Another advantage of this diet is that it soon make unnecessary the many extra feedings that are commonly associated with the hypoglycemic state and so often have consisted of such foods as milk, cheese, eggs, etc. This observation, which has already been hinted at, further confirms the poor energy output from these high fat and cholesterol containing foods.

Pritikin brings out the point that the typical high fat American diet results in the poor oxygenation of the body tissues which is so readily associated with diabetes, arthritis, gout, cancer, and diminished vision and hearing of aging. This problem can be compounded when smoking and relative lack of exercise are part of the lifestyle of the individual concerned.

In conclusion, a diet with a twenty percent fat content, high in unrefined carbohydrates, largely whole grains, fresh fruits, raw or lightly cooked vegetables and containing not over 100 mg. of cholesterol per day is to be recommended. This diet and activity program may help to reverse many cases of angina, hypertension, claudication, diabetes, and arthritis if followed carefully.

## Vitamins

The question "to take or not to take vitamins" has received a great deal of attention. Thousands of unneeded vitamins are being taken today by health enthusiasts, while sales of vitamins are at times pushed by health food stores, with little real public understanding of the role of vitamins and minerals in human metabolism. Too frequently neither the physician nor the patient understands what is meant by the statement that in a "good, well-rounded diet one will get all the vitamins needed."

Prior to 1960, I often made such statements myself. The fault is not the physician's, for this is what he has been taught both in medical school and in his postgraduate education. The fault is in the neglect of medical schools to give nutrition the place it merits in the curriculum. The concerned physicians who, like myself, have discovered the need to investigate this important field of health education have largely had to turn to lay publications to keep up with research in nutrition because of the dearth of material in the medical publications.[8]

Biochemist and pharmaceutical manufacturer Pescetti points out to me that the proper manufacture of biologically active ascorbic acid tablets must be very exacting, since the vitamin's activity can be destroyed by light or contact with metal, air, or heat. Controlling these factors, and using a no-heat process, he is able to process an ascorbic acid with much greater activity and stability than the usual product. In fact, it has been shown stable for a period of five to seven years.

One of the reasons why many researchers have disclaimed the value of vitamins is because they may be using "dead" substances rather than the true vitamins in their experimental studies. As an example, niacin (vitamin $B_3$)—along with other related vitamins—is being used quite extensively to control schizophrenia. The usual starting dose in this program is 3,000 mg. a day. If a biologically active preparation is used, only 400 mg. a day is necessary.

## Minerals

Minerals, relating as they do to the earth's very structure, are of primary importance. Many millions of years ago primitive living structures had to make use of these primary substances to sustain their life processes. Algae, fungi, and bacteria are admirably capable of converting these inorganic minerals into organic compounds which are the natural foods of plant and animal life.

The story of minerals in metabolism is just beginning to be told. Chemist, Dr. John Miller of Chicago has made a most significant contribution in this area via seminars offered physicians on the subject of the role of minerals in the body's metabolism.

We can only scratch the surface in presenting this vast subject. Hair analysis, which is still largely in the research stage, is the most available avenue for making diagnoses in this area. The minerals routinely tested for include sodium and potassium, calcium and magnesium, copper and zinc, iron and manganese, chromium, mercury, cadmium and lead. (I linked most of them in pairs because the ratios between these groups is very important.) Sodium and potassium hold a dominant role in these relationships because of their all-important part in the control of the movement of other minerals and nutritional elements into and out of the body's cells. Let me mention a few direct applications of the role of specific minerals in the health picture. Calcium has a primary function in the support of muscle tone, while its partner, magnesium, is the relaxer. The supporting role of copper and manganese in the metabolism of the red blood cells is being increasingly understood. Zinc, in addition to its role in the formation of insulin, also is very necessary for growth and in the healing of wounds.

May I cite two examples of mineral supplementation. The first instance is that of an educationally handicapped girl in a special school who performed quite well just as long as she regularly took her copper supplement. The second is that of a hyperactive child who stayed calm and presented no particular problems as long as he took his zinc supplement.

Excessively high levels of certain metals noted on hair analysis are also productive of symptoms. In this area lead is of particular importance. Here one might investigate the use of hair dyes, air pollution and industrial sources. This determination is a much more sensitive indicator than lead values in blood. It is frequently associated with brain dysfunction in the educationally handicapped child. Zinc and copper elevations are frequently present in the schizophrenic state. Good results in treatment of these excessively high levels of minerals are obtained with ascorbic acid and particularly with certain magnesium chelates.

### Chelation

An exciting new era in applied biochemistry is the advent of chelation, a process that greatly increases absorption of minerals. Food supplements that are manufactured in this way mean a more concentrated type of supplement and many less pills to take.

Many minerals such as calcium preparations, magnesium, and iron compounds as offered in most vitamins are very incompletely absorbed. The instance of ordinary supplemental iron is a good example. In the chelated form it is absorbed nearly 100 percent with the result that there is no resultant constipation and the tarlike black stool is absent. By way of explanation, the iron molecule is wrapped up inside of an amino acid or vitamin molecule in a form that is very acceptable to the needy cell, and it enters the cell rather than being pushed aside.

## Metabolic Pathways

The body is much more than a collection of organs that operate independently of each other and can be replaced from a parts supply house when they wear out. The group of tissues that make up the body organs share the common purpose of supporting and housing a spiritual being. Interpenetrating and interweaving them are vast energy systems that we have scarcely begun to comprehend, let alone map out.

The fundamental unit of animal life is the cell. The cells of the human body are specialized units all containing billions of the basic atoms: hydrogen, oxygen, carbon, nitrogen, sodium, potassium, calcium, phosphorus, magnesium, and sulfur. Atoms of other elements are needed for the specialized functions of certain cells. For example, iron, manganese, and copper are essential components of blood cells; iodine is needed by the thyroid; zinc and chromium are needed by the cells of the pancreas that produce insulin.

The cell is made up of a central nucleus and its surrounding cytoplasm, all of which is encompassed by a very delicate and discriminating cell membrane that picks up from the blood stream just those particular nutrients it needs.

Cells are the factories where the body's metabolic processes take place—thus the importance of keeping them free hereditary individuality and also direct the individual's metabolic processes. The cytoplasm is the cell factory and food storehouse. One very important element contained within its structure is the all-important mitochondrium. This performs a function like a battery, housing the essential end-product of the breakdown of glucose, which is the basis of energy production.

Cells are the factories where the body's metabolic processes take place—thus the importance of keeping them free of the contaminants that are common in food today and contribute to a breakdown of the metabolic assembly line of bodily processes. Each cell is responsible for supervision of somewhere between 1,000 and 10,000 different chemical reactions. It is also the storehouse for some 5,000 or so enzymes needed to implement these chemical reactions.

Physicians Abraham Hoffer, Humphry Osmund, and David Hawkins and biochemists Roger Williams, Linus Pauling, Anthony Pescetti, John Miller, and others have illuminated the importance of the metabolic pathway in the adequate functioning of the brain. Dr. Pauling has suggested Orthomolecular Psychiatry as the name for this field of study.[10] It has also been referred to as Megavitamin Therapy because of the large doses of vitamins used.

It has long been known that psychotherapy alone is ineffective in the treatment of the major psychotic states, principally schizophrenia. Hoffer and Osmund followed up on a hunch that there was a relationship between the mental state seen in the vitamin $B_3$ (nicotinic acid) deficiency state known as pellagra and that in schizophrenia and began treating a series of schizophrenic patients with increasing doses of vitamin $B_3$. They observed a very favorable response.

Dr. Hoffer observes that, if all the vitamin $B_3$ were removed from our food, we would all be psychotic within a year. He further points out that the similarity between pellagra and schizophrenia only goes as far as the need for vitamin $B_3$. In pellagra there is a failure in the delivery of the precursors of the essential amino acid tryptophane, vitamin $B_3$, and $B_6$ (pyridoxine) in the diet. In schizophrenia there is an internal failure inasmuch as the body does not deliver enough of the enzyme NAD to the brain. In the actual treatment of pellagra and schizophrenia, much less $B_3$ is needed in the former than in the latter state. There are many components situated along the metabolic pathway in the human body that are essential to the delivery of the finished product, which is mental energy. A block at any point in the chain causes the entire assembly line to break down. This block may be due to dietary lack, malabsorption from the intestinal tract, food allergy, toxic chemicals ingested with foods, or even a missing hereditary gene.

Also of prime importance in the function of the brain is the adequate delivery of glucose. This brings up the relationship of the adaptation-exhaustion syndrome and states of mental confusion. It has been estimated that a disorder of carbohydrate metabolism similar to that connected with the adaptation-exhaustion syndrome is present in nearly 75 percent of all schizophrenic patients. A deficiency of glutamic acid, another amino acid, has also been found to play a part in brain malfunction.

The HOD (Hoffer and Osmund Diagnostic) test is highly useful in following the progress of individuals with schizophrenic tendencies. This test consists of a set of 145 cards containing statements worded in such a way that responses enable evaluation of visual, auditory, touch, taste, olfactory, and time perceptions as well as thought and mood disturbances. When the biochemistry of the brain is altered away from the norm, changes in the above-mentioned areas become apparent.

### Intracellular-Level Growth Processes

The research work of famed biochemist Ernest Anderson has been filmed by time-lapse photography and shows growth processes at the intracellular level. It brings out a number of very important points. Proper development of plant and animal cells is impossible unless metals, at least in a large part, exist in combination with organic substances that are acceptable to the cell and in harmony with the thousands of enzyme reactions operating within the cell's structure.

One part of the film reveals the nutrients needed for cell life and the formation of cell membranes. At one point these ingredients are flowing clockwise to get in proper position for absorption, and then a moment later the direction mysteriously changes. One can imagine how the slightest interruption of these movements would change the composition of the cell's interior or how the absence of one ingredient could destroy cellular function.

In another part of the film, a tiny bit of poison—only one part per 30,000,000 parts—is added. Quickly the movement of the cells changes—first speeding up in frenzied fashion, as though trying to escape all contact with the antagonist, then the latter begins to take its toll and the metabolic system slows down. Partly formed cells begin to disintegrate and the approach of death is evident.

Other interesting findings that are comparatively new concepts are coming out of these intracellular analyses. On determination of blood chemistry findings, the values have generally been considered as falling either into a normal range or not, but research into intracellular analyses also reveals that ratios of one element to another are equally important. For instance, the ratio of calcium to magnesium should be roughly 8 to 1, that of sodium to potassium roughly 2.4 to 1.

Most important of all is sodium and potassium balance, since these minerals control the movement of all fluids and minerals into and out of the cells and are responsible for the nourishment of the cells and for the elimination of their waste products. Intracellular analysis is beginning to clarify the role of some of the minerals that have long been known to be necessary to humans but whose role had previously not been clarified.

Let us illustrate the use of the hair analysis with the case of S.D., a thirty-six-year-old married woman who was seen for extremely severe and disabling headaches, allergies, and severe depression almost to the point of suicide. She had been treated for sixteen months for the adaptation-exhaustion syndrome on a changed diet, food supplements, and homeopathic medications as well as adrenal cortex extract. There was considerable improvement, but a plateau was reached at this time.

Hair analysis revealed low sodium and potassium values, but the ratio was nearly normal. Calcium and magnesium were both quite low, though again the ratio was near normal. Iron and manganese were both low. Lead was not elevated. She was given chelated calcium, magnesium, iron, and manganese. She was also advised to increase her use of salt. One month later, she reported that within a few days she felt much more calm and all body odor had disappeared. Within another month, she noted great improvement and had only one headache. This is a very sketchily drawn case, but with the multiple types of treatment that I am employing it is difficult to single out clear evidence in favor of one facet of the treatment over another. This determining of causes needs to be done in a controlled scientific study. But I strongly believe that this new area of therapy will eventually occupy an honored place as a complement to nutrition in aiding human resistance to disease.

## Body Acceptance of Foods and Supplements

The foregoing discussion points to a great importance of the body's ability to be able to accept the foods and supplements we offer it. First, we might ask, Is the food formula balanced and as nearly complete as our knowledge at this time can make it? For instance, does the vitamin preparation contain sufficient vitamin $B_{12}$ (cobalamine), which is quite expensive and, therefore, in many vitamin formulas low in amount, in order to save the manufacturer money? Dr. Pescetti points out, as an example, that if the body is supplied a supplement containing chelated copper, 0.1 mg., the liver will start to put out its own $B_{12}$, and if to this is added 25 mcg. of $B_{12}$, the output of the liver will be increased two to threefold. This is particularly important with older people, whose stomachs may be deficient in hydrochloric acid, or people who have had partial surgical removal of the stomach. Vitamin $B_{12}$ is a necessary part of the chain of agents needed for the conversion of proteins into nucleoproteins, an essential part of the DNA molecule. The chain is never stronger than its weakest link, so that if one part is deficient, the chain cannot carry through to its anticipated end point.

Dr. Pescetti feels that manufacturers of vitamins and other food supplements should approach nature as closely as possible. In his manufacturing of vitamin E, for instance, he has determined the most biologically active ingredients and has arranged them in combinations closely approaching the natural state. He has also discovered that vitamins can be processed without the use of heat and thereby retain a biological potency otherwise not possible.

For the above reasons it would seem that the use of natural foods very high in vitamin content such as brewer's yeast, sesame meal, or wheat germ should usually be used along with other vitamins to make up for deficiencies in the manufactured brands, especially if the latter are the largely synthetic ones.

It is frequently difficult to tell from labels whether a product is made from natural or synthetic sources. However, in general, if the name is a chemical name such as thiamin, it is a synthetic, while if it reads "thiamin (yeast)," it is derived partially from a natural source.

For example, labels reading "vitamin C from rose hips" can be very misleading because in a 500 mg. tablet often 490 mgs. is synthetic ascorbic acid and only 10 mg. is vitamin C from rose hips.

It is a very interesting fact, however, that if even a small fraction of the natural vitamin is present in a largely synthetic vitamin tablet, it enhances the biological value of the synthetic vitamin, according to Dr. Pescetti. This is somewhat analogous to the homeopathic principle of adding milk sugar pellets to a tiny amount of another homeopathic preparation. The newly constituted resulting preparation becomes identical to the original in its therapeutic activity.

In the case of vitamin C, there is increasing evidence that the added naturally occurring bioflavinoids enhance the value of vitamin C. I would think it safe to say that the presence of some of any vitamin in the natural state will greatly enhance the therapeutic value of the vitamin and make the needed doses considerably smaller. When we are using natural sources, we are also using fractions that science may not yet have analyzed. Essentially, the body does not ask whether a vitamin is natural or synthetic, and it has been found that excellent results may be obtained by combining the two.

We conclude this chapter with some practical suggestions about nutrition.

### Bread

Bread has been considered by many as the "staff of life." Modern advertising still likes to present this picture, even though the facts are to the contrary. This is well illustrated by an experiment carried out by Dr. Roger J. Williams on a group of rats.[11] Of four different strains, 1,281 in all, one-half of them were fed on commercially enriched bread and the other half were fed on bread containing a balanced formula of vitamin, mineral, and amino acids. The two breads looked alike.

Among the rats fed commercially enriched bread, two-thirds were dead of malnutrition within ninety days and the others were severely stunted in growth. The rats on the improved formula, which at wholesale rates would cost only a fraction of a cent more to produce, did surprisingly well. Their growth was seven times as fast as those on the commercial bread. Yet we are led by advertising to feed the latter product to our children! This same "enriched" flour is the basis of cakes, crackers, pastries, doughnuts, macaroni, and so on.

In a recent conversation Dr. Pescetti described the making of bread by his mother as she, in turn, had been taught by her mother in Italy. It took all day and was baked at a very low temperature for four to five hours, using home-grown yeast. In his opinion commercial white bread as we buy it today has absolutely no nutritional value and is a far cry from the "staff of life." We should be concerned that the milling industry is so little interested in our national health that nutritional values in the product are sacrificed to low production costs.

## Milk

We have long been led to believe that pasteurized milk is superior to raw milk. In his time Pasteur performed a great service by cutting down the incidence of milk-borne diseases such as typhoid fever, bacterial dysentery, undulant fever, and tuberculosis. However, today with the certification of raw milk, we have a very safe product that is nutritionally far superior to pasteurized milk.

Milk processors today add vitamin D, iron, and vitamins $B_1$, $B_2$, and $B_6$ to their product. In the process of pasteurization and homogenization, the required temperatures are extremely high, and, as a result, very little of a true biological value remains in the product.

The body can assimilate only a trace of calcium (of the type found in homogenized pasteurized milk). Dr. Pescetti feels that dental caries are largely related to the body's lack of the ability to assimilate calcium, magnesium, phosphorus, and zinc in the bone structure. He has seen supplementation of these elements, when administered in a chelated form, restore to normal a destroyed bone structure in six months. Sugar, he feels, is a contributing factor to dental caries when the teeth already are deprived of the above-mentioned essential minerals. This is because the deficiency results in soft enamel that is easily penetrated by sugar.

Dr. Francis Pottenger, Jr., has done many experiments on the effects of raw meat and milk versus cooked meat and pasteurized, vitamin-D-enriched milk on the diet of cats. He reports:

> Cats receiving raw milk and raw meat reproduced homogeneity from one generation to the next. Abortion was uncommon, litters averaged five, and the mother cats nursed their young in a normal manner. Cats receiving cooked meat scraps reproduced a heterogenous strain of kittens, each one having a different skeletal pattern, abortion running about 25 percent in the first generation and 70 percent in the second! Deliveries were difficult and many cats died in labor. Mortality rates were high, often the kitten was too frail to nurse. The females were dangerous to handle and irritable, being more prone to bite their keeper. Many diseases seen in humans, both of infectious and degenerative nature, were present.[12]

These findings were instigated by Dr. Pottenger's observation that there was considerable mortality among cats upon whom he was doing adrenalectomies for the purpose of standardizing adrenal cortical extracts. The reason was found to be the use of cooked meat scraps from their sanitarium. This certainly makes one wonder about the possible relation of this factor to cardiac arrests (heart stops) in modern human surgery. Ought we not investigate to determine if there is any correlation between these near deaths in humans and their high cooked meat consumption?

## Cooking Methods

In general, it is not advisable in cooking or processing to use high temperatures, which are very destructive of the essential nutrients in food. Processing any food with heat profoundly alters the food value. It destroys the enzymes and vitamins and changes the food's nature. The higher the temperature and the longer it is maintained, the greater the destruction. Low-temperature cooking is far superior and keeps the food crisp and tasty. (If vegetables are cut into small pieces, less heat is required in the cooking process.)

It is interesting to note in this connection that the white-cell count of the blood is not altered by a meal of raw foods but is usually raised by a meal of cooked food, as the policeman-like white cells are mobilized to handle the emergency. When the food also contains preservatives, the different types of white blood cells alter their normal ratios, showing a still greater disturbance of human physiology. This well illustrates how improperly prepared foods interfere with the body homeostasis mechanisms. Cooked foods when eaten along with raw foods are more acceptable.

When the source of vegetables and fruits is unknown, thorough cleansing is of the greatest importance to remove, as much as possible, any injurious sprays. The Bircher-Benner clinic suggests scrubbing the root vegetables with a brush under running water, then peeling them and putting them into cold water to which salt and lemon juice have been added to retain the natural vegetable color.

## Bowel Movements

In my own medical practice, I rarely find it necessary to prescribe cathartics or enemas for other than bed patients. Promoting the idea that a bowel movement should occur at a certain time every day misconstrues the truth of the matter. Every individual is different. Some individuals will have a movement every day, regularly as clockwork, others two a day, others one every other day. To skip a day or even two occasionally is certainly harmless and no cause for concern.

Just the worry and fear of constipation or some other imagined consequence, on the other hand, causes a body tension that in itself can have an inhibiting effect upon one's normal daily rhythms. A daily exercise program tends to promote regularity, as does a regular, liberal consumption of raw vegetables. Undiscovered hypothyroidism (thyroid underactivity) is frequently associated with a pathological type of constipation.

### Proper Utilization of Food

Supposing now that one has set up a good nutritional program, we must still consider other factors to assure its proper utilization. Of first importance is the proper crushing of the food so that there will be adequate surfaces for the digestive juices to get at the food particles. Obviously this is a dental problem and means proper opposition of teeth or dental plates that can satisfactorily masticate the food and allow sufficient time to carry out this process.

Next, the absorption of the food intake is of utmost importance and often is overlooked, particularly in the older age group. When should improper absorption be suspected? Possibly one of the first clues is the onset of indigestion soon after eating, which should always raise the question of the absence of hydrochloric acid in the stomach. This acid is one of the essentials in starting the process of digestion.

Also, the person who is habitually underweight and just can't gain, even though he seems to be consuming an adequate quantity of correct foods, should investigate the lack of hydrochloric acid in the stomach as a possible cause. Hydrochloric acid and pepsin are necessary to start the digestion of the proteins and to ensure the retention of calcium in the system. They also have effects on the utilization of vitamins and minerals. Their presence can be easily verified by a simple test that no longer requires the oral insertion of a stomach tube.

As ingested food enters the small intestine, sufficient juices and bile must be liberated from the pancreas and small bowel wall to carry on the individual digestion of the carbohydrates, proteins, and fats and also to emulsify the fats. Another clue to malfunction in this area, besides the indigestion and distention that may follow a meal, is the presence of undigested food particles or whole pills in the feces.

Late distention of the lower abdomen may be associated with the lack of the acidophilus bacillus, which is very necessary for the synthesis of parts of vitamin B and normal large-bowel activity in the normal intestinal bacterial flora. These important bacteria are frequently destroyed when antibiotics are used for any length of time and should be replaced by adding acidophilus culture to milk or by the use of buttermilk or a good quality of yogurt.

Another less common form of malabsorption known as nontropical sprue is associated with stools that are dishwater type (very rarely formed) that float on water and show evidence of oil or fats that have not been assimilated. This is treated with folic acid and a gluten-free diet.

## Attitudes toward Nutrition

Nutrition and food absorption are profoundly related to the state of mind. Many guests coming to Meadowlark have brainwashed themselves into malnutrition by strong prejudices as to what they can and cannot eat. One cannot eat anything raw; another can't eat anything cooked. One can't eat proteins and carbohydrates in the same meal; another can't eat tomatoes, onions, strawberries, and so on.

It is amazing how a complete change from the associations with home, job, certain associates, and a little letting-go of responsibilities and instruction in relaxation techniques can have these people piling their plates with many of the "forbidden" foods within three to four days. Homeostasis in the new context brings about the disappearance of many allergies. A meal of natural, unadulterated foods, taken in a relaxed fashion with new friends who also are seeking solutions to life problems, can be a healing experience!


### Tips on Vitamin Use

Should one take vitamin, mineral, and protein supplements? Here are a few questions that you might find helpful in obtaining an answer:

1. Do you consider yourself in robust health?
2. How closely do you follow the recommended diet of the preceding section?
3. Do you eat an adequate amount of raw fresh vegetables? Are these raised without the use of sprays? how soon after picking are they consumed? Are they raised from a rotated soil using natural fertilizers?
4. Are most of your meals eaten at home where you have better knowledge of the sources of your foods and can control cooking temperatures, or do you eat in restaurants or other facilities where you cannot know about these factors?

If you can give favorable response to these questions, possibly there may be certain times of the year when added vitamins may not be necessary, but for the most part I would not want to be without these supplements. I can only say that in the last year or two, when I have been very aware of some of the information that I have been passing on, much of it obtained in Europe where nutrition occupies a far greater place in the practice of medicine, my energy has been definitely better than in the past.

The decision on choosing your vitamin supplement should ideally be made with the help of a nutritionally oriented physician, biochemist, or nutritionist. In general, if you are in moderately good health, you might refer to the report of the Food and Nutrition Board of the National Academy of Sciences in which are suggested values.[13] Possibly multiply them by three as, in their determination, prevention of actual recognized vitamin deficiency disease states such as scurvy, pellagra, and rickets was the objective rather than the less understood subclinical levels of vitamin deficiency that are so prevalent today.

Then, since they have scarcely admitted that vitamin E is important,[14] be sure to include at least 200 units of d-alpha tocopherol succinate if you are below 30 years old and 400 if over, and 1,200-1,400 if you have had a heart attack or have known heart disease. Do not take more than 100 units if you have high blood pressure or rheumatic heart disease. Also it may be wise to take more vitamin C than recommended, possibly in the neighborhood of 1,500 to 5,000 units a day, divided into four equal doses. If you can get the timed-release formula, that is best.

Remember that minerals, too, are very important, especially in the chelated form, which permits much more ready acceptance by the body. These should include sodium, calcium, magnesium, potassium, copper, zinc, iodine, manganese, chromium and molybdenum; probably others will be discovered to be needed in infinitesimally small amounts. Kelp is a very good source of these minerals.

### Four Tips on Good Nutrition

1. Include as high a percentage of fresh raw vegetables and fruit as possible in your diet. This should at all times be in excess of 50 percent of the total intake, and in case of illness should approach 100 percent and include fresh vegetable juices. Fresh raw seeds (especially sunflower, sesame, and pumpkin), nuts, wheat germ, and brewer's yeast are also valuable.

2. Avoid processed, packaged, or canned foods as much as possible, especially those made of or containing white sugar and/or flour. Vegetables that require cooking (steaming is the best method) should be given the minimum of cooking time to avoid loss of vitamins, minerals, and enzymes. But remember that *most* vegetables can be eaten raw.

*Whole grain* breads and cereals provide good nutrition. Also avoid fried foods, preserves, chemical preservatives and sprays, artificial sweeteners, coffee, tea, cocoa, chocolate, and all carbonated beverages. With proper nutrition, one no longer has any desire or need for stimulants. Herb teas are found to be much more interesting.

3. Begin each meal with a raw food, such as a salad, fresh vegetable juice, or fruit. This has been found to result in the most effective digestion. The proteins in fresh, green leaves, whole grains, and seeds provide excellent nutrition. Research indicates that homogenized-pasteurized milk is of lower nutritional value than certified raw milk, buttermilk, yogurt, cottage cheese, and natural cheese. Avoid processed cheese.

If there has been an allergy to milk as an infant, eczema as a child or nasal allergies with much catarrh and mucous formation, it is well worth trying the effect of leaving milk out of the diet for a month or two and see if there is a general improvement in the picture.

4. Do not be discouraged if changes in health are not immediately apparent. Lasting improvement, however, is the result of patient and persistent following of the new way of living. One is often surprised by the rapidity with which changes sometimes do occur. Although nutrition is not the only factor in high-level physical well-being, it is very important. Maximal health without good nutrition is impossible.

We now turn our attention to the topic of exercise, another factor that contributes in an important way to one's state of well-being.

# 4

## ON EXERCISE

Better to hunt in field, for health unbought,
Than fee the doctor for a nauseous draught.
The wise for cure, on exercise depend;
God never made his work for men to mend.[1]
                                    John Dryden

If you are troubled with too frequent colds or flu, have backaches, are plagued with insomnia, have had heart trouble, high blood pressure, stomach ulcers, arthritis, varicose veins, diabetes, periods of depression, or are just plain overweight, it is time that you gave serious consideration to the kind and amount of exercise you are getting. If you are chronically tired but are not obviously overworking yourself, then it is not more sleep that you need but, among other things, more exercise.

### Muscle Use

Life in a world geared toward maximum physical comfort is costing us dearly. We have already considered at some length what alterations of our foods are doing to today's national health picture. Alongside nutrition is the need for exercise, because of its effect on blood circulation and the supply of oxygen, both of which are essential in the utilization of foods.

Food never tastes quite as good as it does after a long hike in the wilderness when we have been breathing in plenty of fresh, unpolluted air. This type of exercise also stimulates the taste for natural and simple foods. The sedentary type of life, replete with stimulants, alters and perverts the taste sense so that our bodies lose their ability to crave the foods they need.

Automobiles and motorcycles have largely replaced walking. Many modern suburbs lack sidewalks, while city parks have become unsafe places. The brave individual who wishes to take a walk near his home has to dodge automobiles.

As a medical student in New York City, I was fortunate not to have been able to afford a car and to have had parents who loved to walk in the beautiful wooded hills of northern New Jersey. The result was that once a day, for the two years I lived with my uncle and aunt on New York's West Side near the Hudson River, I had the opportunity of walking some five miles each way to school. The other two years I shared an apartment on the East Side a little closer to school. It was on the fifth story and there was no elevator, so that running up and down stairs was a regular source of exercise. Now in my sixties I still make it a practice to run up to the third or fourth floor in the local hospital on the days when I do not have time for my morning jog.

Not only are there indications that leg muscles are atrophying from disuse, but similarly our arms and hands are also getting little exercise. The advent of television has made it considerably more fashionable to sit at home and watch sports than actively to take part in them. Hedge clippers, lawn mowers, and saws are now motor-powered.

This modern, comfort age has even had its effect on sports. A man used to go out on the weekend for nine to eighteen holes of golf and to be refreshed by the exercise it affords.

Today many drive to the club house, rent an electric golf cart, and ride over the course, bravely getting out of the cart at the point where the golf ball rests, bracing their legs to support their gathering avoirdupois. After a few hours they walk back into the club house exhausted by their strenuous morning, to find renewed strength in a couple of cocktails.

In the previous century, daily exercise was demanded by living, and, as a consequence, heart attack, stroke, and other forms of degenerative disease were by no means the threat to life they are today. Neither were mental health problems as prevalent. The percentage of young men today unable to pass a simple physical examination making them eligible for military service is far greater than it was a few decades ago. There is much evidence that today's young men would rather use a motorized vehicle than their own muscles to express their aggressive, adolescent feelings.

There is a very direct correlation between lack of physical exercise and premature aging. Many forty-year-old men today could pass for sixty, and physical examinations reveal marked evidence of hardening of the arteries and elevation of blood cholesterols, both of which indicate circulatory breakdown. Seldom, if ever, do I see any individual with elevated blood cholesterol who carries out an exercise program such as I will describe. It has been my frequent observation that, with adequate exercise, there is less need to observe a low cholesterol type of diet.

When smoking of tobacco is added to the lack of exercise, there is a lessened resistance to disease and a further significant drop in life expectancy. The suggested exercise programs frequently cannot be followed through because of poor tolerance due to lack of stamina, shortness of breath, and troublesome coughing.

Early in my medical career I spent five years working with the fishermen of northern Newfoundland and another two years in the interior of China and found in both places a relative absence of degenerative diseases. The fisherman's life on the stormy North Atlantic was one of hard exercise all day long. In the winter, he had to go out daily ten miles or more on his dog sled to cut enough wood to heat his house. During these seven years I can recall seeing only three cases of myocardial infarction (heart attacks). In Newfoundland, one was the sedentary local magistrate and the second was one of the principal merchants. In China it was the secretary of the local chamber of commerce—again, a very wealthy merchant.

The Chinese in rural Yunnan province were farmers and traders and thought nothing of walking, or practically running, many miles with loads weighing 200 to 300 pounds. They had a very definite feeling of rhythm associated with their exercise, and there is little doubt that this increased their work output. This same feeling can well be applied in our own jogging or running or swimming practice.

At this point one might well ask, "How is all this exercise going to benefit my health?"

In the first place, physical deterioration is most evident in the circulatory system. The food we eat must reach the "factory," that is, individual cells, because it is here that the food will be converted into the energy needed to carry on our daily living. The return circulation from legs to heart and lungs is, to a great extent, dependent on the muscle tone of the leg muscles. An active circulation promoted by a good exercise program and proper breathing habits tends to keep the blood vessels clear and free from atheromatous (cholesterol-containing) fatty deposits, and it also maintains a healthy, balanced tone in the valves and muscular walls of the smaller vessels of our limbs and internal organs.

### Breathing

In addition to food the cells must be supplied with adequate oxygen from the lungs, because oxygen is necessary for any type of combustion and, so, is essential in the conversion of food to energy. While the body can store food, it cannot store oxygen, so good breathing habits are of utmost import. Comparatively few people really know how to breathe properly. They think that to inhale they must throw out their chests and pull in their bellies. The opposite is true, as every trained singer knows. The expansion of the lungs through chest breathing is very limited due to the rigidity of the bony ribs, whereas action by the muscular diaphragm, the movement of which is accompanied by an inward motion of the abdominal wall, allows much greater compression of the lungs and thus far more chance to ventilate air.

Breathing can be much more than a physical exercise, particularly since breath is symbolic of the whole of life. Life is ushered in with the first breath, yet how little attention we Westerners pay to this basic movement of life. One's confidence in life is actually expressed in his pattern of breathing. Physically it is manifested in body control, mentally in increased clarity of thinking, and spiritually it radiates something of one's faith in the Giver of Life.

The breath, too, should be of sufficient depth to supply the oxygen needed to make possible the chemical reactions that are involved in the life processes. The body needs, not only this oxygen, but also the atmospheric ions present in the air. Who can be unaware of the greater healing effects of mountain or sea air as compared with the smog-laden air of cities? Breathing should be accompanied by an awareness of a breathing-in of the subtle energies of the universe (the yogi's *prana*) that are capable of augmenting one's own life's energies.

There are many breathing patterns: the fast, staccato, loud breathing of an angry man; the rapid, somewhat uneven breathing of the anxious, fearful person; the gasping breathing of an unconditioned body under stress; the very shallow breathing of one who has lived on the "surface of life." If these patterns are carried further to the realm of the sick person, we observe the fast breathing of the patient who is ill with pneumonia or with high fever, both of which are associated with extreme anxiety and frustration.

Then, there are the patterns of people suffering from

asthma and emphysema, who appear to have major respiratory problems usually associated with a lack of understanding of the use of the diaphragm in breathing. These are frequently accompanied by the bronchial spasm, which adds to the difficulties of expiration and is associated with emotional problems.

Correct breathing must start in the consciousness, which is under the control of the personal will or the ego and which operates quite apart from the Real Self, with its intimate connections with the life-giving energies and fundamental rhythms of the universe. As previously indicated, all too often the diaphragm is neglected in breathing, with the result that the chest muscles are called upon to assume the major role in this important act. The ribs can only rotate in movement and so allow very little expansion for the lungs in inhalation. Observe your own breathing, with one hand placed with the fingers on the abdomen just below the ribs and the thumb extending around the side. As you breathe in, see how much the abdomen is sucked in and how much the chest moves. With correct breathing, the chest should not be responsible for more than one-quarter to one-third of the motion felt. Exhaling as completely as possible with a real emptying of the lungs requires diaphragmatic muscle power and is an expression of one's life force, or *prana*, and should take longer than the inhalation, which is merely sucking in—a passive act.

Having now observed the phenomenon of breathing in health and illness, let us turn our attention to good breathing habits. The learning pattern may be divided into three stages. The first is becoming concerned with and conscious of the physical act of correct breathing. The second is given over to recognizing one's self in wrong breathing and beginning to breathe without the participation of the will. The third step is a personal relinquishment of the act of breathing so that "I" (ego) no longer breathes but rather "I" is "breathed through."

Breathing exercises should be practiced daily in a quiet place where one may be undisturbed. The position may be in a straight-backed chair, high enough so that the knees are not above the pelvis, and with both feet on the ground. The back should be perfectly straight, yet not forced upward, with shoulders relaxed and arms loose at the sides. Some may prefer the lotus or the half-lotus position. The best time for practice is when the stomach is empty, either in the early morning or just before dinner at night.

It is well to drink a glass of water first to empty the stomach because there should be no gas present to stimulate the vagus nerve in an unfavorable way. A nearby open window is desirable. Begin to breathe slowly and deeply, the lips closed, remembering that breathing is not just a movement in and out of air, but a fundamental movement of a living being that affects the world of the body as well as regions of the soul and mind.

At the outset, counting the breaths in some such manner as this is helpful: "*In*, one, two, three; *hold*, one, two; *out*, one, two, three, four; *hold*, one, two; *in*, one, two, three," and so on. To do this well takes diligent practice.

As one inhales, he will pull the abdomen in, then raise the lower chest, so to speak, with the primary movement coming from the raised diaphragm. Be sure the rib muscles, shoulders, and arms are still relaxed. With exhalation one should thrust the breath down so that the final pressure is felt in the lower abdomen. The attention should be placed particularly upon the exhaled breath. This phase should last longer than the inspiration, the latter becoming a mere reflex sucking in.

During practice, one concentrates completely on the counting, paying no attention to intruding thoughts. Don't even try to get rid of these; just keep on counting. The point of concentration should be directed away from the head to the area of the navel, for this tends to support the solar plexus, which is all-important to the adrenal gland function. After some months of practice, the counting will disappear and the breathing will be allowed to happen naturally. This involves the release of the mental or ego control and the allowing of oneself "to be breathed."

With the gradual handing over of the personal will—and

with it, the surrender of the ego—one hands over as well his fears and anxieties. With them goes much of the tension that is related to shallowness of breathing. The rewards of this relinquishment are tremendous as they usher in a new dimension of living in *faith*, which is the basis of the life lived by Christ and the prophets, or of Paul: "I no more live but Christ lives in me."

### Physical Fitness Program

About five years ago I became concerned about my own state of physical fitness. I was also giving thought to the part that exercise should play in a medicine of the Whole Person. Thomas Cureton's book, *Physical Fitness and Dynamic Health* came to my attention, and I eagerly plunged into it.[2] Discussing the nature and meaning of good physical condition, Cureton gives a Standard Test of Physical Fitness in which he suggests that any score below 100 can be considered a failure and is an indication of poor physical condition. I took it and miserably failed. My score was 65 out of a possible 195.

The next day I started my own physical fitness program, and I am still at it. It is an adaptation of Dr. Cureton's ideas plus those of the *Royal Canadian Air Force Exercise Plans for Physical Fitness*[3] and the suggestions of Dr. Kenneth Cooper in his book *Aerobics*.[4] Fourteen months after starting I once again took Dr. Cureton's test and made a slightly better score of 140. Now, on the average of five days a week, I do the Canadian program, maintaining at present the usual standards for a man ten years younger than myself.

The first two months of alternate walking and jogging for a mile was an uncomfortable experience because of the painful rebellion of my calf muscles. Then this slowly disappeared, and I found that I was able to jog the mile. At first, my time was 9 minutes and 50 seconds. After a month this came down to 8:40, where it pretty well stayed. There would be times,

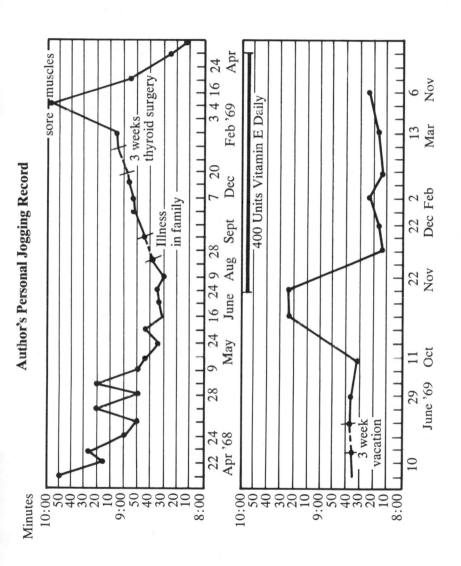

**Author's Personal Jogging Record**

however, when my biological rhythm (see Chapter 5) was such that I would not try to do the usual amount of jogging and would settle for just walking and enjoying the natural beauty of our Friendly Hills ranch.

Knowing the value of vitamin E (d-alpha tocopherol) in making oxygen more available to the heart muscle, I began taking 400 units regularly in addition to a balanced vitamin formula and found that it wasn't long before my time on the mile improved from the plateau of 8:40 to 8:10-8:20, as can be seen on my jogging chart on page 91.

Before entering a program of exercise such as I have described, one should always have the approval of one's physician if one is over 50 years of age or has any heart problem or back condition or if there is any question about one's health. The program should be started gradually and should not be associated with certain types of competition, especially if one is older.

Maybe one can't get enthusiastic about walking or jogging if he lives in the city. Alternately, there is running-in-place, and standards for this are described in *Aerobics* or *Royal Canadian Air Force Exercise Plans for Physical Fitness* for women or for men. Or there are swimming and cycling programs, all of which are useful exercises for improving the heart muscle and circulation.

The question may well be asked, "What about the substitution of other type exercise programs such as weight-lifting, the use of various gadgets to strengthen certain groups of muscles without any actual movement of the limbs?" These may or may not have their place in developing specific weakened muscle groups, but they do not bring in as much fresh supply of oxygen for that most essential muscle, the heart.

### Benefits from the Program

Here is a list of some of the benefits that accrue from this type of program.

1. You will feel generally better.
2. Excess flabby fat will be replaced gradually by more solid tissue.
3. If you smoke, you will probably find that you will cut down on your smoking.
4. If you are nervous and have insomnia, you will become more calm and be able to sleep.
5. Certain heart conditions, notably angina, will improve.
6. If you are diabetic, you will need less insulin.
7. Blood pressure and pulse rates will lower.
8. Cholesterol level will drop.

In the last thirty years, medicine has made a radical about-face in regard to the matter of exercise. Formerly, the patients we operated on were kept practically immobile in bed. After hernia surgery, one was usually kept flat on his back for two weeks. Following childbirth, women were often kept in bed for a week or ten days.

All this has changed. Hernias and most other surgical cases are gotten out of bed as soon as possible, even on the day of operation. Arc thcy any the worse for it? Quite the contrary; they do much better with early exercise. There is much less postoperative pneumonia. Atelectasis (failure of a lung to expand because of a mucous plug in a bronchus), a formerly frequent complication, is now comparatively uncommon. Postoperative embolism is much less frequent, and catheterization of the bladder is rarely needed in those who get out of bed very early.

In the following pages (excerpted from Thomas Cureton's *Physical Fitness and Dynamic Health*) the reader will find a series of ten exercises designed to maintain general physical fitness. If you are in general good health and do not have a heart condition, you should be able to do these exercises, which are arranged in the form of tests.

### Standard Test of General Physical Fitness

Each of the tests is worth a certain number of points, if you are able to pass it. Take the entire battery of tests, and write your scores down as you go along. When you have finished, add up your scores to get your total. A perfect score is 200 points. The average is around 100 points. Any score below 100 can be considered a failure and is an indication of poor physical condition.

## Standard Test of General Physical Fitness

**1. SCORE: 25 POINTS**          YOUR SCORE: ___

Stand with your shoulders back and your chest expanded to the maximum degree. Measure the circumference of your chest just beneath your armpits. Then measure your waist, with your stomach in a relaxed position—not sucked in or forced out. Your chest should measure 5 inches more than your waist. (For women, the difference should be 10 inches.)

**2. SCORE: 10 POINTS**          YOUR SCORE: ___

Sit on the floor with your legs stretched out in front of you, and place an 8-inch-high book upright between your knees. Then, keeping your legs straight and flat on the floor, bend forward and touch your forehead to the top of the book.

**3. SCORE: 15 POINTS**          YOUR SCORE: ___

Stand on your toes, with your heels together, your eyes closed, and your arms extended forward at the shoulders. Stay in this position for 20 seconds without shifting your feet or opening your eyes.

**4. SCORE: 20 POINTS**     **YOUR SCORE:** __

Lie on your back with your hands behind your neck, and raise both legs to a vertical position without bending them at the knees. Then lower your legs to the floor, again without bending them at the knees. Repeat this 20 times successively.

**5. SCORE: 15 POINTS**     **YOUR SCORE:** __

Support your body stretched straight and sideways on one hand (with your arm held straight) and the outside of one foot. Place your other hand on your hip. Raise your upper leg to a horizontal position 25 times, without bending either knee.

**6. SCORE: 25 POINTS**     **YOUR SCORE:** __

Lying flat on your stomach, face down, with your fingers laced behind your neck and your feet pinned to the floor, raise your chin until it is 18 inches off the floor.

**7. SCORE: 10 POINTS**     **YOUR SCORE:** __

From a kneeling position, with the soles of your feet up and your arms stretched forward from the shoulders, swing arms down and up, jump to a standing position, and hold your balance. Both feet should come up together.

**8. SCORE: 20 POINTS**                   **YOUR SCORE:** ___

Lie on your back with your hands behind your neck, your legs straight, and free (not held down). Do 25 sit-ups without pausing for rest.

**9. SCORE: 10 POINTS**   **YOUR SCORE:** ___

Do a standing broad jump. Do *not* take a running start. The length of your jump should approximately equal your height.

**10. SCORE: 50 POINTS**                  **YOUR SCORE:** ___

Run in place for 60 seconds, lifting your feet at least 4 inches from the floor. Then take 3 deep breaths. Then hold your breath for 60 seconds.

How many of the above tests did you pass? What was your total score? A perfect score, as we said, is 200 points. The average is 100 points.

If your total is below 100, you are in poor shape and urgently in need of an intensive conditioning program. If you failed the last test, and any other two, you should seriously consider a physical conditioning program. Even if you did fairly well, a good conditioning program will enable you to hold on to your present condition, and even improve it.

There is always the fear of exercise in patients who have angina or who have had an attack of myocardial infarction. It is a known fact that exercise increases both muscular volume and strength, this being true of the heart muscle as it is of the other muscles of the body.

Many doctors who see numerous heart patients after a heart attack, are carrying out a program of "stress testing," which includes, for the most part, graduated walking on a treadmill with an increasing uphill gradient that is monitored by a continuous electrocardiographic tracing. According to these results, particular exercise programs are suggested. Patients are encouraged to carry out their exercise programs and then check their pulses, bringing the rate up by exercise to specified limits. If any symptoms such as chest pains occur, the exercise must be stopped. I have seen a number of patients with angina who are on this graduated exercise program and who are taking Vitamin E greatly reduce or eliminate their angina attacks.

Other forms of exercise that will fit into an aerobics program might include tennis, rowing, and canoeing. After Sig's and my summer vacation trips to the lakes or mountains, we come back completely renewed—physically, emotionally, and spiritually.

As the body responds positively to good nutrition, so also it responds when the lungs are deeply filled with pure air. Sea or mountain air, along with the emotional exhilaration of such an environment, adds another inexplicable dimension of health. As naturalist John Muir so aptly put it, "Wilderness is a necessity. . . . mountain parks and reservations are useful not only as fountains of timber and irrigating rivers but as fountains of life."[5]

In this and the preceding chapter, we have dealt with practices that lead to good health. Now we look inward to the amazing regulatory system for maintaining harmony known as the endocrine glands.

# 5

## ON THE ENDOCRINE ORCHESTRA

Hence there is then in the system [endocrine] that
activity of the soul, that is the gift of the Creator
to man. . . .

Edgar Cayce[1]

In this chapter we shall deal with what I like to describe as
the endocrine orchestra. Along with the closely allied au-
tonomic (involuntary) nervous system, it takes information
from the brain integrated with subtle signals from Nature's
clock and carries these to the body cells to produce the
rhythmic music of life.

Let us picture the orchestra as follows: First, we must have
a composer. The composer is the midportion of the brain,
known as the hypothalamus. Its job is to contact its surroundings and pick up the appropriate tune. It passes this on to the
conductor of the orchestra, the pituitary gland. Our body
cells, by aid of hormones, are the instruments.

The word *hormone* comes from the same root as the
word *harmony*. Harmony in human beings is very dependent

on the harmonious function of hormones, which depend very much on a mind at peace. Hormones operate through the mediation of our brain. We know that the brain functions both consciously and subconsciously. The conscious functions are under the direct control of the cerebral cortex, and the subconscious functions control the various organs of our body. These are thought to be mediated through the hypothalamus and the nearby basal ganglia.

Under ordinary conditions one does not have control of his subconscious activities, but through training and strict disciplines these can be partly brought under voluntary control. Acts that we frequently repeat—such as many of the maneuvers associated with driving a car—are gradually shifted into the realm of subconscious response.

## The Pituitary Gland

The pituitary gland has often been referred to as the master gland because of its important job as controller of the other glands. It is composed of two parts. One of nervous origin—the posterior lobe—is concerned with water balance in the body and also with the contraction of smooth (involuntary) muscle fibers that are found in such parts of the body as the walls of blood vessels and the uterus. Then there is the very important anterior lobe of the pituitary, which puts out trophic hormones, the stimulators of the functions of the various glands.

A few of these important hormones produced by the various cells found in that portion of the pituitary include the adrenocorticotropic hormones (ACTH), which stimulate that portion of the adrenal gland known as the cortex; the thyrotropic, which stimulate the thyroid gland; the gonadotrophic, which exert their action on the testes and ovaries; and the lactogenic hormones, which stimulate the production of milk in the breasts of pregnant women.

## The Adrenal Glands

These two vitally important glands are situated on top of the kidneys and are composed of two principal parts: (1) the inner medulla portion, which secretes adrenalin, which gives us that spurt of energy so necessary in an emergency, and (2) the outer cortex. The cortex has many and varied functions. Approximately fifty different hormones have been isolated from it, the best-known being cortisol, or cortisone.

These hormones are divided into groups: (1) the glucocorticoids, which have to do with the use of sugars in the body, and (2) the mineral corticoids, which perform various functions including establishing the balance between sodium and potassium—two elements very essential to the body's economy. These two groups of hormones are important to the movement of fluids containing minerals and food into and out of the cells. Deviations from the norm in their proportions can quickly cause a severe disturbance.

Potassium is the all-important intracellular component of the team, while sodium is found in the spaces between the cells, referred to as the extracellular compartments of the body. If their proper ratio, for any reason, is upset, the balance of other minerals important to the vital intracellular processes will be disturbed. Thus, the movement of calcium, magnesium, iron, manganese, zinc, and copper is very significant in sustaining the cell's metabolic functions.

In our present day of deadlines and stresses, we should be very thankful to Dr. Hans Selye for his outstanding research into the understanding of the body's response to stress, which has opened up new avenues of treatment. In his book *The Stress of Life*, he describes the three stages of this mechanism: first, the alarm reaction; then the stage of adaptation; and finally, if the stress is not handled, a stage of exhaustion, which could even be followed by death.[2]

The alarm reaction is responsible for the release of adrenalin by a portion of the adrenal gland known as the medulla.

This, through a typical endocrine feedback system, causes the anterior portion of the pituitary to release ACTH, which, in turn, stimulates the adrenal cortex to release cortisol. The first step of adrenal release is responsible for the liver's conversion of its stored glycogen to glucose. The cortisol is then called upon in connection with the body's conversion of this glucose to energy and, in the process, makes more glucose available through the conversion of protein into glucose.

Each person has his or her own target organ that will bear the brunt of this stress mechanism. It might be the vascular system in those with high blood pressure, or the stomach or duodenum in those with an ulcer.

## The Thyroid Gland

The next gland of great importance to health is the thyroid. This has long been studied by physicians because of its prominent position in the neck and its predilection, in areas of the world where iodine is scarce, to form goiters. Deficiencies of this gland are also very frequently present. People who feel sluggish and, particularly those who have a hard time getting started in the morning, yet can stay up to the wee hours, should investigate thyroid deficiency as a possible cause.

The thyroid is a very important gland in stoking the metabolic fire and maintaining body heat. Some of the common symptoms of its deficiency in addition to sensitivity to cold weather are lack of energy, excessively dry skin, brittle finger nails, falling hair, and puffiness of the eyelids or fingers in the morning.

This gland is a very important consideration when analyzing and dealing with children who are retarded in various phases of their development, such as not sitting up, walking, talking, or erupting their infant teeth at the usual time.

The tests for this condition are many, though none is really completely effective.[3] Unfortunately, there are a number of factors that can cause false readings, such as the birth control pill, estrogens used to treat menopause, certain types of diagnostic x-ray procedures, extraneous sources of iodine in the diet or in vitamin pills, and certain drugs such as aspirin.

In addition, we must realize that what really interests us is not how much thyroid extract is circulating in the bloodstream but how much is active in the metabolic process that takes place within the cell.

Today the salient part of the endocrine diagnosis is a carefully taken history and a few clinical observations. The blood tests have their importance, but they are not primary and should be used only to confirm our clinical impressions. If one relies entirely on the blood reports, he will miss many endocrine problems. When we test the blood and do a urine analysis, it is like trying to determine what is going on in the engine of an automobile by analyzing the gasoline in the carburetor or a sample of the exhaust fumes. Such a test can by no means provide the complete picture. One must raise the hood and investigate the engine itself.

An interesting advance in the treatment of thyroid deficiencies has been made by Dr. Murray Israel in his observation of the relationship of this condition to the genesis of arteriosclerosis.[4] His work has been responsible for inducing a group of doctors to study the process of aging. He has successfully treated thousands of people who needed thyroid but didn't know it. Approximately 80 percent of them had had normal thyroid tests results!

He has had particularly notable success in helping people with diabetes who were heading toward blindness from the effects of arteriosclerosis of the vessels of the retina. This cannot be done simply by the addition of thyroid extract but must be accompanied by supplemental vitamins, particularly of the B complex, whose absorption must be assured. The dose of thyroid must be very carefully titrated because many of these patients will require only a very small dose and may be made worse by taking too much.

Three cases illustrating the importance of the nutritional-endocrine balance are cited here:

## Marion, Age 33

The first indication that something was wrong with my health came about three years ago when I was thirty years old. I began to have "weak" spells, usually around eleven in the morning. I would be going along just fine and all of a sudden I would feel so ill and faint and weak that I was not able to stand. I found that if I ate something sweet right away, I regained my energy in a few moments and then could go on and prepare lunch for myself and my family. After experiencing about five of these spells, I decided it was time to consult my doctor.

It was first thought that I had a tumor on the spine, so I was sent to a large hospital in a town some fifty miles away, where I could have the services of neurological specialists. I was to undergo more tests and examinations, including a myelogram. I expected to have back surgery in two or three days. However, the myelogram test showed no tumor on the spine, so other examinations were made including another gtt. test.

The results of all the tests were given to me at the end of the week by the senior neurological specialist. The diagnosis was uncertain and it was felt that I might have multiple sclerosis or diabetes. I went home to my husband and family stunned. I couldn't even allow myself to think about the diagnosis. Every time I did, it was so frightening, I just didn't know how I could handle it. I felt I was so young, and with a husband to care for and a little girl to raise, it just didn't seem fair. I kept thinking "Why me?"

That evening Dr. Loomis called my husband and asked him to bring me in first thing in the morning. He had my reports, and still was very optimistic. He told my husband we would fight this illness and not to worry.

The next morning both my husband and I sat in Dr. Loomis's office. He told me he felt this was not diabetes. It was true that I had reached a very high sugar reading, but then it had dropped rapidly to a very low point, which is frequently seen in one form of hypoglycemia. The test did show that the low blood sugar situation was much worse than it had been two years before. This time there could be no cheating on my diet.

I was relieved to hear this because I did not want to have to start taking insulin, etc. However, the possibility of multiple sclerosis did frighten me quite a lot. We discussed this illness and what Dr. Loomis intended to do about it for me. He told me that he preferred not to label someone with an illness, like MS, but rather to refer to it as a metabolic disorder of the neurological system. And this is the way we would treat it—as a disorder which we, patient and doctor, would work to put back in order.

I was given a new diet to follow. Basically no meat, just fresh raw fruit and vegetables, milk, cheese, and eggs and natural, unprocessed foods. I also began taking very high dosages of certain vitamins, plus daily injections of certain B vitamins and adrenal cortex extract. I also began taking a homeopathic medicine to combat this illness.

This period was a very difficult time for me, probably the hardest period of my life. I saw Dr. Loomis once a week and always felt very optimistic and encouraged with these visits. But there were also times when I had to face my own private fears of becoming crippled and at times I was afraid that I would not improve, as I hoped I would.

It is hard to look back now and remember all this happened almost two years ago. I tend to forget the pain and the fear I suffered. This period was difficult, as I said, but in looking back it was also very inspiring. I gained much more of an insight into my life because of this illness. I discovered that I could not face any of this alone. I needed the help of my doctor, my husband, and my family. And most of all I needed the strength which only comes from God. I began to improve and I gave thanks each day for the life I had and for the love of the people around me, especially my husband, who was very helpful and protective with me.

I feel most of us take our good health for granted. When this illness struck me, I realized that the most precious thing in life is the very thing we take for granted—our bodies, our minds, our health. During the past year my illness has improved about 85 percent, but it has taken determination and a healthy, positive attitude toward life.

Also, we have made a very definite change in the eating habits of my family. Not just myself and my husband and child, but the rest of my family as well. We all grow vegetable gardens and we eat only natural, fresh foods. The health of the whole family has improved! Dr. Loomis had guided me through all of this and without his special knowledge and enthusiasm, I'm sure I could not have made so much progress.

I am not completely recovered as yet; I still have some problems with my leg and foot. But I hardly ever limp, and I am not in any pain, and I feel that I am continuing to improve all the time. The main thing is that I feel well. I am happy and satisfied with my life, my precious God-given life, which I value above everything on earth.

## Donald, Age 9

Mrs. V. W. (Donald's mother) was on a rather unsatisfactory diet (high in refined carbohydrates) during pregnancy, had pneumonia during the fifth month, and had a forced labor with pituitary extract. The baby boy cried immediately following birth. His development seemed normal the first two years. At two he became acutely frightened by noises, even that of the family's own auto terrified him. He stopped talking, withdrew, and slept a lot. His sentences regressed to only the use of single words, and he became markedly hyperkinetic (an abnormal type of ceaseless activity).[5] He drank a great deal of milk until age two and a half, and then refused it and started craving sugar. Then he had an unidentified virus infection with a temperature of 103 degrees, after which he just lay around for two weeks.

When I first saw Donald, I was confronted with a nine-year-old child who was pale of complexion and very frightened by the examination. Other than a positive Babinski's sign,[6] the examination showed little of significance. His electroencephalogram (EEG) exhibited seizure patterns, and he was thought to have petit mal. His parents indicated that he had been placed on many tranquilizers, mood elevators, and antihistamines without benefit. He sometimes cried and would hit himself with great frustration when, because of lack of speech, he couldn't make himself understood. The dietary history was very significant. Breakfast: beef, bacon, and ginger ale. Lunch: beef or egg yolk, cookie, potato chips or white bread, ginger ale. Dinner: meat, spaghetti, or pizza, bread, and ginger ale.

An attempt to change to a diet of vegetables was made and adrenal cortex supplement with digestive enzyme supplements plus vitamin supplementation was started. In eight months, there was less hyperactivity and some attempts at speech. Treatment was stopped because the parents would not implement the dietary part of the program and insisted that Donald wouldn't eat the vegetables.

## Mary, Age 13

She was seen because of blackouts, six occurring in the previous weeks, and behavior problems. She felt that other people hated her. In turn, she hated practically everyone. She thought people were spying on her. In psychological terminology, she had been somewhat paranoid for the past two years. She was extremely jealous of her sister. Her school work was below average partly due to a poor ability to concentrate and lack of motivation. She had had many headaches, a stuffy nose, itching eyes and leg cramps in the past year. Her headaches started shortly after she went to live with her father, who was a pilot and crop duster.

A physical examination revealed little besides low blood pressure and signs of allergy. The five-hour glucose tolerance test suggested hypoglycemia. Blood count was quite normal; urine showed a low level of vitamin C. The stool examination showed evidence of the lack of absorption of fats in her diet. The X ray of her wrists revealed bone development consistent with her age, a good indication of normal thyroid activity. Because of her exposure to her father's crop-dust-laden clothing, a blood study was made for evidence of agricultural poisons. The tests indicated that this was not a problem. A hair analysis was done that revealed a high zinc and copper level. The high zinc level was felt to have been due to a supplement the child was taking. The EEG was reported as being normal. A Hoffer and Osmond Diagnostic (HOD) test showed definite evidence of schizophrenia.[7]

In view of the above findings, diagnoses of schizophrenia, hypoglycemia with hypoadrenalcorticism, hay fever, and malabsorption were made. A diet was prescribed with a large component of raw and lightly cooked vegetables and fruits and about seventy grams of protein. She was put on weekly injections of adrenal cortex extract, digestant tablets, niacinamide, and vitamin C, pantothenic acid, and vitamin $B_6$, following the megavitamin program of Hoffer and Osmond, and homeopathic nux vomica (poison nut).

In one month she was feeling better, had fewer headaches, no more blackouts, and her school work was improving; in two months she reported only one headache, her nose was much clearer, and her concentration was improved. Three months later, her mother reported considerable improvement with no particular problems. The blood pressure had returned to normal. She had begun to like people and was adjusting much better. There were no more leg cramps, though the nose was slightly stuffy on smoggy days. Her HOD test showed some improvement but was still quite far from normal.

Ten months after onset of treatment, her disposition was reported distinctly improved and her HOD test was completely normal. As of this writing, she is still on adrenal cortex extract weekly, which can be cut down and gradually eliminated once she stops cheating on her diet. She will need the megavitamin program for some time to come. After increasing potencies of nux vomica, she was given Anacardium (marking nut), which provided considerable help.

We have made no attempt to discuss the entire field of endocrinology. These remarks only scratch the surface. The important role of the pituitary gland in problems of obesity, menstrual difficulties, and water retention in the tissues has been discussed at length by other authors.

Calcium deficiency at the cellular level has an important endocrine aspect. Muscular twitching and leg cramps are especially important symptoms in this area. Osteoporosis, or the loss of calcium, particularly from the spine and hips, is a frequent cause of precipitating fractures in old people and is gland-related.

I would like to plead for the use of natural extracts of glands in treatment and for the avoidance of the cheaper and all-too-readily-available synthetic substitutes. It took the vastly superior Creative Intelligence of the Universe millions of years to design this complicated endocrine system about which we still know very little. Chemically, many of these synthetics show a similarity to the natural occurring hormones, but they frequently are not even chemically identical. The endocrine orchestra is far too delicate to be tampered with in this fashion, and the long-range risks are too great. This especially applies, in my opinion, to the use of the birth-control pill.

Another important point is that nature combines certain substances intended to be man's food. Thus vitamin E is likely to be associated with vitamin A, which enhances its activity, as does the important ingredient of fat known as lecithin. These natural interrelationships worked out by Nature during the course of millions of years are still largely unexplored by our scientists.

In the case of synthetic hormones, thyroxin is a good example. The levo-thyroxin seems to be the most active principle, but we know that we also get thyroid effects from tri-iodo thyronine, which is present in thyroid extracts. There is no doubt in my mind that certain life energies are present in human beings that cannot be duplicated synthetically, and it seems reasonable to suppose that these natural extracts of the endocrine glands are more suitable vehicles for these energies.

### Rhythms

An essential part of any orchestral work is rhythm. In closing this chapter, I would like to speak briefly on the subject of rhythms. It usually takes a good part of five to seven days for most vacationing city people to unwind and let go of their tensions. Then the renewing process starts. Guests coming to Meadowlark often go through a period, toward the end of the first week, that we refer to as the "muddy stream." They become very tired and discouraged as the body and mind begin to release the old, unnatural stresses under which they have been living, and they begin to discover their own natural rhythm.

There are three basic human rhythms, sometimes referred to as biorhythms: a physical twenty-three-day cycle, an emotional twenty-eight-day cycle, and an intellectual thirty-three-day cycle. Undoubtedly the best understood of these is the woman's menstrual cycle. A twenty-eight-to-twenty-nine-day recurring cycle is a good sign of homeostasis (organic equilibrium).

The regulation of this cycle once again looks to the hypothalamus and pituitary glands, which through hormones direct the various responses. It is a common experience for a girl going away to college or summer camp or having a boyfriend and under emotional strain to stop menstruating. Usually this imbalance will correct itself in two or three months. If the stress is great and prolonged, a period of cessation may last for many months and even years and need endocrine stimulation for its reestablishment, but particularly necessary is elimination of the specific stress.

Then, again, the stresses and changes in life-style of the menopause period are frequently accompanied by menstrual problems. The use of hormones in such cases is like priming a pump, and they can often be discontinued when appropriate psychotherapy and/or spiritual counseling is used concurrently to change life situations.

## Biorhythms

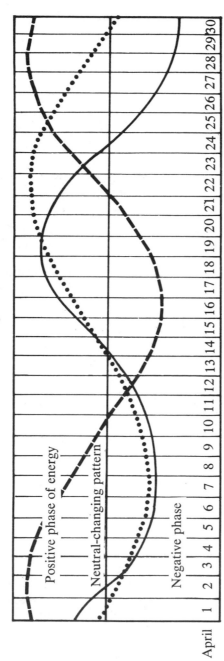

April | 1 | 2 | 3 | 4 | 5 | 6 | 7 | 8 | 9 | 10 | 11 | 12 | 13 | 14 | 15 | 16 | 17 | 18 | 19 | 20 | 21 | 22 | 23 | 24 | 25 | 26 | 27 | 28 | 29 | 30

Positive phase of energy

Neutral-changing pattern

Negative phase

——— *Physical Cycle (23 days)*

•••••••• *Emotional Cycle (28 days)*

– – – – *Intellectual Cycle (33 days)*

These three cycles have their onset at a common point at birth, and a chart for any month may be calculated from tables.

Critical or accident-prone days are those where the physical or emotional curves cross the central line from a positive phase or from a negative to a positive.

On the above chart such a phase is seen on the 24th for the physical and the 30th for the emotional. A doubly critical or accident-prone day is the 14th, where both the physical and emotional are crossing on that same day.

Everyone has surely noted that he or she has "good" and "bad" days. Many women have noted periodicity in their moods that are associated with the week or ten days before the onset of their menstrual period. Thus there is nothing new to the observation of a twenty-eight-day periodicity to emotions. Viennese psychologist Herman Swaboda became interested between 1890 and 1902 in the rhythmic cycles of human beings and went on to describe a twenty-three-day cycle in certain aspects of illness, which he considered to be a masculine rhythm in contradistinction to the twenty-eight-day female rhythm. He was very much aware of the bisexuality of human beings, each male and female having component parts of the opposite sex in their make-up.

Some years later in the 1920s, an instructor of engineering, Alfred Telscher, made note of the fact that his students' mental high and low peaks had a thirty-three-day periodicity. As other professionals in Europe took up and furthered this study, it was observed that, by taking advantage of these circadian rhythms, surgeons could cut down on postoperative complications, athletes could time their days of best performance, airlines could keep pilots off duty on their critical days, which were the days when the physical twenty-three-day and the emotional twenty-eight-day curves of the performance pass closely together from the positive phase into the negative phase.[8] This is truly a fruitful area for further research.


### Rhythmic Eating Habits

Good eating habits should follow a regular rhythm, both daily and seasonally. For most people to start a day with no food makes about as much sense as starting out on an auto trip with a practically empty gas tank. This habit is particularly destructive of health when it is followed by several coffee or cola breaks during the day. Heavy physical, emotional, or mental stress will disturb all the rhythms. At these times, good, natural, unrefined food should be used, and stress factors should be reduced to the lowest possible levels.

In hot summer weather, food needs differ from those in winter. Raw, uncooked salads, vegetables, and fruit should be the mainstay in the warm season; while an increased amount of dairy products, meat, fish, and oils may be needed in cold weather. Nature has planned it this way. The Eskimo can raise very few vegetables and fruits in his cold country, while the natives of the tropics live on fruits, vegetables, and fish.

Loss of appetite may be associated with an undiscovered illness or a lack of interest in what one is doing, in associations, or in life in general. It is often associated with boredom, discouragement, or a feeling of spiritual emptiness.

Obesity, on the other hand, is associated with malfunctioning of our built-in time clock. It may manifest itself as compulsive eating when, due to feelings of frustration, one too frequently visits the refrigerator. Or it may appear as a perversion of appetite, or be associated with hypothalamic or pituitary gland dysfunction in relation to food balance, since many people with such conditions have waterlogged tissues.

The craving for sweets or alcohol is a sign of imbalance and is regularly associated with the hypoglycemic state.

The venerable father of medicine, Hippocrates, was very much aware of the relationship between rhythms and healing. He realized that the patient could not be observed apart from his environment; that certain foods were for certain seasons; that certain climates were helpful to certain patients; that phases of the moon affect human rhythms. Indian medicine men today still are taught to pick the healing herbs at very specific times of day and seasons; Rudolf Steiner has discussed this subject in relationship to the life-giving quality of certain plants.

If we physicians knew as much about health as we do about illness, we might better serve our patients. To see man in health would increasingly appear to mean to see him in his total environment, including the physical, mental, and spiritual atmosphere in which he daily lives.

In the past, the healing professions have tended to turn their research inward to certain areas of evidence of malfunction and become quite expert in reproducing disease states in animals. As Dr. Phillip Norman, former consultant nutritionist to the New York City Health Department, wrote:

> For centuries, physicians have been breathing the miasmic odor of biological decay in the dismal swamp of pathology. We are more proficient in the detection of biological decay than we are in the recognition of biological health.[9]

A central theme of this book is that there are subtle life rhythms throughout the universe with which man is linked, and a proper, holistic philosophy of medicine must take this fact into consideration. There is little that would lead me to believe that synthetic chemicals, particularly those derived from coal-tar products, which are an end-product in the death process of nature, would be a likely source of new life and health.

We have already referred to the yogic concept of the chakras and its apparent relationship to the glands. We have had much to say about daily and monthly rhythms as they relate to the output of hormones. We know that breathing can affect our body chemistry and, therefore, our glandular function.

The yogis who have spent a lifetime mastering the art of breath control, as it relates to meditation, may very possibly be able in the not-too-distant future to show us much about the regulation of our entire endocrine system. Possibly, scientists and philosophers from India may lead us into new and unexplored vistas involving some of the vortices of human energy that directly animate our glands and reinforce our total homeostatic structure.

# 6

## HARMONY AND BALANCE
## IN MEDICINE

In the body every motive force is balanced by a
retarding force, and this nice equilibrium is quite
essential to the proper regulation of the numerous
cellular functions. Should one of the two factors
gain ascendency, disorganization may be expected
at once, and the extent of this disturbance can
hardly be confined to the single area in which it is
initiated.

Henry R. Harrower[1]

Any discussion of harmony and balance in a human being
must involve the physical, emotional, mental, and spiritual
dimensions in all their complex and varied relationships. And
it soon becomes apparent that the Law of Love, a central
theme of all major religions, is the great balance wheel in all
aspects of the life processes. When love is absent, disharmony
inevitably appears. As the late sociologist Pitrim Sorokin so
well said:

Love raises man as a biological organism to the level of
divinity, infinitely enriches the human self and empowers a

mastery over the inorganic, organic, and sociocultural forces, up to the potential rescue of an individual and mankind from even biological death.[2]

## The Two Approaches to Medicine

There are two fundamental paths of scientific research: one starting from the center of a problem and working out to the periphery and the other starting from the periphery and working toward the center. The former deductive method proceeds from the general to the precise; the latter inductive method proceeds from the precise toward the general. When applied to medicine, the deductive method is the path of the physician who endeavors to integrate the whole person: body, mind, and spirit. He reinforces natural immunity and the natural tendency to recover and gives great attention to nutrition and psychosomatic medicine. He respects natural herbal remedies and recognizes the valid field of homeotherapeutics (homeopathy). He employs his academic medicine and surgery only wherever and whenever these are rationally constructive.

The inductive method has been the more prevalent of the two in the last 150 years. This is the course followed by the experimental determinist who is largely controlled by the findings in the laboratory. If nerves are malfunctioning, he will cut them; if the thalamic drive disorders the body, he may use surgery to remove a part of the brain or extirpate the pituitary gland or the adrenals. In case of infection he may use large doses of antibiotics as his first recommendation.

He tends to deny the basis of psychosomatic medicine and may likely be unaware of the body's restorative powers. The so-called inductive physician may be compared to the chess player who observes the last two moves in a chess game and from that observation infers the first moves.

It is heartening to find an increasing number of physicians moving away from this orthodox rigid inductive view to explore the relatively forsaken path of the deductive physician. This tendency has been responsible for at least five new medical societies: The American Holistic Medical Ass'n, the International Academy of Metabology, the International Academy of Preventive Medicine, the International College of Applied Nutrition, and the College of Orthomolecular Psychiatry. The emphasis in these groups has been toward the establishment of a homeostatic, balanced condition in the patient rather than toward describing new diseases and treating them as though they existed as independent entities, instead of as symptoms of imbalance in the patient. Their studies are taking the form of extensive research into nutrition, biorhythms, intracellular chemistry, and the nature of these basic energies that make a human being "tick."

One might well ask, "Why the need of these studies? Isn't medicine making great advances today?" Certainly, medicine is making great advances, particularly in the control of infectious diseases and in certain aspects of surgery. We can be very thankful that immunization procedures and other public health measures have, in the Western world, nearly wiped out such deadly diseases as plague, cholera, dysentery, smallpox, malaria, and polio, to name just a few.

Pneumonia is not nearly the threat to life it used to be. Surgery is much safer than ever before. Both these latter advances are largely due to the use of antibiotics. But we have by no means answered the question as to why some people are much more susceptible to infections than others, nor why a certain type of cancer will linger in one person and go on to a rapid termination in another.

We have made very little real progress in the control of the degenerative diseases such as coronary thrombosis, strokes, and the other conditions associated with arteriosclerosis, or hardening of the arteries. And arthritis, many neurological and skin diseases, cataracts, the problem of the so-called brain damaged or retarded child, and the great problem of mental illness still plague us.

There has also been a steady increase in so-called iatrogenic diseases (diseases resulting from the doctor's treatment). Drugs when prescribed in improper combinations are turning out to be incompatible and even harmful.

## Nature's Doctors in History

As a background to the new thoughts in medicine, I would like to recall some of the great doctors in history, men who had vision beyond that of the narrow traditionalists. The acclaimed father of medicine, Hippocrates, had a keen sense of man's partnership with the natural world. That he believed in the theory of homeostatis is evident from his studies of the balance of the four humors: fire, air, water, and earth.

Let us compare these views with those of workers in the new areas of medical research. The *Earth* element relates to the new studies in nutrition. *Water* relates to circulation and the intra- and extracellular fluid exchanges. *Air* relates to the breathing capacity, and rhythms in general, which increasingly we find are of great significance in our physiological processes. Finally, *Fire* relates to the metabolic process and the intracellular enzyme chain.

Next, let us go back a century-and-a-half and look at the great physician Dr. Samuel Hahnemann, whose work has had a profound impact on my own practice of medicine. Quoting from his *Organon*:

> In the healthy condition of man, the spirit-like force that animates the material body rules with unbounded sway and regains all the parts of the organism in admirable, harmonious, vital operation as regards both sensation and functions, so that our indwelling reason-gifted mind can freely employ this living, healthy instrument for the higher purposes of our existence. . . .
>
> No organ, no tissue, no cell, no molecule, is independent of the activities of the others, but the life of each one is merged into the life of the whole. The unit of human life cannot be

the organ, the tissue, the cell, the molecule, the atom, but the whole organism, the whole man.[3]

In a similar vein the noted surgeon and medical researcher Dr. Alexis Carrel reminds us that

> As soon as a portion of space containing living cells becomes relatively isolated from the cosmic world, there is a modification causing congesting waste products to stagnate, thus altering the cells' surroundings and recordings of time. Resistance creates residue, the residue of toxin.[4]

This statement has great relevance for us today in our studies of the ever increasing problems of aging. To prolong life, we must deal with living processes and get away from the internal use of chemicals taken as drugs. Also, environmental pollutants are sure to produce effects that are damaging to the human system.

Our foods should be "living" and not "dead" foods. It would seem that this fresh and new approach is also particularly important in cancer therapy. For too long we have been led to believe that only surgery, radiation, and chemotherapy should be considered valid for this process. While it is true that we may be able to remove the primary site of cancer, which frequently slows down the process for a time, there is the constant fear of a metastatic cancer showing up at a later time.

In our own country during the nineteenth century, a small number of physicians, starting with Isaac Jennings in 1822, rebelled at the unnatural practice of orthodox medicine and began a medical movement based on natural laws.

This was the beginning of the Natural Hygiene Movement, which recognized that every organism has an innate force acting in it that attempts to heal the organism if given the opportunity under proper circumstances. It was discovered that these proper circumstances included the presence of fresh air, pure water, natural food, rest, exercise, and a proper mental attitude. The value of fasting as a natural method of rest and detoxification was also rediscovered.

The concept of toxemia in its broadest sense was considered the cause of illness. The signs and symptoms were merely the organism's method for dealing with or eliminating the toxicity. With this understanding, according to Jennings, nothing should be done that would suppress the symptoms because that would interfere with the natural process of cure.

The cause of toxemia is understood as the result of not living in accordance with natural laws, and in this view illness is a manifestation of the organism's detoxifying itself. Treatment is directed at allowing or aiding this process. This is followed by discovering what the person has been doing that is wrong and teaching him how to live correctly according to his needs.

This movement was the beginning of an organized approach to preventive medicine and optimal health. The healing profession could now view the nature of man and his requirements for health in a more comprehensive context. The healer became both a researcher and a teacher.

It is important to reiterate here that human rhythms bear a close relationship to the rhythms of the universe about us. In this connection let us take a look for a moment at the Taoist view of life, one of the major contributions of ancient China.

The Chinese character Tao is commonly taken to mean the Path or the Way. On analyzing its various components we see the head and the foot, or heaven and earth. Also there is the suggestion of stepping forward with the left foot and then pausing. This implies that if I am to find my way along the path of life, I must first find the balance between my physical and spiritual self. Then as I move forward on the path I must go

one step at a time, taking time to assimilate each forward
movement.

Descending into the physical world with its duality, we find
fluctuations that are necessary to maintain the balance between health and disease. Chinese medicine pictures this in
the symbol of the yang and yin, the male and the female.

This symbol is so arranged that the two elements are indis-
tinguishable. If you turn the figure upside down, it looks the
same, because one side is no more important than the other,
and each is in a sense the shadow of the other. Where there is
one, its mate must be close by.

In the atomic and molecular kingdom, we discover positive
and negative charges in dynamic balance. In the plant and
animal kingdom, male and female are the counterparts. This
rhythmic sequence is everywhere around us, and on its balance depends the stability of the system. The positive sunlight
of day is the major time of regeneration and is complemented
by absence of sunlight at night.

### The New Medicine

Health is dependent on balance. The balance between acid-
ity and alkalinity of the blood is delicate and allows only
slight variation, for the human body is a finely tuned instrument. In addition to daily rhythms, the human being also finds
involvement in the outer universe in the monthly rhythms—

the most notable, of course, being that of the female. Much further study is in order to understand better these cycles and their relation to medical practice.

As an example of the importance of rhythms, Edson J. Andrews, M.D., reports that "It has often occurred to me, as it has to many eye, ear, nose, and throat surgeons, that at certain times the human body has a greater predilection to excessive bleeding than at others. There are days in the operating room when hemorrhage is of no import; at other times, persistent and annoying bleeding is the rule of the day."[5]

He goes on to report further that as a result of a two-year analysis of all his tonsillectomy cases that had severe and troublesome bleeding, 82 percent occurred in the interval between the first quarter and one day before the third quarter to the moon. He later compared his results with those of another surgeon, Dr. Carl McLemore. These two surgeons plotted curves to illustrate this phenomenon better and found their two curves were practically identical. They both also observed that hemorrhages dropped to near zero at the time of the new moon. He then went on to analyze hemorrhages in his hospital occurring in ulcer patients and found the same result. While I have not done as extensive a survey in my own local hospital, I have alerted our operating room supervisor to make similar notes, and it looks as though our findings are practically identical.

What we have referred to as the new science and the new medicine must be much more inclusive, or the human being will continue to be lost. The physician or the minister will need to find more time for his own healing inherent in the words "Physician, heal thyself," as found in the Book of Luke 4:23.

On the emotional and mental levels, there must be a coordination of function between the thinking and feeling areas. Many people today have, from childhood, so inhibited their emotions that they are unable to weep or to express the anger they feel. The resulting tension is an important factor in many illnesses.

On the spiritual level there is the all-important struggle between the self-directed ego and the self-effacing Real Self, or Oversoul. The reestablishment of peace between mind and soul is all-important for high-level well-being. We lose our sense of peace repeatedly in this world, and what we need is an inner sense of peace and strength to meet the many problems that confront us. I hope that the recent trend emphasizing research in human ecology will help to relate man more closely to Nature, to his surroundings, and to his fellow humans.

Possibly we might compare the scope of changes in thinking regarding medicine to the profound change that took place in physics from the time of Newton, who viewed the world as made up of tiny corpuscles (units of mass), to that of Einstein, who envisioned great interweaving systems of energy. The great electrical and mathematical genius Charles Steinmetz wrote,

> I think the greatest discoveries of the future will be made along spiritual lines. Here is a force that history teaches has been the greatest in the development of man through history. Yet we have merely been playing with it and have never taken it seriously and studied it the way we have physical forces. If such a study were embarked upon, what would happen? The laboratories would be turned over to the study of God and prayer and spiritual forces which have scarcely been scratched. When this day comes, the world will see more advance in one generation than has been seen in the last four.

The concept of relationships is of great significance to our study. Its very mention seems to take us away from the idea of thrusting a patient into isolated diagnostic pigeonholes. According to the uncertainty principle proposed by the great physicist W. Heisenberg, one cannot separate the observer from the entity that he is observing, because each has a measurable effect on the other. And the philosopher Martin Buber tells us also that the true human relationship is not one of "I-

It" but rather one of "I-Thou," where I see myself in respectful relationship to the other person as a person—a Thou rather than as a Thing or an It.

In the field of religion we find this same concept of relationship in the words of Jesus: "I and My Father are One" (John 10:30); "I am in the Father and He in me" (John 14:11); and still again, "As you did it to one of the least of these my brethren you did it to me" (Matthew 25:40).

As surgeons we have placed great stock in the pathologist's report of the surgical biopsy.[6] Perhaps this has too often sealed the fate of the unfortunate patient. I find that I am increasingly able to say to my patients, "This is what the pathologist finds to be the case at the present time. But we will change your nutrition, give you food supplements to make up for the insufficient vitamins, minerals, or enzymes in your diet. If it seems necessary, we will refer you to a psychiatrist, psychologist, or ministerial counselor who has a working relationship with his own mental and spiritual self. With this combined approach, I believe your whole picture can change."

Practically every honest physician who has practiced medicine for twenty or thirty years has seen people with cancer or other so-called incurable diseases get well when they were given up by our profession to die. We have in the past attached a great deal of finality to the difference between so-called organic and functional disease states. What determined this difference was only the fact that, in the first instance, the pathologist could see tissue changes under the microscope, while in the second he could not. In other words, what the pathologist is able to observe at the autopsy table is what distinguishes the two. In the former instance he can see cancer, tuberculosis, arthritic changes, and so on, but he cannot tell that the patient has been subject to migraine headaches, bronchial asthma, or schizophrenia.

All that we see with our own eyes is one "octave" of light energy in the electromagnetic spectrum. There are approximately seventy-five known octaves of energy in this spectrum extending from the low frequencies of electrical waves with the ever ascending frequencies of radio, television, and radar waves; the infrared, visible, and ultraviolet bands of light frequencies; up through the X-rays, gamma rays, and ultimately to the extremely high frequencies of cosmic rays. Many of these other energies in the spectrum beyond that associated with visible light affect our bodies. There has frequently been a tendency in medicine to feel a sense of finality associated with the visible organic changes of diseases such as cancer and advanced arthritis as though these were streets of no return. They have usually been regarded as something to be surgically cut out where feasible or suppressed by irradiation or chemotherapy. The latent healing energies of the human mind and spirit have scarcely been tapped. Many cases of instantaneous healing have been reported and well documented by the medical board of the famous healing shrine at Lourdes in France.[7] Many churches today are having regular healing services. The healing ministry of Kathryn Kuhlman is particularly worth noting in this regard. It is time that we physicians make a much more thorough study of this whole area.

There are still many physicians who succumb to the temptation to tell the patient that there is nothing wrong with him, or that it is all in his head, when a diagnosis fails to identify a specific organic disease. I must confess I have been guilty of this, but today I am making a real effort to be more honest and admit it when I can *find* nothing wrong.

When one glances through a modern medical textbook, many conflicting stories of physiochemical relationships are apparent, but human relationships are rarely mentioned. Because there is only a relatively small amount of literature available on psychosomatic medicine, should we conclude that the person is not responsible for his illness, that somehow the person and his body are only vaguely connected?

As a case in point, recently a patient in our hospital died. He was a seventy-one-year-old man, whose autopsy revealed atherosclerosis of the coronary vessels and aorta, pulmonary emphysema, anemia, and kidney infection. Are these just a few rather isolated facts? What message lies here if we are perceptive enough to receive it?

While this patient was living, three specialists and I could find no explanation for his anemia. The bone marrow biopsy was quite normal; the pathologist could say only that it looked as though something was inhibiting the release of the normal blood cells from the marrow into the circulation. Blood transfusions were ineffective.

The attitude of the patient was "I just don't care." This was reflected by his resisting the orderly's attempt to change his position in bed or to set him up in a chair each day. He had given up!

Is it possible that this attitude, in some manner, prevented the release of red cells into his circulation? Why had he given up and succumbed to depression? Is it enough to call this an endogenous depression, or could there have been factors of spiritual dimensions?

Perhaps he no longer saw a reason for living, for hoping. Perhaps he no longer felt loved by those formerly close to him. Was the torture of his diseased body too great for him to hope for healing? Had his disappointments in life been too great? Was his feeling of relationship to God nonexistent? Unfortunately, in his case we will never know the answers.

An autopsy presents me, the physician, with a group of somewhat unrelated observations. Am I to conclude that these are a set of disconnected phenomena or should I look further for a pattern that has been disrupted, resulting in illness and death? It could be that I do not sufficiently understand what is meant by "wholeness." As a physician, perhaps my understanding does not even encompass what it means to be a truly human being!

Doctoring the whole person as a medical student some thirty-five years ago, I was fortunate to attend a medical school that was one of the first institutions to teach psychiatry, the Cornell Medical School. At a time when some schools were scarcely even recognizing psychiatry, we had a four-year program in this relatively new field. In our first year we had a course called "psychobiology," which, I confess, was taken very lightly by me and most of the other students. We had to go through this rather dull preliminary to get on to the more meaningful course in psychopathology the following year. With this latter course we felt we were back in our field of medicine because we were concerned with disease, the real function of becoming a doctor.

Now, after these many years have elapsed, I ask myself with increasing frequency, "Am I qualified to treat people who are ill if I don't really know the meaning of health or wholeness? How can I plot the therapeutic course of a human being so that he may find health and wholeness if neither he nor I know precisely where he is going?"

During the past few decades, it has been the custom that students who get into medical school have been selected on a scale that is heavily weighted toward technical competence in academics and reflects minimal concern with humanistic aptitudes. This is the case despite increasing evidence that society has a desperate need for "physicians" who can assist in coping with the anxiety-producing problems such as the following (compiled by E. Grey Dimond) that face its members in the years immediately ahead:[8]

a. Birth control
b. Genetic manipulation
c. Euthanasia
d. Environmental pollution
e. Physical disuse
f. Nourishment
g. Psychological trauma
h. Narcotics
i. Alcohol
j. Venereal disease
k. Highway trauma
l. Murder
m. Suicide
n. Boredom, from leisure and old age
o. Sex
p. Divorce
q. Juvenile delinquency
r. Prison reform
s. Mental deficiency
t. Neurosis
u. Psychosis
v. Transplantation
w. Resuscitation

Each of these problems generates the need for the medically trained professional who also has psychological sensitivity, moral and ethical perspective, and compassion. Medical education is sorely remiss if it continues to focus primarily on technical excellence, as important and as necessary as it is, to the exclusion of these other factors.

It is encouraging to see some evidence of change, even to the thought of including some philosophy and ethics in the medical curriculum. This is certainly desirable in light of the medical-ethical questions implicit in the above list of problems. It is a step toward uniting the fractionized way in which we now approach our patients. Perhaps in days to come the physicist's references to cosmic energy, the physician's references to the healing process, and the minister's references to the activity of the Holy Spirit may be viewed merely as different modes of description of the same essence.

### Homeopathy

There is a branch of medicine that was influential in the nineteenth century and is again experiencing a small resurgence.[9] In many respects it takes a contrary view to that of the medical establishment, but this may well be in the best interests of the healing art. This branch of medicine goes back a century-and-a-half to the German physician Samuel Hahnemann (and slightly later in America, James Tyler Kent, M.D.), who described the fundamental principles of a medical therapeutics system referred to as homeopathy. This form of medical practice makes certain basic assumptions:

> 1. There is a "vital force" or "power of recovery" which is manifest in the rhythmic alterations of the body's normal healthy functions.
> 2. A disturbance of this normal basic rhythm is the basis of disease.
> 3. The symptoms and signs of disease are the reactions of the body's attempts to restore the normal state of homeostasis.

4. In contradistinction to the more common allopathic approach to medicine, homeopathy holds that these changes are not the essential elements to be studied and classified in disease. They are rather the end products of the disturbance in function.

5. Accordingly, the man who is sick should always be studied as a whole, not as some diseased tissues.

6. Homeotherapeutics accordingly is based on an analysis of the symptoms of the individual patient. Of primary importance are the patient's mental symptoms and his attitude toward life, as this has a profound effect on recovery.[10]

After all, the mind controls the person. As already stressed, our body type is determined by our personality. Thus the various organ symptoms must be taken into account, and their subjective quality is of great importance.

In the usual (allopathic) medical practice a patient has pain, and he is given a pain pill, the type depending largely on the degree of pain. The homeopathic physician, on the other hand, must learn the quality of pain. Is the pain aching, boring, cutting, constricting, shooting, throbbing, pressing, and so on? The remedial medication must take into account this description. The remedies must be simple and in a form in which they occur in nature. Otherwise, they will act as so much poisonous matter and may interfere with the homeostatic process and the body will reject them. If it does not, they will be injurious to some body organ in particular, most frequently the liver, kidney, or bone marrow.

Basic in treatment are the principal elements of which the body is composed: namely sodium, potassium, iron, calcium, magnesium, phosphorus, sulfur, and iodine. Also bearing an importance that medical science is just beginning to appreciate are some of the elements present in trace amounts such as manganese, copper, zinc, fluorine, molybdenum, and lithium.

Another important group of elements includes some of our principal metals, which in ordinary usage we would consider quite poisonous. These include gold, silver, platinum, mercury, tin, lead, and arsenic. In a dynamic and nonmaterial state, not yet clearly understood, these metals may be very essential to health and to the reestablishment of harmony in our body energy-systems.

A second and large group of homeopathic drugs come from the plant kingdom. These include Aconite (monkshood), Arnica (leopard's bane), Belladonna (deadly nightshade), Chamomilla (chamomile), and Pulsatilla (wind flower). These plants have an internal clock much like the human clock, to which reference has already been made. This fact is an important consideration in relation to the timing of the human symptoms as related to our previous discussion of biological rhythms.

The father of biological classification, Carolus Linnaeus, described a plant time clock from his observation of plant circadian rhythms back in the eighteenth century:

6 A.M.: Spotted cat's ear opens
7 A.M.: African marigold (Calendula)* opens
8 A.M.: Mouse ear hawkweed opens
9 A.M.: Prickly sow thistle closes
10 A.M.: Common nipplewort closes
11 A.M.: Star of Bethlehem (Ornithogalum)* opens
12 NOON: Passion flower opens (Passiflora)*
1 P.M.: Chiding pink closes
2 P.M.: Scarlet pimpernel closes
3 P.M.: Hawkbit closes
4 P.M.: Small bindweed closes
5 P.M.: White water lily closes (Nuphar)*
6 P.M.: Evening primrose opens (Primula)*

It is also interesting to find that even the seemingly lifeless minerals have their rhythms. This fact is very evident to the homeopathic physician. Arsenicum album (Arsenious oxide) finds its greatest use for symptoms occurring near and within two to three hours after midnight. Many heart patients, prior to their first dose of Arsenicum album have had to get out of

* Where the scientific genus is placed in parenthesis the plants are used homeopathically.

bed around this time and spend the rest of the night sitting in a chair in order to breathe. After the first few doses of Arsenicum album this frequently is no longer necessary.

It would seem that there is an invisible thread of continuity along the trunk of the evolutionary tree leading through the mineral, plant, and animal world and out into our own human structure. This, too, is suggested by the human embryo, which traces our early development through the preceding forms of animal life to culminate in the human being. Many of the characteristics of these earlier states of life linger in the human form.

One of the most dramatically useful emergency drugs for the person who appears practically lifeless, who is cold although his head is hot, whose color is poor, and whose pulse is thready and weak, is Carbo veg. (vegetable charcoal). This description may be that of a patient in acute heart failure, or in what looks like a terminal pneumonia. To see such a patient, after he is given Carbo veg., have a return of pulse in a few minutes, develop color in the face, and sit up and look alive, is indeed a rewarding experience!

Pulsatilla (Windflower) is one of the most commonly used remedies for the woman who, like her flowering counterpart, is riding high and upright one day and who is flat on her back the next when the winds of adversity begin to blow.

Then we come to the drugs that are drawn from the animal world. From the sea comes a particularly important drug, Sepia, the black substance from the ink bag of the cuttle fish. It may be the treatment for the individual who feels he is walking around in constant darkness. He is likely to be indifferent to his family, his work, and is constantly and silently depressed. Nothing is right. He may be constipated, bloated, and just generally slowed down in most of his functions.

For example, R.D., a sixty-four-year-old housewife, had experienced considerable pain and some swelling below her right ribs. She related at great length and in a very monotonous tone how uncomfortable she had been and how little her doctors had helped her for the past two years since she had been ill with hepatitis. Her husband just didn't understand her, and then the children had their own problems. Somehow, her mood spoke louder to me than her symptoms. Following a dose of Sepia daily for a week, she came back reporting that she felt considerably better, and I noted that the gloomy shroud didn't seem to be surrounding her. On subsequent visits, she received ascending doses of Sepia for swollen and tender arthritic finger joints, bloating, and recurrence of the original pain in her side, and each time she reported improvement. Her mood also improved, and I no longer dreaded her visits, with their accompanying tales of woe.

From the insect world, a useful example is Apis, the genus from which the common honey bee finds its origin. This is a drug for more acute symptoms, such as the prevention of the toxic effects of bee stings in those who are peculiarly sensitive. In general, it is used for certain acutely piercing types of pain, weltlike swellings of the skin that are rapidly progressive, and for acute and life-threatening allergic reactions where the patient becomes drowsy, mentally dull, awkward, listless, tearful, or at times stuporous.

### Administration of Homeopathics

The homeopathic prescription is given according to four principles: (1) the Law of Similars, (2) the Minimum Dose, (3) the Single Remedy, and (4) the recognition of certain basic and underlying chronic disease states. It may be given in the form of any one of some 2,000 remedies, 800 of which may be chosen from regularly in medical practice.

The value and symptomatology of these has been described by hundreds of homeopathic physicians and patients in what is referred to as "provings," which are tests under controlled conditions. The crude substances are ingested orally, and all the various symptoms and signs that are experienced by numerous individuals are described in detail. This information is then sorted out and catalogued in a manual referred to as repertory. The regularly used homeopathic drugs have had thousands of "provings."

In contrast to the homeopath's 800 remedies, the allopathic physician is not likely to use regularly more than some fifty drugs. The homeopathic physician has allopathic training in his background since homeopathy can only be studied as a medical postgraduate course. There will be occasions when he may decide a case warrants use of such drugs as digitalis or an antibiotic.

In the case of the usual drugs, very few are derived directly from nature, as is digitalis. This is not to imply that synthetic drugs do not have their place in medicine. In many instances they do away with the undesirable side effects of natural drugs, such as vomiting. However, the homeopathic physician stays as close as possible to natural remedies, since many synthetic allopathic medicines are toxic and cause allergic reactions.

### The Minimum Dose

The various homeopathic potencies are prepared by combining one part of the original substance with nine parts of the material used for the dilution, which might be milk sugar, alcohol, or water. The starting point might thus be a grain of bark of a tree, the root of some medicinal plant, the powder of sulfur, or a drop of mercury. This would be placed in a suitable container such as a mortar and would be very thoroughly ground with nine parts of milk sugar and a drop of pure grain alcohol to make the first dilution, referred to as a lx dilution. Another method of preparation is to dissolve the original substance in alcohol and water as the starting point. One part of this mixture would then be mixed with nine parts of the milk sugar in a small vial and shaken vigorously thirty times, holding it in the hand and striking the closed fist against a semifirm surface. The result is a 2x potency. This process is then similarly carried through a number of combinings and successions to obtain the desired strength. Commonly the 12x trituration is considered low potency, while 30x and above is considered high.

While it is beyond our comprehension to understand how these high triturations seem to increase the remedial strength in these very high potencies of M, 50M, of CM (100,000), it can only be said that the proof is in the result. It is to be expected that many who have had no homeopathic experience would say that such therapy is merely the application of the "placebo effect."

However, thousands of homeopathic physicians around the world have been, and are, curing some of the most resistant and stubborn types of illness. It is of particular interest to note that the lower potencies deal more specifically with the physical complaints and, in ascending order, the XM, 50M, and CM doses have more effect on the whole personality. This will be illustrated in some case histories from my own files.

*Lorraine*—aged seventy—on April 27 noted some discomfort with swallowing and became aware of a lump in her neck. She was seen three days later and on examination was found to have a stony hard mass, measuring 3 cm. by 2 cm., in the right lobe of her thyroid.

The usual tests of thyroid function were normal, and I had planned to do a radioactive scan. However, in order to save her the expense of that test, I first gave her a homeopathic dose of iodine. Three weeks later she no longer had the throat symptoms, and the mass was only 1.5 cm. in diameter. On June 1 it was down to 1 cm., and then I prescribed the homeopathic, Lycopodium (club moss) and Psorinum. Two months later the mass was difficult to find and was about the size of a pea.

On September 19, approximately four months after it was first noted, the mass could not be found. Whether it was a benign tumor (adenoma), a cyst, or a cancer we will never know. We do know that it was a great relief to the patient to be spared the surgery that otherwise would have been mandatory.

*Harriet*, a fifty-nine-year-old divorcee working actively as a nurse in a doctor's office, complained that she had not felt well for thirty years since a severe automobile accident. She became quite hysterical while relating her story. She went on to explain that at times her mind stopped working.

Ten years earlier hypoglycemia had been discovered, and she showed some improvement following a dietary change. However, she still suffered from splitting headaches, periods of mental confusion, a poor attention span, and at times suicidal impulses.

Her physical examination revealed nothing else, and diagnoses were made of relative hypoglycemia, nervous colitis, and anxiety with depression. Slight changes in her diet were made. In view of the marked fluctuations from day to day in her moods, she was put on Pulsatilla.

One year later she reported, "It's a miracle; I no longer have a fuzzy brain and I'm not as sleepy as I used to be."

*Ben* had had a sore throat for a week and was still running a temperature. His throat and tonsils were an angry red, and many small pus pockets were to be seen. Several doses of Mercurius iodatus flavus (the yellow iodide of mercury) were given. In twenty-four hours all symptoms were gone without the risk of possible side reactions that might have accompanied the use of an antibiotic.

*Alan* was a ninety-two-year-old man, brought in by his wife. She complained that her husband was so mentally confused that he would get lost in their home and would not be able to find the room he wanted. He spent much time just wandering about in this confused state. Baryta carbonate (barium) was given as a single dose. A month later his wife reported that his appetite had improved and that there was no more confusion. He was now playing golf regularly once more with his friends.

*Elsie*, a thirty-five-year-old married woman, complained that she had to urinate very frequently, and could not really empty her bladder. She had been visiting a urologist every six weeks for dilations, which would give her temporary relief. I prescribed a few doses of Cantharis (Spanish Fly) to be taken every fifteen minutes. Her bladder pressure pains were relieved immediately. Subsequently, specific doses were advised, and in a week she reported that the results were unbelievable. It is now two years since this first dose, and she has needed no further instrumentation. One to two doses of CM strength will now last her for three months.

*Archie*, a seventy-four-year-old man, had been troubled for several years with a draining sinus in his leg, following an accident that left him with a bone infection (osteomyelitis). Following one dose of nitric acid the abscess healed, and at last report a year later there had been no further trouble.

*Norman*, age twelve, had had grand mal (epileptic seizures) since the age of ten months. He was treated in a major clinic with different combinations of anticonvulsant medications but developed undesirable side effects, and this had to be abandoned.

There was a history of epilepsy and diabetes in his family. Therefore, a glucose tolerance test was run with the following results: fasting 96; one-half hour 106, and subsequent hours up to five, 92, 78, 83, 65, and 91. This very slight rise after ingestion of glucose and the drop of thirty-one points below the fast level indicated a hypoglycemic state.

Other aspects of his laboratory and physical examinations were unremarkable. The electroencephalogram showed evidence of a focal convulsive disorder, which was initially local motor in type and was later generalized. The neurologist had no other recommendation than the anticonvulsants that had already been tried unsuccessfully.

On the basis of his symptoms and a very detailed study of the nature of his seizures and the premonitory signs, homeopathic prescriptions were suggested. The important points or guidelines used in the choice of the homeopathic remedy included nocturnal seizures, jerking motion of the eyes during seizures, unconsciousness, excessively violent shaking, clenched thumbs, alternate sweating and coldness, and blueness of the lips. Metallic copper in homeopathic high dosage was found to be the most effective medication used. It was very interesting to find, on hair analysis, that high values of intracellular copper was the outstanding abnormality. According to the basic homeopathic Law of Similars this would be the way of treating toxic amounts of copper.

At last report, while it is too early to draw final conclusions, the seizures had stopped. This report is indicative of the possible connection between hair analysis findings and homeopathy.

## The Single Remedy

Only one medication should ordinarily be given at a time so that the medication's individual effects may be observed. In some cases, there will be a steady state of improvement within a few hours or a day. In other cases, patients will have provings, meaning that they will experience symptoms—which may last from a few hours to several days—in the reverse order in which these symptoms originally appeared. If a second medication is given concurrently, it confuses the symptoms picture; this latter is essential in finding and determining further therapy.

### Chronic Illnesses

Homeopathic theory postulates four underlying chronic states that often may be related to chronic and frequently recurring illnesses. Three of these Hahnemann referred to as psora, syphilis, and sycosis. Later, tuberculosis was added to this group of "miasms" or chronic pathological areas of weakness, which are only very indirectly related to the diseases suggested by the names.

The first-mentioned, psora, is extremely common, and it underlies many functional and organic illnesses, in particular chronic allergic states, epilepsy, ulcers, and diabetes, to mention a few. But again it must be emphasized that it is not the disease but rather the person who is treated.

One of the outstanding homeopathic teachers of the past century, J. T. Kent, M.D., described psora as follows:

> . . . An underlying cause . . . or primary disorder of the human race. This state expresses itself in the forms of varying chronic diseases or chronic manifestations. If the human race had remained in a state of perfect order, psora could not have existed. The susceptibility to psora opens out a question altogether too broad to study among the sciences in a medical college. It is altogether too extensive for it goes to the very primitive wrong of the human race, the very first sickness of the human race, the spiritual sickness, from which first state the race progressed into what may be called the true susceptibility to psora, which in turn laid the foundation for other disease.[11]

The other three states are mentioned only in passing. Not infrequently, people may have two or more of these types of weakness and must be treated for these before they fully regain robust health. Dr. Kent hinted that, while the homeopathic medication for them will help restore health, the whole person must be involved in the cure, which necessarily involves renewed orientation toward a life of greater meaning from a personal, interpersonal, and spiritual standpoint because the mind and the accompanying spirit determine the wholeness or health of the person.

## What Is Meadowlark?

The entire atmosphere at Meadowlark is one of peace and beauty. The citrus trees provide fruit and the pool offers refreshment to all who wish it. Guests may be found chatting in the living room, reading in the library, or just lying quietly in the sun or shade, alone or by twos or threes. Roses are in bloom, and the vines on the house are a shiny green. The chapel is a lovely, cool oasis, filled with quiet, comfort, and healing love. The staff quietly and efficiently keeps the wheels turning so that guests are almost unaware of the motivating power behind it all.

So . . . what is Meadowlark? First of all, it is a place to be. All of us must have a place to be, and for some who come here their "place to be" no longer exists, or being in it has become intolerable. Meadowlark becomes for a time their home; their place to put strong roots into the ground, to feel the sun warm on their backs, to look up to the stars.

This is a place of healing—physical healing. Before making great music, the instrument must be tuned, and so must we. The Meadowlark experience starts with the tuning of the instrument. All the tools of modern medicine—diagnostic and curative—are focused on the individual. We also use our knowledge of healing as practiced in the Eastern world. No avenue is overlooked merely because it is not of our present culture. There is persistence here, too, and hope. There is always something more that can be done.

Meadowlark does not wait for the completion of the "tuning of the instrument," however. A guest walks through the massive entrance gates, across the spacious grounds, through the wide front door. Staff members hold out welcoming hands. Other guests extend friendship and understanding. One is at home.

The total program swings into action. Here there is no feeling sorry for oneself if ill or tired, no withdrawing into loneliness. Here is healing—healing for one's whole being. Guests may freely participate in as much or as little as they wish.

It is morning. Chimes ring out to greet the day. Get up! Get up! New life awaits you.

Again the chimes. Do you wish to meditate? To pray? To calm your spirit? To be? The chapel waits for you. Now, or at any hour of the day or night, it waits for you. Come and be enfolded in its peace, sustained by the strength that you find there, guided by new insight.

The chimes, always the chimes, announce each new activity. This time it is breakfast—quite possibly the best breakfast you have ever eaten, certainly the one most planned to meet your body's needs. What is served? I shall not tell you. You must come to see for yourself. But I am confident that those who cook and bake here would be welcomed in many of the great restaurants of the world.

The day progresses, and soon you will be called to "Body Balance," a time for getting acquainted with yourself, your weary back, your aching knees, and learning how to be kind to them. At times you will take part in the gentle, rhythmic exercise. When you feel like it, you will rest. Sometimes you will only watch. Some surprises are in store for you. You will get acquainted with that heart of yours that has beaten so faithfully—how many times? You will rest while music washes over you like waves at the seashore.

What does the music say to you? What do you want to get out of yourself? What do you see that is beautiful; what is ugly? What feelings of resentment do you have, what gratitude struggling to be born? What fears come out of the past, what hopes for the future?

This is the time for bringing it all out on paper, in color. No work of art, perhaps only a scribble of ugly colors—sharp jagged lines, raw feelings. Someday these will all be out of you, and you will hesitantly, then eagerly, reach for the bright, the hopeful, the beautiful, and you will know that a new you is being born.

Lunch. Again the nourishing food, the friendly conversation. Then, rest time, reading time, do-what-you-like time. At four o'clock the chimes call you for tea—on the patio, or by the pool, or by a crackling fire in the living room. The gracious atmosphere of tea time will soon become a part of you.

Dinner is a work of art and prepared with love. You will be begging for recipes to take home.

Several psychosynthesis techniques, especially the "waking dream," as taught by Roberto Assagioli, are being used extensively with the guests at Meadowlark. It is a real joy to see a guest who has come bowed down with problems and who is uptight emotionally begin to relax, unfold, and make a new self-discovery, finding his identity. More guests are staying a little longer now—from two to four weeks or more—and this gives more time to build a rapport and help them find themselves by closer association with the staff member working with them.

To many of us, evening programs are high points that we would not want to miss. Here we are introduced to a wider world than we have known before. Staff members have been chosen with great care for their own maturity and ability to be good listeners plus the capacity to accept people as they are and without prejudice. They have been trained variously in techniques of analysis, exercise, free expression in the arts and crafts, and meaningful group experiences of various sorts. Sometimes the doctor explains to us new concepts in medicine. Sometimes he speaks of the wisdom of the ancients. Here we have as guests great people, great ideas. Here we take part in experiences of fun, of sharing, of catching glimpses of whole new areas of living opening up to us.

What else is available at Meadowlark? Instruction in Zen

meditation, Tai Chi Chuan, experience in toning, psychosynthesis, workshops in many areas, a fine library, a hi-fi recording system, a 600-acre ranch with trails to walk and hills to climb, and much, much more.

The following case histories illustrate what often takes place in the lives of guests at Meadowlark.

When *Marcia* came to Meadowlark, she was only thirty years old, but she had been ill with a variety of ailments for six years. Her energy was so low that she frequently had to leave work. She had suffered for the past three years from throat infections and had undergone a course of autogenous vaccine treatments without result.[13]

She became pregnant a year before we saw her and had been violently upset when her obstetrician failed to arrive in time for the delivery of her child. Following this, she had become extremely nervous, annoyed by the baby's crying, more exhausted than ever—indeed some days unable to perform any of her duties as housewife and mother.

Five months after the birth, she had become deeply depressed and fallen into a panic. She was hospitalized for three days and put on tranquilizers, which helped her for only about six months. After seeing another physician from whose advice she did not benefit, she came to Meadowlark.

She was found to have a multitude of symptoms, including low energy, headaches, hay fever, a chronic cough, depression, palpitations, feelings of faintness, and periods of disgust for life in general. She was also extremely sensitive to hot weather.

Her five-hour glucose tolerance test had not been completed when she arrived, but she showed clearly a diabetogenic-hypoglycemia type. Accordingly, she was put on a diet of no refined carbohydrates or stimulants, with frequent feedings. Her symptom picture best fitted homeopathic Calcarea carbonate, which she was given daily, with daily injections of adrenal cortex extract (ACE), which were to be spaced further apart as her energy increased.

She remained at Meadowlark only a month but continued with ingestion of Calcarea carbonate and ACE injections in addition to taking a daily walk. In three months her energy was 50 percent better, and she reported that she was finding her way out of stressful situations more easily. By this time her ACE injections were down to two a week, self-administered. Her blood pressure had risen from 75/60 to 90/75.

Two months later she had a setback with depression but came out of it much faster than in the past. For this she was given Pulsatilla, followed a few days later by the M potency.

She recently wrote:

> Before I came to Meadowlark I didn't even realize God had lessons for me that I hadn't already learned. As a matter of fact, I wasn't certain there was a God. I'm grateful for the patience and love shown me at Meadowlark. When I was acting my worst, you loved me into loving myself enough to allow God to enter my life and make some necessary changes.
>
> After much prayer and rebellion, and then obedience and acceptance, God revealed to me *His Very Real Presence* and concern for my life. Since then, I'm happy to say, He has been able to use me to reach others. Praise God!
>
> I know that the health and nutrition program at Meadowlark has been extremely helpful in keeping my body functioning properly during times of heavy stress through this very important period in my life.
>
> My family has a new, happy, conscientious, loving wife and mother, ready to meet and accept the challenges set before her. I thank you for the greatest of all gifts shown to me—that of love!

*Marian* was thirty-seven when she arrived at Meadowlark. In fifteen years she had had three major operations, many illnesses, and multiple allergies. She suffered from migraine headaches, dizziness, and considerable indigestion. There was also arthritic pain with swelling in several joints and an extreme sensitivity to sunlight, which caused her facial skin to break into eruptions at the slightest exposure. During each of her four pregnancies she had gained fifty pounds and had become so sleepy that she took quantities of dexedrine.

She had consulted three doctors without result, and a major clinic had diagnosed Lupus erythematosis and prescribed cortisone. By the time she got to Meadowlark she was also in the throes of divorce.

Accommodations were made for herself and her four daughters. She has written of that period:

> I felt terrified and lost. I did not expect to get better. The children were very troubled and disturbed, but they were helped in subtle ways of which they were unaware, but which made a noticeable change.
>
> I was not allowed to become dependent on the doctor, but led to search out and develop my own strength. The reading material to which I was directed put me on a path toward an inner realization of myself and toward spiritual awareness.
>
> In my case, although there was no remission, there was a long, hard road of medical care and spiritual development. Adrenal cortex extract replaced the cortisone. The "green drink" [high protein] and the whole nutritional program played an essential part in my recovery.
>
> Prolonged stress of any kind results in adrenal insufficiency. Whatever the ensuing illness, it must be healed without further damage to the body before emotional growth can be begun. Meadowlark's approach is wholly constructive, aiding the body to heal itself by building it up, strengthening it further with the use of adrenal cortext extract.
>
> For six months after I got home I was in bed much of the time, but gave myself five cc's of adrenal cortex extract daily, and I still adhere strictly to the diet prescribed for me. In two months my vision improved and my joint swelling lessened, as did the accompanying pain. In six months I was sleeping considerably better and doing much less of it during the day. I was less sensitive to light and was able to reduce my adrenal cortex medication to twice a week.
>
> A month later both my headaches and my arthritis disappeared. And in eighteen months I was able to take up work as a waitress and still care for my home and children with-

out help. I now use adrenal cortex extract only when I need
it—that is, in times of unusual stress.

*Dolly's* story covers a period of about three months at
Meadowlark and begins with some background material. She
tells it in her own words:

> I have worked for eighteen of the twenty-four years since I
> married. I held a responsible position calling for maximum
> effort, but I abused my body terribly by not eating on time, or
> properly, and by working long hours under heavy pressure.
> On top of this, my husband, Ted, is over-emotional—it was
> not I who cried, but he. Every discussion or confrontation
> ended for him in a burst of tears and a slam of the door. He
> would return full of remorse for whatever he had said or
> done; he had no idea why he did it, etc. And I would be left
> with a lump in my stomach.
>
> When our daughter arrived—she is now 20—I felt that the
> last thing she needed was *two* crying parents, so for nearly
> 20 years I hardly shed a tear. I didn't know it at the time, but
> I was working myself up into a good case of hypoglycemia.
>
> Two years ago came the day of reckoning. I consulted my
> physician of nine years, owing to headaches, crushing depres-
> sion, and physical weakness. He took an electroencephalo-
> gram, which, incidentally, did show something out of balance.
> He concluded that I needed psychiatric care. But I knew my
> body itself was out of balance, and I eventually found a doc-
> tor who gave me a tolerance test and diagnosed hypoglycemia
> and peptic ulcer. I followed his directions to a "t," but two
> years later I was still slowly dying inside. Life had lost its
> meaning. I was withdrawing from people. Thoughts of taking
> my own life came more often.
>
> My doctor said, "Dolly, I can't do anything for you until
> you get your problems with your husband straightened out."
> I felt desperate. Then a friend gave me a brochure on Mea-
> dowlark and one of their books on hypoglycemia. I called our
> minister's wife, who is a psychologist, a teacher, and a friend.
> I had not consulted her earlier because of my husband's heavy
> involvement in church affairs. But now I needed help.
>
> She talked first with me and then with Ted, and after she

had read the Meadowlark brochure, we agreed that it sounded like the place for me to go. In just a week from the day I first heard its wonderful name, I was at Meadowlark. To describe it to anyone who has not had this experience is almost impossible. You can only say it is filled with beauty, love, peace, and serenity. Finding myself surrounded by people who cared, and who understood what was happening to me, it took me only three days to begin releasing the torrents of damned-up tears. The staff offered me a listening ear to pour it all out to, and also provided the spiritual help I needed so desperately.

After a physical examination, I was put on adrenal cortex extract and vitamins $B_{12}$ and $B_6$. I had stopped all the medication I had brought with me and put my full faith in Dr. Loomis' knowledge of homeopathy, which I must confess, I had never heard of before.

My body began to respond to nutritious foods and medication, and I felt many curious changes taking place. But I was reassured and enabled to accept them. However, after two weeks my mental condition remained the same. I had even refused visits from my family.

Now I was into my third week, and I realized that I would soon have to find the strength to face Ted. I could not do it, but two of the staff talked with him and planted the seed that eventually bore fruit when he decided to see a psychologist. This I could never have accomplished, for he believed that it was only I who needed help.

At the end of the third week I really felt I should go home, but even though he did not think I was ready, Dr. Loomis let me make my own decision. Just then Velma joined the staff, and convinced me that she saw something in me that I could not see myself. She spent many hours with me. Other guests shared their experiences with me. There was always someone I could trust and communicate with. The result was that good music, poetry, and spiritual values were brought back into my life.

By the time Dr. Loomis left on a speaking tour, something strange was beginning to happen to me. I was sleeping only two and a half hours a night, spending the rest walking all over Meadowlark, where there is no danger in the dark. And then suddenly there came a day when I felt as if something was ablaze in my abdominal region. I asked my family not to visit me that weekend.

In the evening, filled with despair, I went out and sat beside the pool. I had still found no reason for living. Velma joined me and did her best to help. I know she was reluctant to leave me there alone in such a dangerous frame of mind, but I insisted on her doing so. She said: "I am leaving you in God's hands and I have to believe you will be taken care of." I sat there about three hours, and slowly the inner fires subsided. I became quiet and calm. Then I said: "God, I can't handle this alone. You'll have to take over." I know now that that prayer was the first step upward.

The next day Sue, one of Meadowlark's wonderful friends and neighbors, asked me if I would like to stay in her house while she was on a month's vacation. My mouth must have fallen open. All I could think was: "God, You certainly came through. You are giving me some breathing time."

That night I was still awake at one o'clock. I was lying on my left side, eyes closed. Then I felt as if someone was lifting my lids. I saw a white, filmy light floating toward me. I felt a Presence in it as it wrapped itself around my body.

I looked intently for a face. I saw none, but my eyes were overflowing with reverential tears. Then I seemed to be forced to turn to face the room. It seemed to vibrate and to become filled with warmth, and I felt prayer filling it. I know now that this was all the praying being done for me by countless people. My eyes closed. I fell asleep.

I was startled into wakefulness about 3:30 A.M. by a strange stirring in my body. I felt panic; then a voice said, "Fear not. I am with you always, even unto death." This calmed me and I lay awake for two hours remembering the words, "Be still and know that I am God." At half past five I got up, showered, and prepared to go out. I wanted time alone to think about all that had happened.

As I stepped outside, everything seemed to take on a new meaning. Instead of just looking at the mountains, sky, and trees, I was now suddenly *realizing* them. I came to a tall eucalyptus and lay down beneath it, gazing up into the serene sky filled with God's wondrous clouds. A branch hung low and I grasped it. It was like taking hold of the hand of God. I was bursting with awe and thanksgiving. I had put aside my intellect and stopped asking "Why?" and now I knew that God loved me and I accepted Christ's Presence within me. Later I learned that many people, especially those who had prayed for me, dreamed about me that night. I remember particularly one letter, mailed the following day in another country by a friend I hadn't heard from for years, who wrote that she had dreamed about me the previous night.

Shortly before this my appetite had simply left me. I had unintentionally begun a fast, confining my food intake to a protein drink and not much more. I was getting less than three hour's sleep a night; yet I was able to function, doing lots of walking and participating fully in the Meadowlark program. I forgot my physical problems; my headaches left me for the first time in years. Somehow I was being sustained. Intuitively I felt I was on a mountaintop from which I would soon have to come down to earth. Once I heard the voice of Amy, Meadowlark's spiritual inspiration, saying, "Dolly, when you descend from the mountain bring your godliness with you." I was to understand this warning within 24 hours.

The next night I was given some pills to relax me at bedtime, but I had a terrifying dream in which I could not walk and when I called for help, there was no answer. I woke up to find my legs as heavy as lead, and yet I was able to struggle to the intercom outside my door. I called the staff member who had the master box with her that night, but I could not stand long enough to get an answer. Somehow I got back to bed, feeling that my dream was becoming a reality.

However, she came to my room within a few minutes and she and a second "staffer" poured hot milk down my throat and did not leave me all night. Oh, how thankful I was for those selfless people who understood what was happening to me! I myself did not, until Dr. Loomis and Velma came at daybreak. Then I learned that I was being born into self-realization. It is a traumatic experience and it continues to amaze me, although I am no longer frightened.

I am now devoting myself to building the body I shall need to serve the newborn Spirit within me. My domestic situation is not resolved, but I know that with God all things are pos-

sible. I do not know what plans He has for me. I do know
that I am available for whatever they may be. I am learning
to live in the "now."
      And meantime I keep remembering the words of Martin
Luther King: "Free at last, thank God Almighty—free at
last!" Free to realize that God loves me and that I love Him,
and to share this glorious certainty with others.

*Walter* arrived at Meadowlark after he had suffered for
seventeen years from arthritis—the bone-eating type—which
had shortened one leg, fused his spine, and twisted his outlook
on life. As an engineer, disciplined to avoid irreversible situations, he had become a perfectionist. Secretly fearing people,
he had sought safety in "having no feelings."
      In 1969, while helping to perfect a missile warhead, he
realized that what he was actually working for was the killing
of more people for less money. This so depressed him that he
quit his job, and he had been a virtual recluse for six months.
      In 1970 he attended a meeting devoted to prayer for spiri-
tual healing. At that conference, he met with me, and I took
the opportunity to fill him in about the basic thinking behind
medicine for the Whole Person.
      After some hesitation he adopted the program of homeo-
pathic remedies. After three days he found himself free of
arthritic pain. He became aware of a new vitality and stamina
as a result of adhering to the Meadowlark menus of natural
foods with no stimulants. His body grew stronger and more
supple as he did isometric and isotonic exercises.
      In 1972 he wrote that he had been obliged to abandon a
plan for a radio documentary on medicine for the Whole Person. He felt that the varied "program-for-the-day, the good
companions, delectable food, and Meadowlark's beauty" could
be conveyed partially, but "how to tape-record its natural
peace, the flow of the day, the coming of self-knowledge and
the simple caring that permeates the very air?" His letter continued:

Flat-out on the lawn, I am aware of sun on closed eyes, of bird song and stray zephyrs, and I become merged with the warm earth beneath. Then gently "coming to" there's a wondrous knowing that I'm one with the humans, too, and only One Life flows through all, warm and good, blending, moving . . . freeing, *being* . . .

In a more recent letter he adds:

At present the situation is this: pain is a thing of the past; a dozen ailments are fading or have already disappeared; atrophied muscles are being restored; faith is full and the prospect is exciting. . . . For there is that which works for wholeness in our lives, if we let it, and Medicine of the Whole Person is programmed to help bring wholeness—physically, mentally, and spiritually. . . . Medicine of the Whole Person combines sudden miracle with slow, steady progress and all of it works for good.

# 7

## THE THERAPEUTIC FAST

And the word of the Lord came unto me in the tenth
month in the government of Oliver Cromwell, in the
year 1653 when I was walking among my sheep,
saying, 'Thou shalt not eat nor drink for the space of
14 days anything but water. But fear not for I will
feed thee with the dew of heaven and with the sweet
incense of my love, and my word shall be unto thee
sweeter than honey, and I will make thee to know that
I am able to keep thee fresh and strong, and able to
do my work without the creatures as well as with it!

Miles Halhead[1]

Surely one of the most overlooked and yet most valuable
modes of healing that will be rediscovered in the future of
the new medicine is the fast. This is because of the increasing interest in looking to oneself for healing powers. For the
fast is an inward process and cannot be entered upon only
from an outer approach with any expectation of a lasting
benefit. The person must invariably be involved with the
overall results. This therapeutic encounter is in direct con-

trast to the usual non-involvement in the physician-directed, disease-oriented medical practice of today.

In this chapter consideration will be given to a review of the medical literature from 1967 to 1977, in which approximately 160 papers dealt in some way with the aspects of the subject. Fifty-two of these, which were felt to be the most pertinent, were reviewed by the author. For several reasons, not much information could be gained from them. Much was too scientific for the general reader, and almost exclusively the subject dealt with obesity and the disease concept[2], not with the healing of the whole person, which is our overriding concern here. Also in this chapter is a brief consideration of the fast as it has been practiced through the ages; and there are extensive comments on the use of the fast in the therapeutic setting at Meadowlark, where several hundred guest-patients have been involved.

Few physicians have seriously considered the fast as a technique worthy of study; and most of those who did, concentrated on its used only in the treatment of obesity. Two notable exceptions, however, are psychiatrists Allan Cott, M.D., and Robert Meiers, M.D. The latter was associated with my work at Meadowlark for a period of three months and initiated my interest in fasting. Dr. Cott spent time in Russia studying the program[4] of Professor Serge Nikoliav of the Moscow Psychiatric Institute where, as of 1972, 6,000 patients had fasted under Nikoliav's direction, resulting in a very high success rate for treatment of chronic refractory schizophrenia, and without a fatality. These patients had not responded to the more usual types of psychiatric therapy. Their fasts were on water, lasted 25 to 30 days, and included much aerobic exercise in the form of long periods of daily walking.

Most attention to the medical fast has been given outside the United States. Paavo Airola's studies of the European clinics cite many successful fasts for a wide variety of human ailments. My own acquaintance with the Bircher-Benner Clinic of Zurich has been a strong incentive toward the use at Meadowlark of vegetable juices and the role of raw vegetables and fruits in the therapeutic armamentarium. The notable work in this country has been carried on by a small group of Naturopathic physicians. Especially useful is the work of Herbert Shelton, who has been employing this modality in his center in Texas for 40 years, guiding many thousands of patients through fasts. His book, *The Hygienic System, Fasting and Sun Bathing,* Vol. III, is the most complete discussion of the physical aspects that I have encountered.[4]

### The New Health Model

Nuclear physics and the new health model view human life with its supporting energy systems as a part of a great continuum. Health is thus seen as a mark of one's resonance with great and universal systems of energies. Disease is a sign of being out of touch. It has always been of interest to me to note that the sicker the individual, the more isolated he or she has become from family, friends and business associates. Thus the role of the physician must be to become increasingly aware of these discordant energies and their sources.

This new challenge is being met by individual physicians, most commonly outside of university settings where they are individually investigating such alternative therapies as acupuncture, homeopathy, polarity therapy, yoga, clairvoyance and psychosynthesis.

These modalities, and I now add fasting as one of the most important on the list, require establishing a contact with the patient, and the future physician accordingly must see his new role as being involved in this interpersonal relationship. He must become absorbed to the limit of his ability in the problems of his patient by listening to the words of that patient and learning even what is behind those words that possibly the patient cannot yet share. Only through this type of empathy can one get beyond the usual objective view of the results of a disease process and begin to get down to causes, many of which are frequently buried in the patient's subconscious. But by being aware, the empathetic physician can gain evidence from the tone of speech, the look in the eyes, in the gestures of the hands, and in those tears that are so obviously being held back. How often in such a time of attunement has a patient said, "I have told you what I have never before shared with anyone, not even my spouse."

To help his patients regain resonance with the universal system, the physician of the new medicine may have to look to areas not often enough considered. He should study the patient's environment, for one example. The physical body's loss of sensitive attunement may be due to such external causes as environmental sources of pollution. These might include chemicals in the air, fallout from atomic testing, more than minimal diagnostic x-ray exposure or other forms of medical radiation, long hours in front of television or microwave ovens, or under fluorescent lights. It might come from drinking fluorinated and chlorinated water, from medically prescribed as well as psychedelic drugs, from synthetic foods along with additives, and in the cases of quite a number of people, even from the artificial materials used in the clothing they commonly wear.

The fast can be most helpful in treatment of patients whose problems have such causes, for it tends toward freeing the body from having to ward off these conflicting sources of energy, and toward freeing the mind from the power of much of the negativity that is all about us today. Once freed, the patient is in a far better position than he was to use his vital energies in a constructive way and so restore homeostasis.

A person needs all of the energy he can healthfully derive, for much is required simply to break down food into its nutritive components, convert the carbohydrates and proteins into glycogen for storage in the liver, and to provide the ready energy needed for healing and optimal physical and mental functioning.

All of this should be within the awareness of new medicine, both for the physician who accepts the new challenge, and for the person who is learning to look within for his own healing powers.

We speak of the fast as being a part of the new medicine. It is a rediscovered part, for the fast as an integral part of life is as old as life itself, and its healing power is to be seen all along evolution's pathway. In the insect world, the feasting caterpillar is followed by the fasting butterfly. Then there are the hibernating reptiles and the bear who take their annual prolonged fasts. If nothing more, this indicates that fasting and starvation are not the same things. Many animals when sick know enough to stop eating, but few humans have retained this healthy insight that intuitively bids one eat or fast as the proper occasion arises and in its natural timing. As William Wordsworth so beautifully comments:

> The world is too much with us,
> Getting and spending we lay waste our powers,
> Little we see in Nature that is ours . . .

Yes, we are out of touch, and the fast provides an ideal setting for renewing this all-important contact. Allow me to quote from one of Meadowlark's recent fasters who began the recontact:

> I am awakened in the morning full of quiet expectation which was deepened by an experience as I sat on the lawn after my simple breakfast of fruit. A honeybee settled on my knee and set about his elaborate grooming of his small person. I was pleased and touched at its confidence in me and extended to him the same. I was struck by his kindness and appreciation showed in every part of his body. I watched with interest and amusement at his insect version of body awareness (referring to an exercise program of that name employed at Meadowlark).

Throughout history, at some time fasts have been used by practically every culture to bring man back in touch with his source of BEING. But unfortunately, Western religion with its only occasional use of fasting has become more and more separated from actual life on an hour to hour basis and needs once more to become interwoven into life's innermost experience, as is still taught by the Shaman of Africa and the Indian medicine man.

Reviewing briefly some aspects of the fast as seen in history:

Jesus—"This kind (referring to the cure, probably of epilepsy) can come forth by nothing but prayer and fasting." (Mark 9:29) Before his period of temptation, Jesus fasted for forty days in the wilderness.

Pythagoras—He commanded his disciples to abstain from all things that had life, and from certain other meats which could interfere with mental perception, and to abstain from wine, to eat sparingly, and to sleep little. (Manly Hall)

Moses—In a time of drought, he fasted for forty days on Mt. Horeb.

The Ethiopian Orthodox Church—Among its tenets, it views the stomach as the seat of the emotions and thus as having a marked effect on the personality. Strong foods such as meat are felt to strengthen emotional reactions and thus are seen as being related to violent behavior.[5]

Gandhi—In his autobiography, he describes his use of the fast and dietary restriction and its great influence on his life's work. It was his observation that passion and the hankering after pleasures of the palate were best brought under control through this means. He goes on further to elaborate that when the senses are subordinated to the rule of the mind, the special relish disappears and man can truly function as it was intended he should.[6]

It would seem that these illustrations reinforce the idea that in times of life's real need to find new sustenance, the fast with its physical cleansing, mental clearing and spiritual mountaintop experiences can open up new vistas on the path of life.

## The Type of Fast and Its Length

The true fast is without doubt the water fast, but experience reveals that this is by no means desirable for all would-be fasters. Accordingly there are many modifications, some suitable and others that are of very questionable merit or even potentially injurious. The fast from both food and water will not even be considered because of the grave dangers that may be associated with its use. In the medical literature, as has been mentioned, the major, almost sole, subject of fasting has been in relation to the control of obesity. Here it has an important role, especially when used along with daily group therapy under staff guidance. When used on an outpatient basis, however, we would tend to restrict it to the overweight patient who has had previous experience with fasting and has been medically evaluated by a physician. Even in this instance we would feel that the patient should have available telephone contact with the guiding physician and a weekly evaluative office visit.

The water fast may also be used for patients other than those with weight problems if they have an adequate fat reserve, that is to say if the skin and subcutaneous tissues of the upper arm when pinched with a caliper measures no less than 20 mm. in the case of women and 15 in that of men. If less, consideration may still be given to a juice or a raw foods fast. In all the above instances, the fast should be supervised by a physician familiar with the procedure. Some of the problems most commonly well handled with fasting include hypertension, arthritis, allergies and headaches along with the detoxification from the use of multiple drugs or tobacco. In our experience this is a very valuable method of handling the problems of the undesirable side effects from long term cortisone therapy. However, in the latter instance, the procedure must be done very slowly, milligram by milligram over a period of time and usually will not be completed in the first fasting experience.

As cited in the medical literature, fasting for obesity has frequently been continued for sixty days and at times considerably longer. The most usually prescribed fast at Meadowlark lasts from two to three weeks. The maximum was 34 days. In that instance the patient was suffering from severe anklyosing arthritis of the spine, such that she had no possible neck motion and had to turn her body to look to the side. There was also associated moderate obesity. This particular guest discovered during the fasters' group therapy that her body stiffness bore a striking parallel to a very unbending religious system in which she felt enmeshed. Toward the end of her fast as she was increasingly allowing herself to express pent up feelings, she began to notice a beginning of motion in the upper spine.

A further use of water fasting is in the emerging field of medical ecology pioneered by Doctors Coca, Randolph, Philpot, Dickey and others.[7] This is in the nature of what is referred to by them as presumptive food testing. That is to say, after four to five days of water fasting when symptoms have quieted down and frequently been accompanied by a drop in the pulse rate, a large meal of the suspected food is given as a single meal, symptom return is noted and the suspect food either discovered or eliminated as a source of symptoms. A case to illustrate:

P.U., a 35-year-old housewife, was seen by me a few years ago complaining of depression, irritability, excruciating headaches, rapid heartbeat, a tremor of her hands, sinus congestion and urinary problems. After a four-day water fast at Meadowlark her symptoms were relieved. Presumptive food testing revealed that following the ingestion of milk her sinuses became congested; following a meal of corn her tremor developed; a headache became evident subsequent to the ingestion of a meal of bananas, and her bladder symptoms followed both rice and strawberries. Two months later she reported no further headaches, bladder trouble nor depression and her marital relationship was vastly improved. The subsequent month, as often happens when one feels much improved, she became lax with her dietary restrictions and practically all her symptoms returned.

The most common of the reacting foods are those which are consumed most regularly, frequently on a daily basis, giving the impression that this frequency of ingestion probably exceeds the body's ability to supply the vitamins, enzymes and minerals required to ensure proper absorption and assimilation. The results often are the cited symptoms of toxicity. Also, life's stresses that are not adequately being handled seem to play a role in these events. And symptoms certainly may also be brought to light by pesticides and other chemicals in the foods, water, the air, clothing, or elsewhere in the immediate environment. While all of these factors play an important role in health, let us not for a minute become imprisoned in a world seemingly controlled by the environment. A hundred years ago a leading homeopathic physician, Dr. James T. Kent, gave good counsel in this regard:

> The internal state of man is prior to that which surrounds him. Therefore environment is not the cause (of disease); it is only, as it were, a sounding board.

The partial or juice fast also finds a place for all the conditions previously recounted and is less threatening to many. Needless to say, the time needed for results may be longer, but the patient's emotional attitude will be superior, particularly if there is a lack of self-confidence with its frequently accompanying feelings of self-deprivation. I prefer the patient to have a choice in the type of fast and the length of fast. For some, even a juice fast is too severe, and in such cases there is a real place for a partial fast, limited to raw fresh vegetables or fruits as practiced at the Bircher-Benner Clinic.[8]

### Fasting, When and for Whom?

In the past the progress of life and the consciousness of one's relationship to the universe as a whole was mirrored in the observance of the fast. Man was very conscious of the fact that he was part of a whole that far surpassed the boundaries of his physical body. He intuitively knew that if he lost sight of his own body rhythms and got out of step with the seasons of the world about him he would likely fall ill. It is of interest that we are only recently rediscovering the importance of these rhythms and their part in everyday life.[9]

In accordance with this principle, times of fasting have in the past coincided with the seasons and the solar system's inherent rhythm. Note the Lenten fast in conjunction with the full moon of Easter in the Christian tradition, and the corresponding Passover fast associated with the same full moon of the Hebrew month of Nasar. Certain cultures have timed the planting and harvesting of their crops according to similar time schedules. Moses and Jesus were both aware of the needed season for a fast and each picked a period of forty days. In Islam, where the fast is adhered to more strictly than in the Judeo-Christian culture, Ahmad Sakr reports that the faithful Moslems all over the world are required to fast throughout the month of Ramadan, the ninth month of their calendar. In his words:

> Fasting is considered to be a training period for controlling one's needs and desires, in restraining from self-indulgence, and a time for deepening one's spiritual life. The fast is started with prayer and reading.[10]

Further, not only does the season of the year but also the exact time of day have significance. When the human body approaches a state of homeostasis, it once again picks up these universal rhythms. This is obvious in the case of menstruation. It may also be observed in many blood determinations such as the pituitary clock and its maximum output of ACTH between 4 and 8 a.m. And even further, observation will reveal the relationship of the human endocrine system to this all-pervasive timepiece. The endocrine clock in association with the advent of puberty has been a time for a fast for the American Indian.[11] I would like to think that once again we may discover the influence of these natural rhythms and their effect on health and their relationship to times for fasting.

It is the person who has become aware of his inner environment, its discovery and cleansing, that usually benefits the most from the fast and its attendant therapy. It was from this standpoint that Moses, Jesus and Gandhi were led into their fasts. During the last decade, approaching as we are the so-called Aquarian Age, there is much evidence of a new hunger to obtain sustenance capable of replacing the spiritual vacuum so prevalent in the materialistic world. The heart is sick! Through all eternity, this centrally placed human organ has symbolized the all-powerful role of love. Could this be the reason for the increasing number of deaths from heart disease? In spite of coronary care units in hospitals, by-pass surgeries and trained resuscitation teams, the long-term results have been to accomplish little toward increasing the span of human life. And so it is not only the outward aspects of health that prompt people to come to Meadowlark, and once there to choose the fast as an aid to finding new avenues of meaning in their lives, to finding fresh contacts with their spiritual natures. This desire for the fast often comes to them as an inner feeling of guidance.

But if considering only the traditional manifestations of health problems, who should avoid the fast? The medical literature is by no means clear cut when considering the possible relative contraindications to fasting. However, I would like to list these with my own feelings:

1. The hypochondriacal patient with deep emotional needs
2. Pregnant women, and for the most part, children
3. Severe bronchial asthma
4. Diabetes
5. Epilepsy
6. Malnutrition
7. Ulcerative colitis
8. Terminal illness

I have purposely referred to the above as relative contra-indications as there will be instances in all the above mentioned states when fasting can be considered.

In the first instance, as related in the book, *Some Unrecognized Factors in Medicine,*[12] the anonymous physician authors state that the hypochondriacal, hysterical patient, as we have also found, is a poor candidate for the fast. So often these persons have never really lived a life of their own. They have tended to live at the beck and call of some other individual and as a result have never truly felt fulfilled. To ask them to make the sacrifice of their food for a period of time can be just too devastating for their inner development and growth.

Concerning pregnancy, I can see a juice fast with juices being prepared daily under a skilled nutritionist (and I am not referring to the usual hospital dietician) as a possibility in toxemia or marked obesity. Such a patient should also be evaluated daily by the physician.

A similar, partial fast may also be appropriate in the case of a child. From the physical standpoint, juvenile onset diabetes or adult type where there have been spells of coma or severe acidosis, severe asthma, frequently necessitating hospital admission, and epileptic seizures might be considered contraindications to the fast unless carried out in a suitable hospital setting. I have in the past found this possible in our own local hospital.

Ulcerative colitis can be handled but presents a number of problems and needs much emotional support for it to be successful.

Near terminal illness where fasting might lead to a starvation would not seem an appropriate line of therapy, although I feel that there can be exceptions when the patient feels a strong sense of inner guidance in this direction. However, in this instance, the relatives and the patient should be well acquainted with the risks involved, and the physician conscious of his risk of censure by his medical peers.

## The Time of the Fast

The time of the fast should be a very special time. Many of our Meadowlark guests have told us that it was the most significant event in their lives to that time. To begin with it is a time of tearing down the old and the onset of building a new body temple. What better words to occupy the mind at the beginning of the fast than the words of that well known physician-poet, Oliver Wendell Holmes in "The Chambered Nautilus":

> Build thee more stately mansions, oh my soul,
> As the swift seasons roll!
> Leave thy low vaulted past!
> Let each temple, nobler than the last,
> Shut thee from heaven with a dome more vast,
> Till thou at last art free,
> Leaving thine outgrown shell by life's unresting sea.

It should be a space in one's life for reorientation and self assessment. It only makes common sense that in this age when the internal and external environments are filled to overflowing with synthetic imitations of the stuff that evolution took a few million years to design, the body and mind need to have periods for an all-important time of cleansing.

The state of mind and its activities can be most significant for the faster. For some it can be a time of self-discovery, a time to stop playing a role and to begin living the real person. Thus, it can be a time for releasing the ego and discovering the Transpersonal Self. In this frame of reference, the late psychiatrist, Roberto Assagioli,[13] speaks of starting to LIVE rather than just to exist. Because these crises in personal development will frequently be met during the fast, it is essential that the person guiding the fast recognize them in their full significance.

Assagioli describes the stages of the unfoldment of the True Self: 1) Crises preceding the spiritual awakening: 2) Crises caused by the spiritual awakening; 3) Reactions due to the spiritual awakening; 4) Phases of the process of transmutation.[12] If these important signs along the road of life are not recognized, a great injustice can be done the person involved. In the process of unfoldment, there may be midnight emergencies as the dying ego manifests itself through a dream or through the frightening experience of the so-called dark night of the soul. It is then that an understanding nurse should be available, one who is thoroughly trained in the process of the fast; and a psychologist or physician trained in and familiar with the areas of transpersonal experience.

For these reasons, and others, the special event of the fast should not be carried on in the usual setting of home or business if anything of lasting value is to be anticipated, other than perhaps temporarily taking off a few pounds of body weight. The setting should be a place of natural beauty, removed from newspapers, radio, television, phone calls, visitors (even including contact with the immediate family). If at all possible, the spot should be self-chosen rather than decided upon, *a-priori*, solely by a physician, friend or family member. Since the fast can be a time of real enrichment of one's inner life, preparation can well lead to some research ahead of time into books that would have meaning for the coming events. Especially significant can be biographies of men and women who have been a source of inspiration or religious writings that have a place in structuring and bringing significance to life.

The importance of the timing of the fast is beautifully illustrated in these words in the Aquarian Gospel of Jesus Christ:

One man may fast and in his deep sincerity of heart is blessed;
Another man may fast and in his faithlessness of such a
    task imposed is cursed.
You cannot make a bed to fit the form of every man.[14]

Chapter 119:23-25

## The Fasting Process

A careful history and physical examination should precede the fast for any person other than one in optimal health, and in that case an office visit is recommended with the guiding physician assessing the desirability of the fast. This is particularly true when any fast is expected to last more than two or three days. Included in the preparation should be blood tests for uric acid, blood sugar, creatinine, cholesterol, total protein and some evaluation of liver function. An electrocardiogram should be considered.

To better explain the fasting process, we will divide it into four stages that also reflect those set down by Dr. Cott, who made a study of the format used in the Russian model, to which reference was made. *Stage 1* is a time of general excitation of the involuntary nervous system, lasting one to three days; *Stage 2,* a time of inhibition, continuing from day two or three to the end of the first week and sometimes even into the second week; *Stage 3,* a time of gradual recovery, which most fasters do not go beyond during their initial experience; *Stage 4,* full recovery.

It is most interesting to note the close parallel of the stages of fasting to the stages resulting during the healing process accompanying administration of homeopathic remedies. In fact, it can be very beneficial to use the two therapeutic modalities concurrently.

From the physiological point of view, during *Stage 1* the general excitation is manifest through the increased electrical activity observed with the electroencephalogram, while the blood picture reveals a mobilization of the healing agents as seen in the increased number of white blood cells being poured into the general circulation. *Stage 2* is heralded by increasing evidence of acidosis, the presence of hypoglycemia and a psychomotor depression. There is generally a loss of appetite, and the tongue is likely to become coated. Gradually the excitation gives way and is superseded by inhibition.

During the first few days, usually all of *Stage 1* and the

beginning of *Stage 2,* the patient is pretty much occupied with cleaning the gastrointestinal tract. This includes the liver, which is relieved of the responsibility of having to handle its usual daily load of imitation foods that have much to do with chronic degenerative diseases. At the same time, the cleansing releases much of the body's innate energies formerly concerned with handling this metabolic load, thus allowing the body a chance to restore natural health and bring about a state of homeostasis. During this period, the cleansing process is very evident in marked signs of toxicity, the return of former physical symptoms, and a marked dulling of mental processes, and not infrequently an overwhelming sense of fatigue and the need to rest.

*Stage 3,* then, is one of normalization with its accompanying feeling of well being, usually far surpassing the state pre-existing the fast.

Weight loss during the early days of the fast can be dramatic, especially in women who have a water retention problem. Sometimes the loss can be as much as four to seven pounds in a single day, and 10 to 20 pounds in a week is not unusual. By the end of the first week, however, this will have leveled off to an average of three-fourths of a pound a day, and there will be days of no loss, and perhaps even days of gain. This need not be viewed with alarm. Factors reflected in the fluid retention may have been too liberal use of salt in the diet, the use of birth control pills, the use of tobacco, the overuse in the diet of refined carbohydrates, or in some cases certain foods may be associated with the problem. When foods are suspected, they may be evaluated by presumptive testing following the fast, as described by Phillpot. Pyridoxine (Vitamin B₆) and Vitamin C also may be helpful in dealing with this problem.

(Very frequently at this time there will surface an unresolved emotional problem and the need to release long dried up tears. Often we have observed this interrelationship. Many times there has been observed a marked diuresis following a counseling session that produced a flood of tears.)

As is common knowledge, the hypothalmic portion of the brain and the closely related posterior pituitary have a major role in controlling water balance. In several patients where there was further evidence of such a deficiency, therapeutic use of posterior pituitary in minimal dosage was of real value. There will be a rapid increase in weight following the fast in these patients if they early bring the refined carbohydrates into their diets and if they do not adequately avoid sources of salt. Closely paralleling large losses of fluid in the early fast will be symptom-producing losses of potassium and occasionally sodium. The latter loss peaks on about the fourth day, while the former loss is evident and rapid during the first few days and gradually may taper off between the tenth and fourteenth days. The most common symptoms related to these losses include weakness, postural hypotension, diarrhea, nausea, vomiting, vertigo and leg cramps. All will be greatly ameliorated by a potassium supplement.[15]

It is well to bear in mind that the early days of the fast also are marked by an acidic condition of the body with the release into the urine of considerable acetone, which can be monitored very easily by test papers available at any pharmacy and used in the control of diabetes. As the fast progresses, another reliable indicator of the body's return toward homeostasis is the use of pH testpapers on the saliva, checked morning and night due to the body's circadian rhythms. Ideally one would like to see the papers register pH values between 6.4 and 6.8.[16]

The breakdown of toxic tissue products during the fast will frequently be reflected in blood chemistry values, which can be rechecked during its course. To be expected is an early rise in uric acid due to the breakdown of tissue nucleoproteins. In this connection there will be on rare occasions an attack of gout. However, this is, in our opinion, no excuse for the use of antiurogesic drugs during the course of a fast. Should gout make its appearance, it could much more safely be managed with homeopathic remedies or herbs.

Fatalities during the fast have been reported in the medical literature when drugs were used, when tests were made requiring intravenous administration of chemicals, and when alcohol or tobacco were used.[17] Patients desirous of getting off drugs, alcohol, tobacco should always do so only under close medical supervision. During the course of the fast there will frequently be an elevation of the enzymes associated with liver function, reflecting the increased involvement of that organ in the detoxification. These will gradually return to normal as the fast continues into *Stages 2* and *3*. There will frequently be evidences of the added stress on the kidneys but in this instance, too, there will be gradual improvement as reflected in the blood urea values. More often these may be late manifestations after the fast if the patient stays on the new diet and keeps away from the use of drugs and foods containing additives. There will also be a return toward normal levels of elevated cholesterol and triglycerides. These later findings will be enhanced by the coincident use of a good program of aerobic exercise.

## The Fast at Meadowlark

Let us now turn attention to the actual program for the groups of fasters as carried on at the Meadowlark rehabilitation center. An average group of fasters might include an arthritic seeking to reduce the amount of medication; two with obesity problems who in the past have not been able to keep their weights down; another guest with migraine headaches; a guest with lupus erythematosis keen on getting off cortisone, and another guest wishing the spiritual benefits of a fasting experience. At the initial meeting the guests are asked to share individually their reasons for wanting to fast and are made to see the seriousness of the discipline and the need of the involvement of their whole person in the process. They are also informed that the discipline is going to be strictly adhered to.

Each faster is then instructed by the nurse as to the measurements that will be recorded daily, most of which the faster will take for himself and record on special forms. These records include a.m. temperature, pulse twice daily for evidence of ecological factors related to illness, blood pressure, water intake and urine output during *Stages 1* and *2* for evidence of water retention, check of urine for ketones and Vitamin C level, and twice daily salivary pH readings.

Vitamin C supplementation is routinely carried on throughout the fast to aid in the detoxification program. If a water fast is carried on longer than a week, a general vitamin supplement is added to the regime. If diuresis seems to be imcomplete, diuretic herb teas are frequently suggested. These might consist of goldenrod, chamomile, watercress, parsley or rose hips.

When the fast is merely for reducing and physical evaluation and there is no evidence of disease, the faster's progress could be watched on the basis of weekly office visits with interim phone calls.

Concerning the role of exercise, opinions vary all the way from those who advise bed rest to those who make a great point of long periods daily of walking, cycling or swimming. It would seem that a middle of the road policy is generally applicable, with individual variations to suit the particular faster. For those who are most toxic and are not troubled with excess weight, initially, much rest best suits their condition, to be followed by a program of gradually increasing exercise as tolerated. In general it is probably wiser not to include jogging, other forms of strenuous exercise and certainly no competitive exercise, yet fasters are frequently surprised by the physical strength they find as they move into *Stage 2* and by the ease with which they can endure long periods of sustained exercise.

Concerning the use of enemas, colonics, or of their avoidance, opinions are very controversial. Once again we have taken a middle of the road position, starting the fast with an initial purge, using phospho-soda, and following on the next three days with self-administered enemas, unless diarrhea occurs or the stool becomes clear. Further enemas are not regularly employed unless there would seem to be discomfort due to the collection of feces.

It is important to keep dental plates in the mouth, biting on them to keep the gums in condition or there may be such shrinkage that by the end of the fast the plates no longer fit.

Personal hygiene is particularly important during the fast, for there may be considerable body odor due to the detoxification taking place. A shower is suggested for each morning. Water temperatures should not be extreme because too long in hot water can be ennervating. To follow a shower with a good body brushing is a good procedure. Cosmetics and deodorants should be avoided during the fast, for they tend to drive the impurities back into the system. An absorbent material or cornstarch under the arms could, however, be used in addition to frequent cleansing. The coated tongue can be brushed and thus cleansed, which will partially alleviate frequent bad taste in the mouth.

In the case of the water fast, spring water from a known good source is preferable; but if this is not possible, distilled water is the second choice, if appropriate minerals are added to approximate a natural source of water. Approximately 70 ml. of water or other liquid per kilogram of body weight should be drunk daily, with the occasional substitution of herb teas if desired.

Inasmuch as we like to see our fasters learn to flow with life, we never tell them ahead of time how long they will be fasting. Instead we encourage them to get in touch with their INNER KNOWER and allow that to be their guide, with suitable comments or suggestions from us when appropriate. This is a day to day decision and not preordained.

In the instance of juice fasts, the juices should be prepared daily as nearly as possible to their time of use, in any case not more than a day before. Preferably, juice is produced with a pressure-type juicer, rather than a centrifugal type. Grapefruit or apple are the usual juices we employ for the start of the day, changing to vegetable juices for the rest of the day. Orange juice is avoided because of its high sugar content and due to the fact that many people have the problem of hypoglycemia. The usual amount of juices for the day is one liter to be divided into four glasses frequently diluted and sipped throughout the day rather than to be drunk solely at meal times. For specific suggestions as to variations on juices see the books of Paavo Airola and those from the Bircher-Benner Clinic, available through health food stores. Favorites among our group have been a mix of carrot and celery juice and Bieler broth.[18] The latter has the advantage especially for people who have multiple allergies or maladaptive reactions to certain foods, for zucchini is very rarely a culprit. Bear in mind also that the green leaves of vegetables restore a favorable acid-alkaline balance after the combustion of foods more rapidly than anything else, so that a plain juice from green leaves has a unique place in the fasting purification process. Supermarket vegetables, if used, should be washed thoroughly to remove any vestiges of pesticide sprays. Organically grown vegetables are preferred.

The first week of the fast is in every way the hardest, for gradually one after another the symptoms of detoxification become manifest. These are generally related to health problems of the past and make their appearance in reverse order of the time of life when they were originally present. This follows the same law that will be observed when using homeopathic medications. One of the most frequently recurring symptoms is the withdrawal headache of the coffee addict. Other commonly encountered symptoms include extreme fatigue, dizziness, nausea, vomiting, palpitations, nasal mucous, visual disturbances, muscle pains and cramps, diarrhea, flatus, irregularities of the heart and increased body odor. (The latter should never be handled by the use of deodorants as this will block the pores of the skin and drive the toxins back into the body.) Symptoms can be greatly ameliorated by the use of the potassium supplement to which reference has already been made. Nausea can often be handled by the addition of lemon juice to the faster's water, or by the use of homeopathic Nux vomica or Ipecac. If vomiting continues for more than a day, it may on rare occasions be necessary to give intravenous fluids. When there is intolerance to ascorbic acid (Vitamin C), magnesium oxide or bicarbonate of soda may be given along with it. Inasmuch as magnesium deficiency is reported at times, it has been our custom to give magnesium oxide in equal parts with the bicarbonate and ascorbic acid. If, however, this is followed by diarrhea, the amount of magnesium oxide should be decreased. When there is considerable evidence of toxicity, that is to say the liver has a large load of work ahead, to help the individual get back into a state of health the liver flush has frequently been used, as recommended by Harold Stone, the father of polarity therapy. It consists of a mixture of olive oil, lemon and grapefruit juice, and garlic.

Although at Meadowlark we have ample evidence that the psychological benefits of the fast, the attunement to the inner life, are equal in value to the improvement in outward health, I have found scant information in the literature reviewed on the use of psychotherapy in conjunction with the fast. Nor is there scarcely a mention of the bonus of transpersonal experiences which are often accompaniments of the group process that I will describe. I will mention one study done by Wine and Crumpton[19] that does make a few good points. In their work they divided 37 men into three groups. In group one were placed the men who had a negative attitude in their hospital surroundings, became irritable, demanding and spent much time making accusations. In the second group were those judged as not being successful in life; as might be expected, neither were they particularly successful in fasting. The third group worked together as a unit sharing each others' problems. This was the one group that truly profited from the experience, gaining insights into their reasons for overeating, the realization of how superficial their lives had been and the discovery of their need to find a new way of life.

At Meadowlark we have the advantage of a setting of great natural beauty in the mountain-girded valley of Hemet, California, which is truly a space apart from the noisy structured life of a large city or hospital setting. This is no doubt a factor in making our group therapy more effective than the study just mentioned. There is also the advantage that our group makes no distinction as to who is included; thus those with poor self esteem have the support of the others. The addition of dream analysis not only helps one to discover the real person but it also frequently takes an individual who has never visited the realm into the dormant area of transpersonal reality. Too, our program takes the faster through exercise programming, biofeedback, psychosynthesis, various types of group encounter, and art therapy, often relating to dream experiences (as related in the chapter on dreams). Lastly but by no means least, much stress is placed upon the keeping of a personal journal.

Certainly one of the greatest benefits of the fast is the mental clarity that accompanies it, and another is the opportunity to discover the value of daily meditation. The group experience always adds to every aspect, for it gives support to each member; and the sharing, loving concern between members and staff frequently strengthens the faster's personal image.

Membership in a Meadowlark fasters' group is something that is taken very seriously, assuredly a factor in its success. To enter it is the guest-patient's decision rather than the physician's. No one is accepted for the group who is to be in residence for less than two weeks, and it is made very clear at the start that fasting is a discipline, that certain rules will be strictly adhered to. For instance, daily attendance at group meetings promptly at 7 a.m. is required, and sampling of food from the refrigerator is absolutely forbidden. Violation of either rule is grounds for asking the guest to drop out of the group. There are other, less rigid rules. To those who cannot meet the requirements, and it happens that some guests do ask for a less strenuous regime after a few days' sampling, it is suggested that another, more appropriate time will come when they will feel more emotionally fulfilled and able to undergo the necessary discipline. This strictness has a salutatory effect on those who do succeed, for the accomplishment seems even greater.

## Coming Off the Fast

The length of the fast has already been discussed, so we will turn directly to the plan of withdrawal from the fasting state. As a rule of thumb, approximately the same length of time should be given to the withdrawal phase as was spent on the fast. It should be remembered that at the end of the fast, the amount of digestive juices available is limited and the stomach may have considerably shrunk. Thus the initial feedings should be in small amounts at frequent intervals. Breaking this rule and gorging after a fast as some occasionally do, or eating highly refined or spiced foods, can have serious consequences, such as severe abdominal pain, diarrhea and vomiting. Deaths have even been reported from such impulsive behavior.

The longer the fast, the more care is needed in its method of termination. The usual procedure is to break it with fruit or vegetable juices. Meadowlark's routine is one glass of fruit juice for breakfast and two to three of vegetables juices during the remainder of the day. In the case of fasts that have continued longer than a week, the juices should at first be diluted. These are sipped at intervals throughout the day and not gulped down as a substitute for a meal. The juices used have already been described under the discussion of the juice fast. The water intake should also be kept up so that a total daily fluid intake should average thirty milliliters per kilogram (one ounce per two pounds of body weight.) For a one-week fast, I would suggest two to three days of juice; for two weeks, double this. However, in case of obesity, one can stay considerably longer on the juice if it is so desired. From juices the next step is the introduction of a breakfast of fruits or Muesli,[20] and the other two meals of vegetables, largely raw or very lightly cooked. If there is a suspected reaction to foods, this is the time for presumptive food testing as already described. Lastly we would add dairy products and wheat, carefully noting any possible change in pulse rate or other symptoms that might suggest a reaction to either.[7]

If chronic illnesses are evident, such as arthritis, malignant states, ulcerative colitis, asthma, cardiovascular diseases, it is very advisable to stay permanently away from red meats such as pork, beef and lamb and consider the vegetarian way of life. If this is too difficult after a period of really good progress in overcoming the signs of the previous disease, it might be permissible to add fish, shell fish and chicken. There are several reasons for the use of vegetable proteins rather than animal that have already been discussed in the chapter on nutrition. It is also of interest to note how many people lose their appetite for meat on completion of the fast. Another benefit is that the appetite can once again discriminate between foods that are health building and those that destroy the body. The latter are very likely to leave a bad taste in the mouth that may persist for as long as several days. The so called junk foods destroy this discriminative sense and induce cravings for sugar, salt and other harmful foods.

### The Significance of the Fast

Returns from a follow-up letter Meadowlark sent to fasters who were in a position to evaluate their fasts after a period of three or more years, reveal these remarks: "was able to eliminate most of my migraine problems" . . . "for at least six months there has been no evidence of hypoglycemia" . . . "exhaustion gone, no depression" . . ."the sustained weight loss was certainly helpful" (10 pounds lost on 11-days' water fast still sustained) . . ."malabsorption problem is lessened" . . . "It cleared my excess mucous problem" . . . "able to stay off prednisone" . . . "blood pressure now normal."

Most of the fasting guests have noted that they have made permanent changes for the better in their diets with a greater feeling of health and well being; this usually means far less use of meats, refined foods and a greater consumption of vegetables in particular. The majority have kept on a regular, increased use of exercise as a part of their ways of life. Several have made a practice of finding time for daily meditation.

In conclusion may I share the comments of a housewife/ psychologist who captures the meaning of her fast through reviewing her personal journal and sharing it with us:

> My fast of 14 days at one time and 21 on another occasion, drinking only water and herb teas, took off 25 pounds. I have kept 10 to 15 off since then. It is like leaving one country and going to another. I still fast one day a week. My blood pressure is now normal, the blood sugar has leveled off, exhaustion is gone and I no longer have periods of depression. I came to fasting exhausted from too much concentration on my job, home, friends, children, community activities . . . Fasting is a place removed from daily toils and has allowed me to open up the emptiness inside of me . . . I have wept freely, I feel no regrets and desire to go deep inside so that my steps in the future represent the path the Real Me wants to tread, not just continuing on with the conventional pattern that is not an expression of my life. I am renewed and invigorated by finding my inner resources and goals and dreams are still there and in good order. I fasted 11 days at Meadowlark, then two week of reflection at home, eating again and now my second fast at Meadowlark . . . I am feeding my long needed

hunger. I shall leave here in a few days much more in tune with the beauties of nature, the joys of my life and with strength, courage and resolve to change the things that must be changed. As I make the needed changes, I know the empty places will be filled with joy. For I saw sign in my first dream that said, 'the joyous Spirit of God is within you.'

# 8

---

## THE FASTER AND HIS DREAMS

For God speaketh once,
yea twice, yet man perceiveth it not.
In a dream, in a vision of the night,
when deep sleep falleth upon men,
in slumberings upon the bed;
then he openeth the ears of men,
and sealeth their instruction . . .
Job 33:14-16

As so often happens, a faster's dreams come with startling clarity. "I just didn't know how clear dreams can be," is the frequent comment of the new faster. And those who have been in a Meadowlark fasters' group for a few days knowingly nod their heads. Dreams are reviewed daily in the fasters' group, with instructions to write down dreams upon awakening, and Meadowlark has dream counseling for those who choose. Very often non-fasters, hearing the fasters discuss their dreams with great enthusiasm, also seek dream therapy.

To me, the most fascinating part of guiding a group of fasters has been the time spent with them reviewing the revelations they have had through their dreams. At the onset of the fast quite a few comment that they do not dream or that the dreams they do have are inconsequential. Following instructions to ask in prayer or meditation for instruction each night through a dream, they are amazed to find within two to three days that dreams start revealing a guiding path for their own evolvement. If after that time the dreams still are not recalled, the use of Vitamin B6 will almost invariably start the dreams in such a manner that they can be recalled. Daytime dream-like visions may come to some, others may have more meaningful experience through an art form, while others may find poems coming through to them. I would like to share such a poem, in this case from an automobile salesman:

> I rode to war on my steed last night,
> To meet my enemy in savage fight.
> I stormed up the hill with anger and ire,
> To put out the fire that consumed my whole being,
> To finally find my enemy unseeing.
> Oh, the years I had waited to crush this one,
> This enemy that tortured and damned me and always won.
>
> I could never catch a glimpse of my foe,
> He came and he left so quickly with woe.
> He seemed to be smiling and I could never fathom
> How this could be, when he was my sworn enemy.
>
> When I reached the scene of the fight,
> A light broke out from sky to ground
> And I was engulfed by the absence of sound.
> The world stood still and I was astounded
> By the feel of air that was love surrounded,
> And peace and love and harmony so dear.
> I wondered what was happening here,
> When a voice exclaimed so clear,
> "You have been looted with love by your enemy, ME."
>                                        F.D.

The fast with its added insights through dreams and relationships with new friends on a new level of sharing opens up scarcely envisioned vistas of experience. The senses become acute so that colors may become intensified, sounds enriched, and the sense of smell enhanced.

Assisting with the editing of the chapters on fasting and dreams has been particularly meaningful for me. I am an alumnus, so to speak, of both, and the lasting effect on my health, on my life, is profound. I came to Meadowlark not with any prior "faith," but because my distress was such that I was prepared to try anything. Success is doubly sweet when you have no expectations, only hope. That was two years ago. These chapters have served as a renewal for me. —*Wayne E. Webb*

A word about dream revelations may be appropriate at this point, as they serve as portals to new areas of consciousness. Some of the common dream symbols will be mentioned below to serve as a guide to anyone unfamiliar with the use of dreams. Note, however, that the *best* interpretation is always that of the dreamer, and that guidelines as indicated are only suggestions for consideration as to feeling of appropriateness. Repetitive dreams are particularly significant and should be studied. If dreams are still unclear as to message, the following night there can be a prayerful request for further insight through another dream.

### Frequent Dream Symbols with Suggested Possible Interpretations

a road or path—the road of life
a building—one's consciousness
rooms—different areas of conscious experience
water—cleansing
aerial experience—ascent toward transpersonal experiences
the color white—a spiritual color
the black person—the dark and unrecognized side of one's personality (only true for light-skinned persons)
fire—purification, destruction of the old

corpses, funerals—death of the old personality to make
way for the birth of the new consciousness
large bowel movements, cluttered rooms—the old consciousness
housecleaning—getting rid of the old
men—the reasoning side of the person
women—the intuitive side
animals—the animal or emotional nature which is either
threatening or in control
child or youth as seen by an adult—movement toward the
innate wisdom of a child

Verily I say unto you, Whosoever shall not receive the kingdom
of God as a little child, he shall not enter therein.  Mark: 10:15

Mary dreamed that she saw an airplane coming in on a
collision course. She found herself in the control room and
was able to guide the plane in safely. "That's the way it
was", she remarked, "but things are really different now."
Susan found herself walking by a police car and going
down into a subterranean room where there were two large
tables covered with dead birds; one with wild turkeys and
the other with pheasants; except that one pheasant wasn't
quite dead, for its tail feathers were moving slightly. There
was a hunter with his gun not far away. She had a feeling
that she should report this to the policeman. As she thought
about this dream and shared with the group, she decided that
the policeman was her inner supervisor and guardian. The
birds symbolized her own past when she had been more
aware of her own intuitive knowing (higher consciousness).
The hunter was her reason, which in recent years had made
her mistrust her former intuitive use of that faculty. However,
she commented, "You know, two of the pheasants weren't
quite dead!"
Earl didn't believe in dreams, except for amusement, he
told the group at his first fasters' session. But he had had a

vivid dream and shared it. Perhaps, some among the experienced fasters said, the objects you dreamed about could mean . . . Earl was silent. Later he confessed, "That hit too close to home. I wasn't admitting those things to myself, let alone to anyone else." He had a session of dream counseling, then psychosynthesis counseling. He had four recurring dreams, the first that same night after the fasters' session and the rest after beginning counseling. At first he felt too overwhelmed by the discovery of the accuracy of his dreams to relate them to the fasters' group, but into the second week of his fast he had wrestled them to the point he could talk about them. His four dreams had dealt with various authority figures, always uniformed, and also with a cat and different male figures. In the fourth dream, he stopped fighting the uniformed figures, literally, and was on equal terms with them. He had only one more significant, related dream. The authority figures were gone, and in that dream the cat and female figures blended into one in a flash of light. The cat and the female figures were his intuition, his creative side, and the problems in his subconscious were settled when the cat, Earl's emotions out of control, was taken over by the female figure. Earl was a writer who had run into so many obstacles that eventually he became quite ill, physically and emotionally. Later he returned to work, but he never had those dreams again. He did say, "I just didn't think it possible that I could become a believer in dreams that rapidly. But they were so very true. That insight was a major turning point in my getting well."

Phillip was at Meadowlark for help for relief from intractable angina. He dreamed repeatedly of a corpse that wasn't quite dead. In consciousness he was rediscovering his own need of love. He came to realize that the corpse was his old impersonal executive image that he was still holding on to in his struggle to rediscover his own true identity.

It is quite commonly recognized in the literature dealing with life's journey into the realm of spirit that there are several significant signpaths along the way, or so called initiations. Possibly we might refer to them, as we regularly see them recurring in dreams, as the death of the old self, the time of cleansing or purification, finally the cosmic rebirth. This is often physically paralleled in the fast.

The first stage in that journey, one that may be associated with something of a so-called "dark night of the soul", can be a very frightening experience with its vivid dreams of dying or of the death of a close friend who may be visualized in a casket or being lowered into a grave. The individual may actually feel he or she is dying and call out for help. It is of extreme importance that a person, preferably a physician or nurse with understanding, be available and on call.

The second or cleansing experience may be symbolized in a number of ways, including housecleaning, bathroom and laundry scenes. The third phase, especially in women, frequently envisions a beautiful baby coming into the life of the dreamer. It is also not infrequently accompanied by intense visions of light.

The housewife/psychologist who shared portions of her personal journal with us concerning her fasting experience, had written this about her dreams:

> Before I came to Meadowlark, if asked, I would have said that I dreamed very seldom and almost never remembered my dreams. I have dreamed all the 21 nights here and recorded the same. I am amazed to find that the dreams deal with my personal life problems . . . indecision, fear, and being literally choked with loneliness. I am an extrovert; I did know that repression was a word that applied to me. Yet now I see how my dreams go into my personal agonies. I took part in two dream workshops. I stood naked in my own anguish . . . I know I must stop kidding myself and change my life. More of my personal needs must be met. Twenty years of bottling me up to make a happy home is sickening and I am going to get off this treadmill and will recover the lost child and her real life aspirations.

In holistic medicine we learn so forcibly over and over that the spirit and mind must heal right along with the body.

When a dream is born in you
  With a sudden clamorous pain
When you know the dream is true
  And lovely, with no flaw or stain,
O then, be careful, or with sudden
  clutch
You'll hurt the delicate thing you prize
  so much.

                              Robert Graves

# 9

## THROUGH ILLNESS TO SELF-REALIZATION

Man comes out of unity into diversity,
The ego appears, has to be recognized,
Then transcended and return to Unity
In a higher octave of consciousness.[1]
    Karlfried Graf von Dürckheim

Illness can be our golden opportunity. For a few days, weeks, or months, we have to step out of the mad race and watch the world go by. This is the time to look at the instrument we call our body and to the condition of the brain that controls its every action and to the larger concerns of our mind and emotions. Before we are ready once more to play our part in the symphony of life, the instrument must be tuned.

For several years I have asked many of my patients two questions. Why do you think this illness came to you at this particular time in your life? Do you suppose this illness has certain lessons for you to learn? The answers have been many and varied. Usually, at first, the answers are not known, but if and when the patient is ready to accept the challenge of responding to the questions with candor and complete honesty, from that point on his life will not be the same.

*Martha* had just come out of the hospital, having had treatment for a low back strain, and was extremely resentful of her treatment while there. One trouble seemed to follow another. At this time she was suffering from a severe burn from a sensitivity she had developed to adhesive tape.

For fifteen years I had been trying to get her to look at herself and see some of the psychosomatic aspects of these various problems, but she had been unreceptive to such suggestions. Someone else, or something over which she had no control, was always to blame. Then, one morning during my period of meditation, I had a strong feeling that she was ready to talk. Later on I approached her, and she opened up, telling me of her need for sex, of her feelings of unfulfillment. She spoke of her inability to communicate with her husband on anything more than a very superficial level.

"I wonder," she said, "if, in my need, I haven't brought this illness upon myself."

The beginning of real therapy takes place when we recognize that we are on the great path of life and that everything that happens to us has significance.

*Clifford* was in the hospital for two and one-half months in traction for a severely comminuted and compound fracture of his leg. He had ample time to ponder the questions. One day he came up with these comments:

"I decided I have been getting too big for my britches. I belong to too many organizations. I'm too spread out. I need to give more of my life to the consideration of others. I have become very conscious of the goodness and kindness of many people who come to see me, some of whom I had never met previously. I am going to be more concerned with things that reach out to others and less with myself. I have realized how fortunate I am. I have seen so many worse off than I. How my leg comes out is of no consequence because a person can always overcome a handicap."

*Mary* was a thirty-five-year-old woman who was recuperating from a hysterectomy for cancer of the uterus. The questions had been asked, and after several days of deep reflection she broke down one morning and said, "At the age of sixteen I was married for the first time and had a baby. When he was a year-and-a-half old I gave his care over to my parents. I guess I was too immature to really mother him. I can never forgive myself for this."

There are many instances of this sort involving young women who became pregnant before they were able to face the responsibility of motherhood, had an abortion or had to put their children up for adoption, and finally, years later, developed cancer. It is as if the malignant process involving their deep sense of guilt germinates in the mind and gradually takes form in the body. A very interesting study of these deep-seated psychophysiological aspects of cancer appeared in the *Annals* of the New York Academy of Sciences a few years ago.[2]

These examples indicate that one's life orientation bears a significant relationship to his state of health. This insight should be presented to the patient by both the physician and the psychologist.

Dr. Artur Jores of Germany reports on a flu epidemic in Hamburg that hit a peak in December and over the Christmas holidays, with a subpeak a month later.[3] On a review of the cases it was discovered that practically all the patients in the latter group were post office workers who, during December, are very busy and play a very significant role in the eyes of the public. Perhaps they were too busy to be ill.

Further supporting this point of view, a medical writer describes the duration of illness in cases of flu among a group of 1,000 patients, 500 of whom, according to psychological testing, were normal and 500 of whom had a high degree of psychoneuroticism. The former group were well within a week, while the latter's illnesses lasted on the average of three weeks.

Why the difference between these two groups of persons? What is psychoneuroticism? The dictionary defines the psychoneurotic as the person with an emotional disturbance less severe than a psychosis, suffering from a mental disturbance due to unresolved, unconscious conflicts, and typically involving anxiety, depression, and somatic disturbances.

## Anxiety

If we wish to become whole persons, the true causes of anxieties, periods of depression, and psychosomatic types of illness must be discovered. We cannot be honest with ourselves and believe that the huge group of illnesses falling under this heading comes from outside of ourselves.

Anxiety is probably associated with illness more than is any other mental state, and to ignore it would be most unrealistic. The word comes from the Latin, *angere*, meaning to choke. In other words, we are choked with emotion. Certainly if a choking person walks into the emergency room of a hospital, the doctor first would examine the patient's throat and remove the object producing the symptoms. So, too, it is the role of psychiatrist and psychologist to remove the cause of the unconscious emotion that is quietly choking the patient and filling him with anxiety.

Most illness states are accompanied by varying degrees of anxiety that should be recognized and rooted out before they so alter the blood chemistry and the hormonal balance as to cause more manifest disease.

Ensuing alterations of the body chemistry, which vary from one patient to another, produce a wide variety of clinical pictures. Early in this sequence of events may be the alteration of the person's sugar metabolism with its accompanying high incidence of anxiety and depression. If these disordered emotions are not recognized for what they are, the functional illnesses that follow at times may persist, and organic illness may appear. In other words, a healthy state of mind is the first requisite of wholeness. What poisons the mind must eventually poison the whole body. Far too often in the past there has been only a medical diagnosis, as though the physical illness were an entity in itself and not related to the mind. But every cell in the body has its nerve connection to the brain and is affected by this greatest of all computers. As Dr. Paul Tournier says, in any illness there are always two diagnoses: that of the illness and that of the person.[4]

## Whole Person Medicine

In any medicine of the Whole Person, the primary requirement is to recognize the message of the illness and ask such questions as "Why am I anxious? Why the depression? Why the backache? Why is my resistance so low that I pick up every passing virus?"

Frequently a full response to these questions must wait until the patient is feeling somewhat better and is ready to face himself. This may take months or years. Many people will not be able to make this personal inspection in this lifetime. First there must be some type of relief of symptoms and attempts to approach a physical state of homeostasis.

At this stage, love, patience, and a feeling of acceptance of the patient are the essentials. This frequently cannot be accomplished in an impersonal hospital setting. It will mean a new education of physician, nurse, and technician alike. One who does not truly know himself can hardly be expected to know another. Those involved in the central portion of the healing team today should have had minimal training in the medicine of the Whole Person. This must, in the future, be taught in our medical schools and hospitals, and the teaching must be experiential. Too often, when a patient has said to me, "But doctor, you don't know how terrible I feel," I have walked out the door and gone to the next patient.

In 1964 I attended my first session of the Medicine of the Person, in Woudschoten, Holland, along with some eighty other doctors and their wives. For one week we looked at ourselves in the patient-physician relationship as we considered the subject "The Comprehension and Understanding of Man." During that week Dr. Paul Tournier gave us four of the most meaningful medical lectures that I have ever heard. They were turning points in my medical practice. They dealt with the "Meaning of True Understanding," "Our Personal Obstacles to This True Understanding," the "Suffering of the Misunderstood Person," and "Knowing God and One's Neighbor."

A few thought-provoking statements from these lectures remain with me to this day:

> The noblest and the worst exist in the same heart.
> Man cannot be seized from the outside.
> The verb "to sin" should only be conjugated in the first person.
> It is dangerous to have a noble vocation. It allows me to escape from recognizing my own sin. I may not be able to reach the patient because of my pride, my love of power.
> Love is not natural. I put up the appearance of loving and of not judging rather than really loving.
> It is in the midst of suffering that man feels the least understood. The efforts men make to understand can add to the suffering, the feeling that not only are we not understood, but we are actually misunderstood.
> To understand the place of illness in life is to understand God working in that illness. The Holy Spirit is the capacity to see, understand, mobilize these forces.

For twenty-five years, these annual meetings have been going on. Physicians from many countries join together to examine themselves and see how fit they are to be teachers of their patients.

### Discovery of Self

In this process of self-discovery there are two essential steps —the recognition of the personal self and, later, the discovery of one's spiritual identity, or one's Real Self. Each step is fundamental and must be taken in that order.

The spiritual self cannot be known until one has developed a feeling of real self-worth. Jesus chose, for His own intimate group of disciples, men who were recognized as successful in their own ways of life. They had found their identity in the world of men. They were ready for the next step—the venture into the world of spirit—and were asked by Him to leave all and follow Him.

One cannot leave what he doesn't have. The boy who has always dreamed of being a football hero, the man whose great ambition has been to make a million dollars, the woman whose great goal has been to raise five children to maturity, must all be allowed to fulfill that dream and have the satisfaction of its accomplishment. One does not ask them to cut off their dream and start a spiritual journey. He who is not the master of his own body and emotions can hardly launch out into the world of spirit with its necessary concomitant disciplines.

In the school of life one does not soar from kindergarten into college. It is always one step at a time, with each life going at its own natural pace. Human growth must follow its own rhythm and fit into the seasons of life. When a natural rhythm is broken, illness will eventually follow.

As previously quoted, "Man comes . . . into diversity; the ego appears, has to be recognized. . . ." This is an extremely important step and cannot be by-passed along the road toward personal fulfillment. I must love myself and believe in myself before I can love or believe in another, to say nothing of loving and believing in God. One who has never been conscious in this lifetime of having been loved by another cannot be expected to give love any more than the non-swimmer can be expected to swim at the command of another. Many people today have been brought up in situations where they felt unwanted and unloved. Plastic surgeon Dr. Maxwell Maltz has described how plastic surgery, while improving the appearance of certain individuals, in many cases did not restore their confidence and belief in themselves.[5]

*Caroline*, in her wheelchair for years with multiple sclerosis, has been steadily improving over the past year-and-a-half on a program of strict nutrition prescribed by Dr. Joseph Evers of Germany plus vitamin and mineral supplementation and homeopathic remedies—namely, Lathyrus (chickpea), which helped her regain full bladder control and helped stimulate leg movements, plus nux vomica, which helped overcome stiffness, and other prescriptions made on a monthly basis.

She then participated as much as she could in Meadowlark's body movement and art programs and had daily workouts on a stationary bicycle to build up her small leg muscles. She is now able to live by herself, walk up and down stairs unaided except by a handrail, walk out to her mailbox with the aid of canes, and has taken up dress-making to help support herself. Very important in giving her the motivation to stick with her program was a "waking dream" experience in which she saw herself on a mountain running and walking with no hesitation.

*Trudy*, ill with a chronic condition, was never able to visualize the trips she had hoped to make with her husband, nor could she play the piano, as she had done in the past. In three months spent at Meadowlark she expected our staff to do everything for her. She did not improve.

How do we regard our bodies? How do we see ourselves performing life's role? No great change ever came without vast exercise of the imaginative function and active anticipation. That which we hold in our minds is largely what we will become. Every thought filled with deep feeling that we pronounce or direct toward our person or any organ in our body is a direct command to our subconscious mind and will be involved in bringing about changes, altering the body's homeostatic mechanism for better or for worse.

It is helpful for us to think of the conscious mind as the captain of our ship, standing on the bridge and directing our body. It relays the orders to the subconscious mind, the ship's engineer, who is below deck and has no choice except to follow orders.

There can be no lasting healing without the cooperation and effort of the patient. Anyone who thinks the doctor is going to do everything for him is in for a sad disappointment. At most the doctor can only remove troublesome symptoms. He cannot change the inner and deep-seated causes of disease. He is, or should be, the leader and along with the psychologist and minister can only point out direction along the proper path. The patient must walk the path.

Every cell in the human body has its own level of consciousness and is, as it were, a member of the body's orchestra, responsive to the direction it receives from the mind of the person. The conductor who loves the members of his orchestra has a vastly greater potential to produce great music than the one who is indifferent or actually working at odds with its members.

The following comments frequently made by patients show their attitudes toward their bodies: "I don't know why my stomach never seems to be able to digest any food without a lot of gas." "That back of mine never gives me any peace." "If it weren't for my d—— knee . . ." Such statements are the fuels that keep disease processes alive and well.

When one establishes a retreat center for healing, the first essential is not, as I had previously thought, a few hundred thousand dollars. It is, rather, a small group of dedicated people who are well along on the path of self-discovery and are ready to serve others and able to establish an atmosphere of love.

The guest who arrives with little or no sense of self-appreciation and is thoroughly discouraged needs to be waited on, loved, and appreciated until he or she can begin to feel accepted. Illness of all types is accompanied by great feelings of isolation in the patient; he hurts and longs for understanding. Frequently he is silent and fails to hear words that may be spoken to him, so high are the walls of his isolation.

There are four steps in the opening up and recognition of the self. First, there is the *risk*, then opening the door of *self*, followed by *communication*, and finally *trusting* and moving into the state of honesty and real openness.

The first message of true healing is spoken in silence, with a look, with a touch, all of which carry the message "I care."

Some weeks after leaving Meadowlark, *Susan* wrote to me:

You opened your arms and took me in,
You asked no questions,
You shared your love with no strings attached,
You listened to my confused searchings,
You trusted my goodness, even when you saw none,
You opened vast new vistas for my mind to explore,
You gave the second chance to find meaning and purpose,
You put the stars back in my sky.

I come to you
for with you I know
the exquisite joy of
sharing souls.

For with you I taste
of the substance of the kingdom of God
For with you I can sit around in my bare bones
and just BE.

After the patient has found some feelings of worth, there must be recovery of an ability to communicate. At first many guests must be alone in their own rooms, too much hurt by life to risk contact with others at a common table for meals. It matters little whether the illness is predominantly mental, emotional, or physical, the sense of isolation is very frequently there. In a group experience, in a relaxation class, or an experience in art, it is easier to stay on the sidelines. Then, finally, comes the day when the person allows the first little revelation of himself. Progress from this point is dependent upon how the revelation is received.

In a group, feelings may gradually emerge. "I never would have thought that Mary has had an experience so much like my own." Or "I never would have guessed that our group leader would have had such awful thoughts during his own period of therapy, so maybe there is hope for me." Or "I never realized that dreams could tell us so much about our own personal lives." And so communication gradually builds up, and self-constructed walls of isolation start to crumble.

On the Lake of Zug, in Switzerland, about thirty miles from Zurich, is the Landhaus Murpfli, a small therapeutic community.[6] There, under the direction of Max E. Bircher, M.D., this dimension of the healing arts is carried on. As one enters, one reads an inscription over the door: *Porta Tibi Patet Magis Cor*, which means "The door is open and even more the heart."

One of the important times of day is the *Teestunde*, or tea hour. This is held in the small meditation room. The guests and Dr. Bircher sit in a circle facing a shallow tiled pool. From a chandelier above the pool falls drop after drop of water, each of which disturbs the pool surface and sends out its circular waves that engulf the whole pool and finally disappear. On one particular day the doctor had shown a film of himself and his teacher patiently working at a potter's wheel. Afterward, an American patient attempted to describe a phase of her recovery at this small, yet world-famous, clinic.

> I loved seeing you, also with this sacred concentration, trying and failing and trying again. And then, the masterpieces that you finally had the power and the knowledge and understanding and sorrow and love to create. . . . Then you came to my door, and though I had wanted to shut out the

entire world, I let you in. I don't know what brought you there. I don't know why you thought I would be there . . . in such need. Of what? Answers perhaps—or more questions, maybe—but you came; and once more I tried to draw you out, in your entirety, into me through my eyes.

Sometimes the tears welled up as I spoke to you of the inexplicable complexities. You wiped away a tear with such gentleness that another came to take its place. I tried to talk, but all I could think of was how little I could ever talk to you; how little time there could ever be; of how late in our lives we had met; that there was so little time to learn from you everything of importance and of worth.

I thought again in passing how you looked more tired than anyone I had ever seen. My heart ached for you to carry all that load of tiredness and that you might be too tired to convey to me anything of the great riches you have gathered in your life. But through your fatigue, you answered me with much quiet.[7]

## Psychosynthesis

Until quite recently psychology and psychiatry have been merely content to deal with the discovery and recognition of the *ego* and have been quite unaware of the Real Self. However, Carl Jung and Roberto Assagioli, being eminently cognizant of the transcendent qualities of man, dared to launch out into man's depth dimensions and have profoundly influenced the emerging and widening concepts of human consciousness. In this country Abraham Maslow, Ira Progoff, Robert Gerard, Jack Cooper, and others have done, and are doing, much to broaden the scope of the psychological sciences in this direction.

Here in detail is something of Dr. Assagioli's concept of the human psyche as he describes it in his definition of *Psychosynthesis: A Manual of Principles.*

> Psychosynthesis should not be looked upon as a single psychological doctrine or procedure. It is a dramatic conception

of the psychic life which portrays as a constant interplay and conflict between the many different and contrasting forces and a unifying center which tends to control, harmonize and use them creatively. Psychosynthesis is a combination of several methods of inner action, aiming first at development of personality, then at the harmonious coordination and unification with the self.

These phases may be called respectively personal and spiritual psychosynthesis. The isolated individual doesn't exist. Every person has intimate relations with other persons which make all interdependent. Moreover, each and all are included in and are a part of the super-individual reality.[8]

## The Waking Dream

While many subjects are considered to be within the realm of this vast area of psychology, we shall deal only with the technique of the *rêve eveillé*, or waking dream, first described by Robert Desoille. The diagram below is intended to give a picture of human consciousness. The lower consciousness is the repository of one's primitive urges and his many complexes, fears, anxieties, and obsessions. The middle consciousness is that portion of the mind that is readily accessible in one's everyday life.

1. The lower unconscious
2. The middle unconscious
3. The superconscious
4. The field of consciousness
5. The conscious self or "I"
6. The Higher Self
7. The collective unconscious

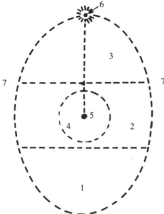

The superconscious is the repository of higher intuitions, aspirations, and artistic, philosophical, and scientific materials. It is the source of altruistic love and the area of genius. The field of consciousness is the part of personality of which one is immediately aware, filled with present thoughts, sensations, and desires. The "I," or center of pure self-awareness, is distinguished from the above-mentioned field of that awareness.

The Higher Self is the immortal aspect of one's being, which never sleeps and relates to the totality of life. It is that presence described by Brother Lawrence in his *Practice of the Presence of God*, the Christ's presence, or the Buddha state of mind.[9] Last, the collective unconscious, a term used by Jung, describes the process of "osmotic" relationship the individual has with his total psychological environment and includes the archetypal images of dreams, psychic experiences, and so on.

In the waking dream technique, following a period of induced relaxation, mental suggestions are presented to the patient, which he may accept or reject at his will, such as the following: Can you visualize a mountain, a lighthouse, a bird? . . . Then the patient has the opportunity to climb a mountain, ascend the stairs of the lighthouse, or even fly on the back of the bird.

If he is not ready for this stage, the suggestion will be refused or accepted then rejected. In the case of the mountain, for example, the ascent may not be completed. One patient who was not ready for the ascent never climbed up the stairs in the lighthouse and instead set up housekeeping on the ground floor.

Perhaps the most useful object for suggesting the spiritual path is the mountain. Here are a few typical responses:

*Monica L.* "Can you visualize a mountain?" "Yes, it is a long way off and snow-covered." "Would you like to go toward the mountain?" "No."

This patient obviously is not ready to make the spiritual journey. The country of the spirit appears cold (snow) and uninteresting to her at this point.

*James T.* "Can you visualize a mountain?" "Yes." "Would you like to climb it?" "Yes. There is no path, so I must make my own way. There are many rocks and the way is steep. I must go step by step. The footing at times is quite insecure. I am tired now and will sit down for awhile." "Would you care to go on?" "No, I think not. I will go down now." Here we have a man ready to make a start, and in subsequent dreams he may go on toward the summit and a spiritual experience, but certain aspects of his life must be put in order first.

*Margaret S.* is being prepared for a hysterectomy for an early cancer, and she is facing the question "What is life teaching you through this experience?" "Can you visualize a mountain?" "Yes, it is far away and somehow I get the feeling that it is made of tissue paper."

On searching further into her background, we discover that her spiritual world was quite lacking in any real sense of significance. It was quite shocking to her to see this, and this area of discovery started her on a very meaningful journey into herself. If one is to make a true recovery from cancer or any other chronic illness, it is essential to find a meaning for life, and this type of experience carries with it such a sense of meaning.

*Edward P.* "Can you visualize a mountain?" "Yes." "Would you like to climb it?" "Yes. There is a good path and it bears around the right side winding toward the top. There are many flowers along the path and a rich loam beneath my feet. As I get higher there are fewer plants. It is interesting that I do not seem to tire, and the cool fresh air seems to really invigorate me. I am nearing the top. I can see off to great distances. Now I find myself immersed in a great white light and what's more, I am that Light. My body seems to fade away and everything is one. There is no separation anymore."

After awhile the descent is made back to the house setting where the dream took place. This type of experience is always accompanied by real changes in life-style and a new sense of values. The dream, of course, has been much abbreviated, to bring out just the essentials.

Birth into a new level of consciousness is life-shaking and life-renewing. The one who has experienced it will never again be the same person. There is a new glow in his eyes, a new lightness in his step, and life takes on a new dimension.

This type of healing is far more effective than can be accomplished by the surgical removal of a diseased organ, the restoration of a blood pressure to normal through drug control, the disappearance of a stomach ulcer through a medical program, or the so-called five-year cure of a cancer. The latter cures are mere suppressions of a certain manifestation of a disease process, but the physician cannot honestly feel that anything has really been done that has restored the homeostatic process, the disturbance of which was responsible for the illness.

## The Role of Art

I cannot conceive of the practice of medicine of the Whole Person without art. Man acting from his brain alone without the symbolic function of heart and his feeling nature is cold, isolated, and sick. Each organ of the body with its related endocrine gland and its corresponding chakra has a deep symbolic meaning, which if investigated in the doctor-patient relationship will enhance the growth experience as the result of having gone through the illness. The heart is referred to here in much the same sense that the writer of the Book of Proverbs intended in these lines: "As a man thinketh in his heart, so is he" (Prov. 23:7). We are referring of course to man's capacity to love. Recalling the discussion of chakras in the second chapter, the reader will note that the center in the heart area of the chest is the love center.

In the total healing of man there is probably nothing more important than the awakening of an all-inclusive ability to love. I may know something very well with my intellect, which operates through the mediation of the portion of the brain known as the cerebral cortex. This center, however, does not affect the brain centers that control my body functions. To do this, it must first be transmitted into my feeling levels (symbolically referred to as the heart area).

The brain by itself cuts others out of its world. It needs the warmth of the heart. Very helpful in this process of the discovery of the self is the employment of some of the free nonstructured forms of art, including the use, under direction, of pastel colors or a lump of clay and music and body movement.

In the Meadowlark program, we think of the visual-art techniques as "heart-to-hand" therapy. Deep within the human heart there is buried a secret center of knowing, always ready to guide and instruct the person. The teacher merely sets an atmosphere or background, makes a few suggestions to initiate the process, or puts on a suitable phonograph record to set a mood for reflection.

Then the colors the individual has a feeling for at the moment are picked, and he allows his hands to move across a sheet of paper (usually about two by three feet on a hard backing) guided by his heart (or feeling nature) rather than by the mind. Colors express predominant feelings; sharp lines may depict the saw-tooth edges of anger; ovals may be tear drops; dark borders around the pictures may depict enclosures that would seem to be confining life. Human figures represent individuals who, by their relative positions and sizes, signify personal relationships and suppressed feelings.

In the ensuing days of art classes, we usually see the softening of lines, new and brighter colors, the disappearance of enclosures, fresh flowing streams of life, young green plants, and other signs of the new life that the guest is beginning to feel in his own being.

Along with these changes there are always significant indications of renewed physical, psychological, and spiritual health. Very frequently there will be pictures of graveyards, burial caskets, and other symbols signifying the death of the old person and paving the way for the new. The new may be signified by symbols of springtime, of the female uterus with the new fetus, or of a baby held in the arms of a madonna. This is also frequently seen in sessions with clay. The instructor of the class may be talking about life or there may be a musical background while each guest, with a lump of clay in his hands, allows his hands to identify with the clay, just allowing the fingers to work in it, scarcely noticing what they are doing. Figures appear, other symbols take form, and as they are taken back into the guest's room at night and reworked, their significance begins to emerge and speak meaningfully to their creators. Literally, before one's eyes, the meaning of Jesus' statement, "You must be born again," is revealed.

When it comes to body movement with music, the average person coming into this type of therapeutic program is frequently frozen, whether it be by a marital problem and divorce, by an increasingly impossible job situation, or by the overwhelming grief from the death of a loved one. He cannot move but can only stand or sit at the edge of the group.

After a few days, possibly the fingers or the toes will start to move to the music. Finally he gets up and lets go, becoming a part of the group. I recall one of our guests, quite schizoid, who just couldn't relate to anyone, but when she danced, she was an angel out of this world. Another guest, not able to function in ordinary life, was an entirely different person in the swimming pool and was the life of the whole group. Thus, the beginning of depth therapy is that initial risk and venturing out of the tight enclosure by the imprisoned self.

### Heart-to-Hand Art

TEACHER: (following relaxation class or yoga). Now that we are so relaxed let's carry this feeling with us as we listen to the following music and just become one with the music. Now choose colors you like and draw your attention to the heart center. Let the colors flow from what you feel there out to your hand. Move the colors over your paper without a thought of drawing a thing. Be willing to let it happen. Let your deeper feelings move in color rhythms onto the paper.

TEACHER: What do those sharp points represent?
GUEST: I am angry!
TEACHER: Are you rebelling because your life seems to be at a standstill?
GUEST: It certainly is!

TEACHER: Do you feel like crying?
GUEST: Yes, but I never could cry.
TEACHER: But why do you hold back your tears?
GUEST: As a child my father would never allow us to cry.
TEACHER: Do you feel hemmed in by life situations?
GUEST:Oh, yes. (Tears break through.)

TEACHER: How do you feel as you look at the pictures?
GUEST: I feel bound and held back.
TEACHER: Let's turn your picture sideways and look at it.
GUEST: Why it looks like a new birth!

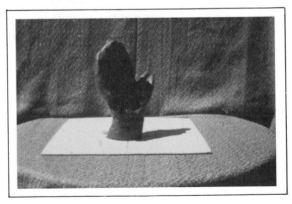

TEACHER: (to a class working with clay). You have in your hands a shapeless ball of clay. As you listen to the music identify with the clay and allow your fingers to play with it and let happen what will. . . . Why do you have a glove on your hand?

GUEST: I guess I am reaching. I want more from life. I guess the glove is my protection.

TEACHER: How do you really feel as you look at this gloved hand?

GUEST: Like my hands are bound. I want to take off the glove and use my hands more creatively. I want to give as well as receive.

## Concentration

Having had a glimpse of one's Real Self, the seeker for true health, or the achievement of Wholeness, is increasingly dependent upon himself, since the search cannot be made for him. Discipline will become increasingly a part of his life. This has already been touched upon in the chapters on exercise and proper nutrition. Now we must consider the all-important discipline of the mind through concentration, meditation, and contemplation. In concentration there is a gathering together of the mental processes to focus on a single point; in meditation, there is a holding of the mind to that point and allowing one thought to develop. In contemplation there is something akin to an actual union of the person and the object he is beholding in the mind's eye.

To start with, the mind is something like a herd of wild horses being broken in by a cowboy; in the beginning of his training, he finds it is difficult to exert control over them. The same situation exists with the untrained mind that flits about from one subject to another and is distracted by bodily sensations, passing emotions, sleepiness, and an attachment to certain life situations or persons.

There can be no progress without concentration. In his book *Concentration and Approach to Meditation*, Ernest Wood describes a fourfold path to concentration.[10] During the first week it is suggested that one pick an object for concentration and hold the mind on that object until the mind wanders. At that point he notes on a watch with a second hand how long a period of uninterrupted concentration was possible. This should be done daily and a log kept, indicating the object of concentration and the distracting thought.

During the second, third, and fourth weeks, Wood suggests that the subject for concentration should be a series of objects observed in a glance around a room. On closing the eyes, the objects should be seen in their ordered positions. If the mind wanders, one uses the will to bring it back. The number of interruptions should be noted.

During the fifth week one opens a book and notes the first name of an object upon which his eyes fall, then turns to another page and notes a second one. The period of concentration is then spent taking a mental trip from the first object to the second one. This exercise in "word bridges" might go something like this: "Millionaire" and "soul" are picked in that order. Millionaire-money-collection plate (in church)-preacher-sermon-saving souls.

For the next three months a very good exercise is a full study of some categorical noun such as wood, cat, book, paint, education, or tree. This exercise comprises the centering of the mind on the object for fifteen minutes and thinking of the various thoughts that the object suggests in the following manner. First, how might the noun be classified and what other things fall into the same classification? Second, of what parts is it made up? Third, what is its purpose and what qualities does it suggest? Last, what familiar experiences have you had with it?

For example, *Cat*:

1. *The cat family:* members—the household cat, bobcats, lynx, ocelot, tiger, lion, jaguar, cougar, and so on.
2. *Parts:* eyes, ears, nose, mouth, skin, tail, legs, claws, teeth, stomach, liver, kidneys, and so on.
3. *Purpose and qualities:* a companion, mouse-catcher.
4. *Familiar experiences:* thought about a particular cat that was an important part of a household.

Such exercises as the above can be practiced, with daily notations as to success, with great benefit and will be very helpful for further progress on any path of self-realization.

Those who would make that next step into the life of the spirit must be strong and disciplined. To quote Walt Whitman:

Allons! yet take warning!
He travelling with me needs the best blood, thews, endurance,
None may come to the trial till he or she bring courage and
    health,
Come not here if you have already spent the best of yourself,
Only those come who come in sweet and determin'd bodies,
No diseas'd person, no rum drinker or venereal taint is
    permitted here.
(I and mine do not convince by arguments, similes, rhythmes,
We convince by our presence.) [11]

What is the answer? While it is as yet largely undefined, it seems to be a search for quality in life and a rejection of the amassing of material goods that has been so prevalent. Courses in comparative religion and classes in yoga and meditation are springing up everywhere. Life must have meaning, or the world will madly go on destroying itself. Let us hope our young people can make the change.

There are many and diverse paths into this land of the spirit, the domain of love-energy. The naturalist may find it in the out-of-doors, the artist on his palette or in his block of marble, the musician in a mystical relationship with his instrument, the astronomer in the starry sky, the church-goer in the silent moments of Holy Communion, the yogi in his meditation.

For a moment the curtain of time drops and one is immersed in timelessness; limitations of the body drift away and one is caught up in the immensity of the universe. He then knows that he is an integral part of the whole and belongs to it. While the experience may fade back into distant memory, it can never be entirely lost. It will always be something of a torch along the path of life.

The following comments are representative of those who have gained deep spiritual insight.

JOHN MUIR (naturalist): "Now all the individual things or beings into which the world is wrought are sparks of the Divine Soul variously clothed upon with flesh, leaves or that harder tissue called rock."[12]

ROBERT HENRI (artist): "I am certain that we do deal in an unconscious way with another dimension than the well-known three. It does not matter much to me now if it is the fourth dimension or what its number is, but I know that deep in us there is always a grasp of proportions which exist over and through the obvious three, and it is by this power of superproportioning that we reach the inner meaning of things."[13]

JOHANNES BRAHMS: "Spirit is the light of the soul. Spirit is universal. Spirit is the creative energy of the cosmos. The soul of man is not conscious of its powers until it is enlightened by Spirit. . . . Therefore, to evolve and grow, man must learn how to use and develop his own soul forces. All creative geniuses do this, although some of them do not seem to be as conscious of the process as others."[14]

GUSTAF STROMBERG (astronomer): "Then we tried to explore the mind and found it in constant communication with the cosmos."[15]

PIERRE TEILHARD DE CHARDIN (priest): Once and for all he understood that, like the atom, man has no value save for that part of himself which passes into the universe."[16]

SRI RAMAKRISHNA (yogi): "As long as one says, 'I know' or 'I do not know,' one looks upon himself as a person. My

Divine Mother says: 'It is only when I have effaced the whole of this Aham (I-ness) in you, that the Undifferentiated Absolute (my impersonal aspect) can be realized in Samadhi.' Till then there is the 'I' in me and before me."[17]

ALFRED LORD TENNYSON:

"I know not, and speak of what has been.
'And more, my son! for more than once when I
Sat all alone, revolving in myself
The word that is the symbol of myself
The mortal limit of the self was loosed,
And past into the Nameless, as a cloud
Melts into heaven. I touch'd my limbs, the limbs
Were strange, not mine—and yet no shade of doubt,
But utter clearness, and thro' loss of self
The gain of such large life as match'd with ours
Were sun to spark—unshadowable in words,
Themselves but shadow of a shadow-world.' "[18]

## Jesus and Wholeness

In His ministry of healing, Jesus was concerned with Wholeness, or homeostatis. If one examines His healings, one will find evidence that there are two principles requisite in the attainment of the healing state of mind—namely, faith and love. Without this state of consciousness it is questionable that there can be any true healing of the Whole Person.

Jesus' disciple John relates the conversation between the man with an infirmity, at the pool called Bethesda, and Jesus. There is no diagnosis of a disease state other than the implication that the man is paralyzed. Jesus simply asks him, "Wilt thou be made whole?"

## The Power of Faith

In true healing faith plays a dominant role. First there is faith in one's self, and then there is faith in the physician. We recall the instance of the woman with the "issue of blood," the account of which is related in three gospels (Matthew 9:20, Mark 5:25, Luke 8:43) and Christ's remark on feeling her touch His garment, "Daughter, be of good comfort, thy faith hath made thee whole."

Then there is the account of the power of faith in the man who sat at Lystra, impotent in his feet. A cripple from birth, he had never walked, but from the inspiration of Paul's words there was an instantaneous healing: "[Paul] steadfastly beholding him, and perceiving that he had faith to be healed, said with a loud voice, 'Stand upright on thy feet.' And he leaped and walked" (Acts 14:8).

If, in the latter part of the twentieth century, we physicians had as much faith in God and in Nature's inherent ability to heal as we have the faith in the destructive power of disease and death, we would certainly see many more recoveries from illness than we are seeing today.

Faith is not something that can be taught in school. It is a self-discipline, and its attainment is only possible to those who are ready to make the necessary sacrifices. The tuning of the body is very demanding and involves a whole new way of life with control of the senses, prayer, fasting, and meditation. It implies carrying on our everyday life, but, at the same time, secretly, at an inner center, touching an inner point of reverential silence. This is beautifully described by the late mystic-philosopher Thomas Kelly:

> There is a way of ordering our mental life on more than one level at once. On one level we may be thinking, discussing, seeing, calculating, meeting all the demands of external affairs. But deep within behind the scenes, at a profounder level, we may also be in prayer and adoration, song and worship, and with a gentle receptiveness to divine breathings.[19]

In the act of faith one drops his mortal limitations, and, merging into a consciousness that transcends his own personality, he contacts an inner source of wisdom. In such a moment the lecturer puts aside his carefully prepared notes and gives the best speech of his life. If you should ask him afterward what he had said, he might well be unable to tell you.

## Love

The other essential ingredient in healing is love. Pitrim Sorokin speaks of this power as the great cohesive force of the universe. Pierre Teilhard de Chardin equates it with cosmic energy. In the touch of a hand, in the look of an eye, a charge of energy passes from one to another and healing is under way.

We are told that Jesus, departing out of Jericho, saw two blind men sitting by the wayside and that he had compassion on them and touched their eyes, and immediately they received their sight. Love and faith of this degree are certainly not common today, and its results rarely speed up the process of healing to this extent, yet there is no doubt in my mind that such acts of love initiate healing.

The role of faith and love in the healing process is told not only in the Bible but also by the Indian medicine man, the Buddhist priest, and in the secret healing agent of all who truly have experienced the power of these two great forces.

In a more recent time, *The Book of Miracles*, by Henry Cadbury, recounts the story of the healing at the hands of the founder of the Society of Friends, George Fox.[20] Many of the individual accounts in Cadbury's book were deleted, for they were then, as they are today, embarrassing to physicians and clergymen. Today more and more of such accounts are being recorded. The healings at the shrine of Lourdes in France have been studied and documented by a group of 5,000 physicians. Dr. Alexis Carrel made the pilgrimage to Lourdes as a surgeon and doubter and came back as a believer, as described in his account *The Voyage to Lourdes.*[21]

The healings are not the symptom patch-up that is so much practiced in medicine today, but healings of the whole person. In this life-stirring process, there is not always a physical healing, but there seems always to be a whole new pattern of life—a change from a life lived to find individual happiness to a life lived in the service of others and a life of far greater happiness and meaning.

The case of Mrs. Eileen Nader, a sixty-seven-year-old woman who came to me for treatment of a lump in her breast, illustrates this type of change. During the preoperative days, she was asked to face herself and search for the meaning of this hiatus in her everyday life. She went through her surgery for cancer with a real and deep knowing that she would completely recover. She described a dream she had as follows:

"When in the recovery room following surgery, something happened to me. I saw myself out of my body, whole and complete like before my illness. Then I turned and looked at myself. There were six tall men, all the same age, dressed in black, standing, three on each side. They were not talking; still I knew they were telling me to follow them. Then I found myself in a very big room.

"The men in black had disappeared and from the west, advancing toward the east, a tall man dressed in a gorgeous white robe and a tall hat like a saint appeared. He was holding a large book in his hand and he strode toward an altar to deposit it. He then told me without words to come to his side.

"Here was a square box with white sand in it. The sand was warm. He told me to shuffle my feet in it. At this point everything disappeared and I found myself alone in the middle of the room. A tremendous white light appeared, like that of the sun, and I heard a loud voice say, 'This is sanctification. You are now sanctified.' I then reentered my body."

From that day on, Eileen was a different person as her life became one of service to others. There was something different about her appearance, particularly the look in her eyes.

For the next five years of her life, before she died of pneumonia, she devoted a day each week organizing rummage sales to aid the program at Meadowlark.

The tremendous role of love in the healing picture can hardly be overestimated. This fundamental ingredient of healing is basic, and its presence is far too often completely overlooked. We physicians are all too ready to take the credit that I am sure we frequently do not deserve. The faithful attention of a loving and encouraging friend, minister, or nurse is likely to be overlooked.

The best medical program, or the most technically advanced surgical operation, is valueless if there is an absence of love in the patient's environment; at most, it can only give temporary relief. First, there must be love for one's own self and a vision of meaningful living; second, a love for one's friends and associates; and, last, a love of the Creator of life —God.

My former teacher in medical school, the late Dr. Smiley Blanton, illustrated well the importance of this love factor in healing in his book, *Love or Perish.*[22] Every act committed without the positive, creative power of love is a nail in my own coffin and implements the degenerative processes at work in my body. Why does one man grow old at fifty while another is still in the prime of life in his late eighties? Oliver Wendell Holmes and Albert Schweitzer are great examples of men who did not age; both were men with a great capacity to love.

Love really cannot be put into words. It is an inner experience, or practice, and is the fruit of meditation. In today's hate-torn, war-minded world, it is scarcely any wonder that degenerative diseases are taking a greater and greater toll than ever before.

No, love cannot be weighed, measured, or analyzed, and so it has not fit into the empirical system of medical teaching, but, as already indicated in our earlier chapters, this situation is gradually changing. As the great physician and philosopher Albert Schweitzer said, "The beginning of all wisdom is to be filled with the mystery of existence and of life." If we Americans are to survive, it is our young people who will save us, as they look to earth, to Nature, and to quality in life rather than to quantity of possessions.

Earlier this chapter dealt with centering of the mind through concentration. Let us now examine the process whereby we approach the wisdom that cannot be tested in schools, and where we experience the mystery of existence and the greater life of which we are a part.

## Meditation

The practice of meditation is a well-tested method of self-help to self-realization. You *can* help yourself, if you will, by this practice. You must have a regular time and place, chosen for the greatest comfort, quiet, and freedom from interruptions. Sit quietly on a chair, or on the floor, with your spine straight, hands resting quietly in the lap or on the knees. The yogic lotus posture is good if comfortable, but it is not necessary. Close your eyes.

Focus your whole attention on your breathing as you inhale and exhale, slowly and deeply, to quiet your random thoughts. All of the air should be forced out of the lungs, followed by a long, slow inspiration, taking in as much air as possible. The chest should be expanded by raising the lower ribs, and diaphragmatic breathing added. When the diaphragm is contracted, it moves downward, drawing air into the lower lungs and causing the abdomen to protrude slightly as you *inhale*. The lungs should be filled slowly and completely, then emptied slowly and completely.

After a few moments of this breathing, it is well to use some method whereby the body, mind, and emotions can be silenced. There are many ways of doing this. Hosea tells us to "take with you words and turn to the Lord." So you can start with such words as "Acquaint now thyself with Him and be at peace."

Think of God as love and then translate the thought into feeling. How does it feel when you are filled with love? Continue with words such as *Life, Peace,* and *Power,* and both think and feel them. And now give yourself this command, "Be still, and know that I am *God.*" After an interval of inner quiet, repeat it, leaving off the last word: "Be still and know that *I am.*" After inner silence, the command becomes, "Be still and know *That!*" "That" is a term used by some to indicate the Nameless—God. And so *God, I am,* and *That* are all synonyms for this experience of stillness.

On the next repetition, the command is "Be still, and *know!*" Next, "Be *still!*" and finally, *"Be!"* As long an interval as seems comfortable should be allowed between statements, or until thoughts begin to interfere. Follow the last statement with an interval of controlled breathing and then repeat the entire series.

Another suggestion for entering meditation is through the first great commandment, focusing the entire attention on God and loving Him with all your heart, with all your mind, and with all your soul and then offering yourself to Him and calling for His will to be done in and through you.

Meditation is the steady, quiet, fixing of the mind on God or on Nature. Plato expressed this in the following words: "The ardent turning of the soul towards the Divine: not to ask any particular good but for itself, for the Universal, Supreme Good."

The practice of meditation will teach us to meditate and will take us beyond meditation, when we are ready, into that state of Oneness with the Father.

### Review

We have merely sketched the path to healing in the sense of attaining a degree of wholeness, and it is not our intention to indicate the whole route, even if we were able to do so. The path is very individual and requires great perseverance. The merger of the self into the larger Self demands a complete change in a way of life. Things that formerly seemed important now become valueless, and a new set of values comes over the horizon. The path into this new consciousness is one through many valleys, which cause frequent loss of view of the summit, but as one ascends the mountain of finer consciousness, the valleys become narrower and more shallow. Self-realization is very demanding. Shedding one's skins of defenses would seem to leave one very vulnerable. However, the old person that one has been is not fit for the new encounter. Walt Whitman describes this journey in his "Song of the Open Road":[23]

> Listen, I will be honest with you,
> I do not offer the old smooth prizes, but offer rough new prizes,
> These are the days that must happen to you:
> You shall not heap up what is called riches,
> You shall scatter with lavish hand all that you learn or achieve,
> You but arrive at the city to which you were destin'd, you hardly settle yourself to satisfaction before you are call'd by an irresistible call to depart,
> You shall be treated to the ironical smiles and mockings of those who remained behind you,
> What beckonings of love you receive you shall only answer with passionate kisses of parting,
> You shall not allow the hold of those who spread their reach'd hands toward you.

Jesus, when approached by Nicodemus, compared the new consciousness, which made possible the miracles he performed, to a new birth (John 3:3). Such a new birth brings new dimensions of being with it. And once its fruits have been tasted, one will never desert the quest for Oneness.

Anxiety and fear give way to a feeling of faith and assurance. Resentment and jealousy are replaced by love. Impatience and irritability dissolve in an atmosphere of patience and perseverance. Love, as one has previously known it, loses its former air of exclusiveness and extends far out to encompass the entire family of man. Every day becomes a new and exciting challenge full of possibilities for growth and increased awareness of one's essential self.

# 10

## SEX AND THE WHOLE PERSON

This is a chapter we have all agreed should be written. Friends and advisors who have been aware of our project and thus, in a very real sense, have participated in it, have so expressed themselves.

There have been many excellent clinical studies on sex. "Sexperts" in all fields of human experience are constantly expounding their views. There are moralistic, legalistic, and labelistic approaches to sex—but as any minister, doctor, psychiatrist, counselor, or bartender well knows, sex continues to intrigue, upset, confound, fascinate, and disturb human beings of all ages, sizes, and shapes.

Judging from the pronouncements one reads and often hears, ministers, doctors, and psychiatrists share the general confusion about the phenomenon of sex. All we can do here is to offer some insights and suggestions that will enable our reader to make up his or her own mind and heart. And, of course, a whole person is willing and able to do that in every area of life; one who is seeking healing or a greater sense of wholeness can often take a step in the direction one wants to go simply by taking a relatively uncluttered look at some of the sexual elements of one's own being. (We might point out that this section is not intended as a "how-to" treatment of sexual techniques and practices, although taking the time to realize the importance and place of sex in the whole person can well work miracles in them as well as in the greater health and joy of living that such a realization can produce.)

It has been observed that "the body is the lamb that takes away the sins of the world." We are thinking now not of the venereal diseases that can be transmitted through sexual intercourse but rather of the unhealthy conditions that show up often in the mental, emotional, physical, and social body of humanity as the result of more subtle sins of fear, guilt, ignorance, and distorted attitudes.

## The Importance of Proper Attitudes

Even in this so-called enlightened age, sex is often treated as a dark and evil subject, as material for coarse and vulgar jokes, as a topic that often makes people feel uncomfortable and embarrassed. Let us assure you that ministers and doctors have just as much difficulty divesting themselves of conventional attitudes toward sex as anyone else.

Let us also assure you that we have seen enough of the insides of all aspects of human relationships to realize that sexual attitudes are instrumental in shaping or distorting the whole person. We can't help but feel that distorted sexual views on the part of ministers, doctors, psychiatrists, and other persons cause the removal of as many female and male organs and portions thereof annually as any other so-called disease.

The reproductive male and female organs, tissues, and functions are the most sensitive in the entire human organism. Guilt, fear, condemnation, and other negative attitudes certainly reap a tragic and destructive toll in this area of human expression and experience. We would go so far as to say that no person can be completely whole until he or she has recognized, accepted, and appreciated individual sexuality.

You might take a look at yourself and then see what would be left if you removed all the elements of sexuality, beginning with the outer manifestations of it in your body and going as deeply as you are able into the mental and emotional and spiritual elements of your being. Or you might take a look at another person in your life and speculate on what would be left if there were no sexuality in that individual.

There is no such thing as a completely neutral state in human sexhood; and we can thank God for that because the whole human experiment would come to a sudden halt if the element of sexuality were removed from human beings. Of course, we could profitably remove some of the attitudes that we have all held toward sex without blocking human progress.

Many approaches to sex seem to be primarily concerned with the physical act of intercourse, the regulation of it, legal questions surrounding it, the intensification of it, the elimination of it; but the genital embrace, important though it is, is only part of the sexual life of the whole person. The sexual act cannot be isolated from the whole of a person's attitude toward himself or herself as a human being and toward the sexual partner—in fact, toward humanity as a whole.

Sexual intercourse, like every other human interchange, is a transaction in consciousness even more than it is a physical experience, and one's attitudes, feelings, fears, and sense of guilt, and one's sense of freedom and love are constant companions in even the most intimate human relationships.

You may wish to do a little inner work before we go any further by asking yourself the following: Am I a whole person sexually? Do I accept my sexuality (masculinity or femininity) without fear, guilt, condemnation, apology, or embarrassment? Do I accept the sexuality (masculinity or femininity) of the people in my life without fear, guilt, condemnation, apology, or embarrassment? Am I honest, comfortable, and relaxed in my relations with members of my sex? Am I honest, comfortable, and relaxed in my relations with members of the complementary sex (there is no opposite sex!)? Am I willing to deepen my awareness, understanding, and working knowledge of the true nature of sex?

As in every other area of human consciousness, most people find they have to drop the old concepts of and attitudes toward sex before any real growth takes place. It is utterly amazing to ministers and doctors, and to others as well, what distorted concepts and painful attitudes and memories about sex supposedly mature men and women carry with them as part of their present living experience. Sometimes an earlier harsh word or judgment from a parent, a teacher, a minister, or another adult will have warped a person's whole life and his relationships with other people.

A child's innocent desire for information and exploration of some area of sexuality can be converted into a living nightmare through the thoughtless, puritanical, or frightened response of an immature adult. Damage to the psychological, emotional, and physical body of an individual is sometimes enormous and very difficult to eradicate. Fear, threats, condemnation, moralizing, or legal action will never make a whole person. Wholeness and freedom come from the loving and understanding acceptance of our true nature.

You may wish to pursue your self-questioning a bit further. The following ideas are suggestions to help prime the pump of your own consciousness: "What am I sexually?" If you are male, you might answer the question in this way: "Sexually I am a man." If you are female, the answer would logically follow: "Sexually I am a woman." If you are familiar with the Bible, these questions and answers will bring you pretty close to the story of the creation of mankind as found in the Book of Genesis—and the beginning of all things is a pretty good place to start in our understanding of the sexual nature of man and woman.

We are told that God created in His own image, "Male and female created He them." If you are not particularly religiously oriented, then all you have to do is take a look at the natural universe and you will see the same great truth.

Our sexuality is a divine gift, the image of God within us, our spiritual or real nature. Small wonder that our sexual attitudes, concepts, and practices shape or mar our whole personality. When we deal with sex we are dealing with our deep, true, inner nature. Once we accept this great truth, we are making a great move toward wholeness—wholeness in thought, feeling, attitude, personality, and individuality. We have come face to face with our real inner self, and that usually is a therapeutic as well as an often shattering experience.

## Learn to Appreciate Your Own Sexuality

You may wish to do a little deep inner work right now in your own attitudes, thoughts, and feelings. This is the only kind of work that is really productive in healing, or the movement toward wholeness. You may wish to move in directions suggested by the following words: "As a male (female) I am a man (woman) sexually—a whole person, a complete individual, the image of God. My masculinity (femininity) is my divinity, my spirituality, my Real Self. I accept my sexuality as my Creator's gift to me. I accept it. I rejoice in it. I am grateful for it. I drop all feelings of fear, guilt, condemnation, shame, or embarrassment concerning sex. I feel a miracle of transformation taking place in my sexual attitudes toward myself and others."

Let these ideas grow and unfold in your own consciousness, and a new understanding and appreciation of your own sexuality and that of others will unfold in its own creative, dynamic way within you. A sense of wonder, delight, and joy in your own sexuality and all its elements and avenues of expression will unfold. A feeling of purity, sacredness, and sexual wholeness will take up residence in your mind, heart, body, and your relationships with others.

A man who, by his own admission, was somewhat less than a whole person, disillusioned by life and by his sexual relationships said, upon hearing some of the foregoing ideas: "My God, man! That's the first time I've heard anything about sex that made any sense at all. I can see why being a sexual athlete, jumping from bed to bed with different partners never brought me any satisfaction. I have been violating the integrity and sacredness of my own sexuality—to say nothing of that of my partners. Thanks for hitting me between the eyes with the truth!"

A woman who had led a very unhappy life that produced three divorces had reached a point where her physical condition was such that a doctor thought she should have a hysterectomy. At her physician's recommendation, she came to see a minister who shared with her some of the ideas outlined above. He added the suggestion that, since her body is a temple of the living God, she should also realize that her reproductive and genital organs and functions are instruments of divine action and that she should bless and love and appreciate them.

Later the woman told a friend that, as the minister was speaking, she felt as if a whole lifetime of unhappy memories, sick experiences, and a mountain of condemnation were draining out of her. She said that as she blessed and loved and appreciated all the organs of her body, she could feel the emotional and mental knots untying and the strain and irritation in her body disappearing. Years later there had been no operation and the women said she was freer, happier, and healthier than ever before.

### The Inner Miracle of Freedom and Wholeness

There is no miracle quite like the inner miracle of freedom and wholeness that takes place as old distorted concepts and attitudes are replaced by a healthy, dynamic, creative attitude toward ourself. No one else can really bring these changes about for us, although we can inspire and help each other in many ways. As you continue the process of understanding the sexual element of your whole personality you may find the following statement a helpful tool: "Right now I accept and establish a healthy, dynamic, creative attitude toward my own sexuality."

As this healthy, dynamic, creative attitude toward your sexuality unfolds in you, a feeling of wholeness will be its fruit. You will find less need of outer rules and regulations to conduct your relationships with others because you will acquire a deep respect and reverence of your own sexuality. You will be less inclined to get into or remain in relationships that adulterate it, distort it, depreciate it, or exploit it. You will experience an ever deepening realization of what it is to be a whole person sexually, and you will joyously preserve that feeling of wholeness.

Naturally your relationships with other people will be transformed also because you will be recognizing, accepting, and appreciating the sexuality (femininity or masculinity) of each one. You will respect the wholeness of his or her personality and sexuality as much as you do your own, and you will seek to establish and maintain relationships that help you and others to be what you are created to be—sons and daughters of the Most High.

You will come to an understanding that, in a very deep and real sense, all human relationships are sexual relationships. If you are a man, then your relationships with men are relationships with those of the same sex. Your relationships with women are your relationships with members of the other or complementary sex. All these human relationships will be on a higher level because you are becoming conscious of the wholeness, the divinity, the sacredness of your own sexuality.

If your relationship with a member of the complementary sex is such that it leads to the physical act of sexual intercourse, then this will be a holy, whole, and sacred sacrament for it will be a joining of two temples of the living God and a deep and intimate exchange of the highest and best elements that are within you both.

A woman who went to see a counselor about her troubled marriage said, in effect, that she felt very much like a prostitute in the sexual act. Her husband provided well for her in every material way but seemed to feel that sexual intercourse was purely an animal or physical act, and he gave her little or no consideration as a whole person sexually. She said that just to have her husband touch her triggered a whole host of negative reactions that made it almost impossible for her to take part in the sex act.

The counselor then asked her if she treated herself as a whole person sexually. She was startled and said she would have to think that one over. Several weeks later she called and said that a miracle was taking place in her marriage and that since she had changed her thinking about herself, her husband had miraculously changed his attitude toward her, leading her to the growing realization that her real problem had never been her husband but the attitude toward men and herself that she had largely picked up from her mother. She said that when she was startled by the counselor's question about her treating herself as a whole person sexually she began to look at her own views.

From as early as she could recall, she remembered her mother's telling her that all men were brutes and beasts and all they could think of was sex. She remembered her mother saying she could just as well be a prostitute for all her husband really cared about her. Apparently this feeling had grown until it became an obsession with the daughter, and all her life she held unhealthy attitudes about sex and her role in it and the brutishness of men. She said that, as she thought deeply about this matter, she realized her own responsibility in the marriage difficulties she was experiencing.

Accordingly, she resolved to change her attitude toward herself and to view herself as a complete woman, to regard sex as a beautiful and natural activity between a wife and her husband, and to free herself from her old ideas about men, which she had accepted as being true. She reported that she and her husband could now discuss their sexual relationship honestly—but she also realized that many of the brutish characteristics she had assigned to her husband did not really exist in him at all, and she knew that he would have been surprised and hurt to realize how she had felt about him in the past.

Men have as many problems as women in the way they think of themselves sexually. It is almost incredible that so-called mature men and women can carry such distorted images of themselves and the other sex and their role in the important sexual relationships.

Essentially, the path to wholeness of the person sexually as well as in all other areas is an "inside job." No one else can really be a whole person for us. That is the continuing, unfolding, freeing responsibility that belongs to each person. Of this we can be sure, however: As we accept our sexuality (even our divinity!), we will see, experience, and share more wholeness of the person in all our human relationships.

As we look at ourselves, we may even hear the voice of the Creator: "You are My Daughter, treat yourself like one." Or "You are My Son, treat yourself like one." And as we look at the many other people in our world, we may also hear the voice of our Creator saying: "These are My Sons and My Daughters, treat them accordingly."

# 11

## THE MINISTER'S VIEW:
## THE UNIVERSAL WHOLENESS

The stage is set for drama. In the physician's office, a man and his wife are conversing in hushed tones. The doctor enters. The usual pleasantries are exchanged, and then the husband asks, in an attempt at bravado: "Okay, Doc, let's get down to business. What's the verdict?"

In the electric atmosphere, the surgeon speaks. He tells them that the wife must submit to a major operation. All the laboratory tests and physical examinations point to the dire necessity of immediate surgery to halt the spread of disease in her body. His words trigger powerful reactions: shock, disbelief, despair, tears, hope, relief, perhaps even uneasy laughter.

### The Power of the Word

No doubt the surgeon has weighed his words long and well, reviewed his diagnosis, and considered his verdict and its impact on his patient. All the power and respectability of his professional status and experience back up his words and give them tremendous import. Often it is no exaggeration to say that the doctor's words mean life or death to his patient—and one is reminded of the Biblical observation: "Death and life are in the power of the tongue" (Prov. 18:21). And we might add, in the mind that operates it!

In another dramatic scene, a woman is seated across the desk from her minister. She has poured out her soul to him— her fears, her sins, her remorse, her doctor's verdict of "incurable," her concern for her family, all that her inner being has held and withheld. Suddenly she is quiet, and in the deafening silence the minister realizes he must speak and exercise the power of the word.

What will the "word" be? Compassion, hope, sympathy, resignation, condemnation, evasion? No doubt the clergyman is well-versed in his profession, deeply grounded in the tenets of his particular faith, motivated by a deep desire to help his fellow man, and, hopefully, conscious of the far-reaching impact of his word.

Once again the power of the word is being demonstrated— for by our words we are forgiven or condemned, healed or sickened, strengthened or weakened.

Not only do doctors, ministers, and counselors employ the power of the word. Great industries pay millions of dollars for the privilege of bringing the power of the word to bear in our minds and lives with the idea of getting us to buy their products. Philanthropic, religious, political, social, and cultural institutions use it to influence our actions and reactions.

Indeed, we are a word-oriented civilization, and we are deluged by torrents of words that vie for our attention and response. For the most part, we remain unconscious, or only semiaware, of the power of the word until a crisis of some kind forces us to seek the solace or inspiration of helpful words. Then we may awaken, at least briefly, to the power and importance of words and what goes into them.

Why are our words, the words we speak or think, so important? Simply because they are our individual use of the One Word, the creative energy that produced and maintains all creation! "In the beginning was the Word, and the Word was with God, and the Word was God. He was in the beginning with God; all things were made through Him, and without Him was not anything made that was made. In Him was life, and the life was the light of men. . . . And the Word became flesh and dwelt among us" (John 1:1–14).

Man is made in the image of God, and he wields creative power through his words, thoughts, and feelings. The creative word becomes flesh—that is, it becomes clothed in form and dwells among us. Our words are always becoming flesh and dwelling among us in our daily experience.

Who has not had the often disconcerting experience of seeing his own words and thoughts come to pass in his world? Probably to some degree every word, and the thought and feeling producing it, becomes flesh in our world. Only our dullness and lack of awareness prevent our understanding this. We are judged for and by every "idle" word—it produces results in our inner and outer world.

A friend of ours, an outstanding atomic scientist, says that, if we had the right kind of instrument, we would know that every time a man opens his mouth to speak, a current of radiant energy flows from his lips into the world and becomes part of it.

We live in a responsive universe, and "the words of our mouth and the meditations of our heart" have a profound and far-reaching influence. Words are living entities. They take root and grow, sometimes fantastically, especially in minds, hearts, and bodies that are weakened or confused by illness, fear, or depression.

Doctors, ministers, psychiatrists, family, and friends of those in need of healing have a tremendous responsibility and opportunity to use the power of the word, both audibly and silently. We are not advocating "Pollyana-ish" verbalizations that pretend all is well—but words of faith and power, words of understanding and appreciation, words that stir trust in the healing power of life itself!

### The Healing Power and Goodness of Life

In a time of crisis, there is no use pretending or mouthing sweet words we do not feel. The crisis we face will strip us naked of pretense, and our words, thoughts, and feelings, and the manner in which we express them will reveal our true attitude and belief.

If we have nothing hopeful to offer, then let us be honest; admit it to ourselves and say little or nothing. But if we have even a "mustard seed" of faith, now is the time to use the power of the word in a constructive, loving way. "When the chips are down," as the saying goes, very few human beings are entirely devoid of courage and faith.

Therefore, when the test comes, speak up. Affirm your faith in the healing power and goodness of life. Do all that you can in thought, feeling, and word to be part of the healing process. Your positive response to the difficult situation may trigger the healing power just as surely as any prescription that is written or any surgery that is performed.

We feel sure the time will come when practitioners of the healing arts will include the power of the word in their practice and prescriptions, for themselves as well as their patients. The healing of the "doctor" is quite as important as the healing of any condition and should be part of it.

When health is spoken of as often and convincingly as disease, we will experience many more dramatic healings in every area of human need. Health is contagious, and many patients "catch" it from their doctor, minister, family, or friends through the power of the word. We know a doctor whose cheery whistle and cheerful words are as much a part of his healing equipment as his skill with medicine and scalpel.

Never pass up an opportunity to speak the word of love, faith, healing, and inspiration. It is part of the healing activity at work in the universe and releases a flow of creative energy that works miracles in mind, heart, and body.

We have often witnessed spectacular changes that take place in patients, their family, and even the doctor and hospital staff because someone had the common sense and courage to speak the word that lifted the whole situation to a new level of experience. It has been said that "talk is cheap," but words can also be invaluable, healing, and inspiring. As you consciously use the power of the word, you will see some great changes for the better in your own world.

## You Are Part of the Healing Team

If you are cast in the role of patient, your own words, thoughts, and feelings may well be the determining factor in your healing. Your own attitudes, beliefs, and desires cannot be divorced from any condition you are experiencing and will help or hinder any professional assistance you may be receiving. You are part of the healing team—not a puppet or inert object of medical or surgical techniques. It is essential that you participate in your own recovery. You can best do this by setting a watch on your mind, heart, and lips and seeing to it that their utterances are acceptable in the process of healing you desire.

The head of one of the largest prayer groups in the world said that when we speak, think, and feel, we have the largest, most important, and most responsive audience in the world right at hand—the billions of atoms, cells, and processes of our own bodies.

Our bodies are not machines, but living, intelligent organisms through which we operate in this earthly experience. They respond to every word we speak, every thought we hold, and every feeling we entertain. We worry, sicken, weaken, strengthen, rejuvenate, heal our bodies through our words and the inner system of thoughts and feelings that produce them.

A woman was told that she was suffering from an incurable disease, that her condition was hopeless, and that she had only a few months to live. She refused this verdict and set about to work within herself to bring about the healing of the condition. The healing did come after a period of intensive and dedicated effort.

She told how she realized that the life force in her was intelligent and responded to her direction. She said she went in imagination to the organs and cells of her body and asked their forgiveness for the inferior way she had used the life energy. She then visualized the pure, healing life force flowing through her entire body—and she soon detected a great improvement in her whole well-being. She recovered from the so-called incurable disease and lived a long and productive life.

Throughout this book you have found reminders of the power of the word, a most important element in healing. It is the power of creative energy that brought forth the universe, including you. In reality, it is the one healing power in the world, whether its agents appear to be medicine, surgery, prayer, or treatment of any kind.

There are simple ways to use the power of the word, beginning right now as you read. If you have a deep religious faith you may say simply to yourself, "God is healing me now, and I am grateful." If your background makes this approach difficult, here is another simple statement: "Life itself is healing me." If you are working with a doctor, you might say, think, and feel, "The treatment I am receiving is effective. I am being healed." That is a minimum act of cooperation with those who are working for your healing.

Once you make a start, you will receive your own direct revelation of additional steps to take. The important thing is that you begin to move in the direction of healing, even if it is only a verbal exercise at the moment. As you persist, the rest of you will follow the healing action—the power of the word is creative, healing, irresistible. Believe it, and get under way!

Remember, words are living entities. Treat them with the respect, confidence, and intelligence they deserve, and they will treat you right!

## The Three D's of Health

The three D's of health are simply these: Desire, Decision, Delight. He who really experiences health desires it, decides that he has it, and delights in it. Our health is the universal activity of wholeness (God, Love, Life) individualized in us according to our desire, decision, and delight!

Most people are as healthy as they desire to be. This may seem like an oversimplification, but let's just accept it for the time being and go on. According to the healthiest One who ever walked the earth, it is our Heavenly Father's good pleasure to give us the kingdom (of health, wholeness), and our response to that divine gift is up to us.

No doubt the kingdom of health offered to us by our Creator with so much pleasure is a way of life beyond anything that we have yet conceived, but the offer is constantly with us. The activity of wholeness is constantly pressing in upon us and we decide whether we really want it or not. Desire is the door in our consciousness through which the activity of wholeness moves to expand its operation in us.

Jesus Christ put the whole issue of health in a simple setting when he asked a man who came to him for healing, "Do you want to be healed?" He projected no complicated religious or metaphysical formula. He simply tested the man's desire for health, knowing full well that unless it was activated, healing would be difficult if not altogether impossible.

It might seem startling to think that anyone who is ill would not desire healing—yet that is often the case, as any doctor, psychiatrist, or minister knows only too well. There are many desires that victimize people and, at least temporarily, overcome their desire for health, wholeness, and life. Some of these desires include desire for attention; pampering; revenge; domination; security; self-punishment; evasion of responsibility; opportunity; the desire to stay in comfortable ruts of thought, feeling, and action; or finally, the desire for death.

These negative desires often start out in small ways, but

unless they are dissolved they may become powerful anti-health factors in the individual's experience and short-circuit or block the activity of wholeness in him.

I know a number of practitioners of the healing art who regularly ask those who come for help if they really want to be healed, to be whole, strong, and alive. The answers received are often startling, sometimes humorous, and in many ways helpful to all concerned. A true answer to the question "Do you really want to be healthy, whole, and alive?" can bring one to a point of self-honesty, which is often therapeutic in itself.

A woman who had spent several weeks in a hospital bed was asked this question by a visiting minister. After an initial flash of resentment at the audacity of such a question, she really began to ask herself if she wanted to be healthy again. She answered in the affirmative and soon left the hospital to return to a more creative and effective way of life.

A man who had been going through a series of increasingly serious illnesses was asked by the doctor, "Do you really want to be healed?" His immediate brusque retort was, "Heck, no! I want to die and get it over with!" The violence of his response startled him so that he started to laugh and said, "That's ridiculous. Of course, I want to be healed!" You know the answer. He was healed because he had taken an honest look at his own desires and was willing to reach the decision in favor of health so that the healing action of the Infinite could operate in him.

Perhaps you don't have the need for a healing of a specific illness, but if you are like most of us, a greater experience of health, wholeness, and life will be welcome. The principles involved are the same. It is always our Heavenly Father's good pleasure to give us the kingdom of health, wholeness, and life, and we can have all of it that we really want.

It might prove enlightening and helpful to check out your answers to this question: "Do I really want to be healthy, whole, and alive?" You can expand the question a bit: "Do I really want to experience the activity of wholeness mentally, emotionally, physically, socially?"

The world expects a great deal from the healthy person, the whole person, the truly alive person. He is expected to shoulder his share of responsibility without complaint. He is expected to be able to stand on his own feet without too much attention, praise, or appreciation. He rarely receives bouquets, either verbal or floral.

I remember hearing one of my first truth teachers say that no one sends flowers to a healthy person. That kind of attention is usually reserved for the sick. As you question your own inner desires, you will probably have an opportunity to reach a decision as to which one will be uppermost in your consciousness. If you cast an affirmative vote for the desire to be healthy, whole, and alive, you may wish to address yourself to the Giver of the infinite kingdom of good in the following manner: "I have decided that I want to experience the activity of wholeness with all my heart, with all my soul, with all my mind, and with all my strength."

This is very close to saying that you love the Lord your God with your whole being. You are responding positively to the good pleasure (will) of your Creator and opening yourself, through consent, to the will of the Infinite, which is abundant life beyond anything you have conceived, comprehended, or experienced.

You are then in the position to expand your desire into an actual experience by putting your faith to work. You might phrase your decision in the following manner: "I believe that right now I am experiencing the activity of wholeness— spiritually, emotionally, mentally, and physically."

The great promise is that according to your faith it will be done unto you, and your decision is your faith. Your faith is now at work, and the activity of wholeness is taking over in your whole being. This means that there are great changes taking place in you from the inside out. Old, unhealthy states of mind, heart, and body are being erased and dissolved. The activity of wholeness, which is life itself, is rapidly expanding its operation in and through you.

This activity leads to a state of joyous appreciation, and you can begin to delight in what is taking place. The three D's of health are being completed in you, and you will find that there are experiences taking place in you that can be described in words like the following: "I delight in the activity of wholeness as it expands its operation in my mind, heart, and body," or "I enjoy the activity of life itself as it cleanses my whole being of unhealthy thoughts, feelings, habits, and attitudes," or "I rejoice in and appreciate the activity of wholeness as it takes over all of my systems of self-expression."

These words are merely offered as guidelines so you won't be too surprised when the activity they describe expands its operation in and through you. To delight in the activity of wholeness is really to delight in the Lord because the activity of wholeness is the activity of God. Once you really welcome this divine action through your desire, decision, and delight, you are well on the road to becoming a new creature. The health that is being established in you is no longer a fragile, transient thing. It is strong and eternal because it is the universal activity of wholeness, the handiwork of God, life itself.

Once again, it is our Heavenly Father's good pleasure to give us the infinite kingdom of health, wholeness, and life. This kingdom comes out of the love that is the nature of our Creator, and it flows into our experience as our health according to our desire, decision, and delight.

Health—the activity of wholeness, the activity of God, the activity of love, the activity of life—is our divinely natural state. Eventually we will all enter this state and never depart from it. Once we have done so, we will discover that even our desire, decision, and delight are part of the activity of wholeness and that it was really our Indwelling Father who planned and executed the whole operation.

Health is yours as the gift of your Creator. Desire it, decide that you have it, and delight in it!

## Counseling

I have often been asked how to counsel people, and I must honestly answer that I do not know how to counsel anyone or to tell anyone what he or she should do. I am willing, however, to listen to others and to try to communicate with them, all the while doing my best to remember that we are communicating in the Counseling Presence of the Infinite One, to whom there is no unknown way or unanswered problem.

To put it in another way, I feel there is no minister, physician, psychiatrist, teacher, friend, or foe who is wise enough to tell another person what to do, although the Counseling Presence may use anyone as its spokesman, usually without his realizing what is being done, in order to save his ego from overinflation.

In my first years as a minister I used to gain some personal satisfaction from dropping pearls of wisdom into someone's ear, either in personal sessions or at a Sunday morning service. Experience, however, the mother of humility, has taught me that others rarely listen to my "gems"—or if they do, are likely to interpret them in ways beyond my comprehension.

I recall how, one morning after a service held in the Waldorf-Astoria Hotel in New York City, a handsome, richly gowned woman came up to me and said, "Dr. Paulson [I'm not a Dr. by any surge of the imagination] I was healed during your service this morning."

"Yes," I replied in eager unhumbleness, "and when did your healing take place?" Her reply taught me more than any instruction in pastoral counseling ever did.

"When your soloist stood up to sing."

She smiled sweetly and waltzed out, and I realized that the Counseling Presence had spoken again, and this time it was to me. Ministers and other professionals sooner or later learn that they have no corner on Truth, for it flows through everyone. I feel that I have never counseled with anyone, no matter what his circumstances, who has not given me something, for the most part unconsciously, that I had been seeking, often for years. I remember asking myself in silent bewilderment, "Who is counselor and who is counselee?" until I finally asked the Counseling Presence and the answer was "*I am* and I am in you both."

Daddy Bray, a Kahuna priest in Hawaii, told me he had never met a man who did not teach him something. I feel he exemplified the attitude of true humility that anyone cast in a counseling role needs to gain and will gain as he listens to the Counseling Presence. Quite often the "patient" counsels the "physician" to the benefit of both, and in a healing, free-ranging counseling session the Counseling Presence works through all involved.

## Wholeness

Healing is our acceptance of the universal wholeness. When we are ill, we have permitted some element of our being to be moved out of wholeness. If we see ourself, or someone else, or some element of the creation as ill or evil, we are denying the universal wholeness. We have removed our consciousness from the stream or ocean or wholeness, and we are subject to separation or unwholeness—an unholy, unhealthy state of affairs!

As a matter of fact, we are always conscious to some degree of the universal wholeness. We couldn't know that we are ill if we do not have some awareness of the universal state of wholeness. Illness is an unnatural state—that's why we realize there is something wrong when we are sick!

I have a spiritual formula that I have found helpful to people in my work as a minister. It is a formula that can be put into words, and I have seen it work wonders in many lives, including my own. One woman, to whom I gave it during a crisis in her life, called it "The Divine Prescription" and I have always liked that title. Here it is:

> The activity of God is the only power at work in my mind,
> body, and life. All false beliefs, all negative appearances are
> being dissolved right now by the loving, forgiving action of
> God. I am whole, strong, and free as I am created to be.

For those whose religious attitudes make them suspicious
of the word *God*, I use the word *Good,* which as you know
comes from the same basic root.

I have often wondered what gave these words such mind-
changing power, but since we have been working together on
this book, I see more clearly what happens when a person
accepts these words and the activity they describe. As a doctor and minister, we would, I am sure, agree that there is only
one healing power at work in the universe, whether it operates through medicine, therapy, exercise, music, prayer, or a
simple, wordless faith.

This power works all the time, but we often forget that,
especially when we are experiencing mental, emotional,
and/or physical stress or illness. In fact, it is our forgetting or
ignoring this pervasive, always active power that keeps us
from being healed. And the work of any healer is to help one
needing healing to open himself to the presence and activity
of the healing power.

The Divine Prescription does this by appealing first of all to
the mind and emotions, quieting them through the realization
that the healing power of the Creator is at work, on the job
constantly. Many times all that is needed is a reminder such as
those words contain. When the import of the idea of constant
healing sinks into consciousness, the mind relaxes—so does
the body—and healing treatment becomes more effective
immediately.

I am sure that many doctors, like ministers, often wish they
had a magic hammer to tap people on the head (not too softly
sometimes) to get them to relax and let healing take place. It
can be frustrating to work with someone right on the brink of
healing only to have his own tenseness, anxiety, or other negative condition block it.

The Divine Prescription works beautifully with those who are so tense that they are "only mouthing" the words at the beginning of treatment. I do not know exactly why—but then I suspect that many drugs and treatments work much the same way. They are part of a movement or return to wholeness, and they trigger a responsive element in the patient—and in the doctor or minister, too.

## Everyone Is His Own Healer

Ultimately everyone is his own healer in that he must be the one who finally lets the universal wholeness into his experience. The words of the Divine Prescription are a cutting edge of a whole process of healing, renewal, and freedom. And once they are taken into the vocabulary and thought and feeling patterns of an individual, the healing process is well under way. I wish that words of this nature might be part of every prescription a doctor writes; they would surely make the prescription more effective.

I recall a woman who had been in and out of the hospital for months, under intensive medication, with no improvement in her condition. She agreed to take the Divine Prescription, without changing anything else, and she started to improve the next day.

The doctor told her she was finally responding to the medicine, and when she insisted on telling him of her additional prescription, he said, "Fine, give it to me. I have some other patients who can use it!" After studying the words a bit, he commented, "That's the whole healing process in a nutshell—all doctors can do is add some window dressing and a few medicines that may speed things up a bit."

A number of doctors have told us that they are delighted to have prayer work done with their patients. They tell me, in effect, that the most important element in treatment is to get the patient back into the stream of life, get him in tune with the idea and process of healing—and, of course, to get "God on your side" is a tremendous boost back toward wholeness. We believe that God is always on the side of wholeness— because God is the wholeness and life of creation.

The Divine Prescription can be the foundation for a new health-promoting attitude regardless of the negative appearance of conditions. Often the gloom and pessimism of family, friends, nurses, and doctors hang like a shroud over and around the patient. A woman told me during a visit to her bedside in the hospital that she felt she could overcome anything but her family's apparent conviction that she was on her deathbed.

In another instance, a young girl was critically injured in an auto accident. The first time I saw her she was in a coma with just about every life-holding piece of equipment the hospital possessed attached to or inserted in her body. Her mother told me the doctor had said there was just no hope, that even if she lived, he was afraid her daughter would never be anything but a human "vegetable."

The mother said, "I don't want to believe that, but what can I do?"

I replied, "Jesus said 'not to judge by appearances, but judge righteous judgment'—so let's take a Divine Prescription for her and us."

For weeks that dragged into months, the coma lasted. Most of the family, friends, doctors, and nurses gave up hope, but that wonderful mother kept her faithful vigil by the hospital bed. I was able to visit nearly every week, and I'll never forget the thrill I experienced the day that lovely young girl's blue eyes opened and a wisp of a smile tugged at her lips and my heart.

Months later she and her mother walked into my office, radiant testimony to a mother's living faith and love—and the working of the Divine Prescription together with the doctors' and nurses' loving care.

This experience also made me realize how important are the words any of us speak around an ill or injured person. Even if an individual is in a so-called unconscious state, seemingly oblivious to all that is going on around him, that fantas-

tic subconscious mind is often right on the job, taking everything in and reacting to it, even to our unverbalized attitudes
and feelings.

A friend who had suffered a severe heart attack and was
unconscious to outer appearance nonetheless heard an intern
or doctor remark, "She'll never make it through the night."

My friend said later to me that when she heard this
thoughtless comment she was at first frightened, but then
something within her rose up and said (silently, of course,
because her lips and tongue wouldn't function) "Oh, yes, I
will. I'll show him. I'm not ready to go yet!"

Since most people in this type of experience do not gener-
ate the spiritual spunk my friend did, it would be more helpful
to speak and think some variation of the Divine Prescription.
My friend is "back on the job" in an exacting assignment, an
inspiration to all who know her.

I am constantly amazed and delighted by the capacity of an
individual to rise out of all types of difficulty when he attunes
himself to his source—the activity of God that produced, sustains, and renews him. Even a simple statement can be
enough to trigger the whole healing process.


## A Life Treatment[2]

This can be the beginning of a life treatment, and I invite
you to read it in as lively a way as possible. You will feel the
flow of the life current as you read briskly, confidently, vigorously, expectantly.

There is one life in the universe—flawless, diseaseless, in-
exhaustible, indestructible, eternal. This life is the creative
energy that made and sustains the whole universe and every
living creature, including, of course, man. Every man is a self-
expression of this creative energy and builds his world—his
mind, his body, his relationships, and all his affairs—by the
way he uses that energy. His contribution to humanity is determined by the way he expresses the infinite life energy avail-

able to and through him. The Master Life Advocate, Jesus Christ, who came to bring abundant life to all who will accept it, called this life energy a spring that would well up into eternal life in those who believe in Him enough to demonstrate it.

In man, life finds its greatest potential of expression. Through his faith, his thought, his feelings, his words, his actions, and his reactions each one expresses life, and not only expresses life but expands or inhibits its flow into ever greater expression.

The following courses of action described in words will, if followed, give you an immediate personal demonstration of the responsive life energy available for self-experience and self-expression through you. Grasp the words firmly in your mind, penetrating through the letter to the spirit, the deep inner meaning, so that you lay hold of life itself.

Here is the first exercise in a life treatment:

> *I rejoice in the marvelous way the life current lifts and clears my vision as I believe in eternal life.*

Remember that to believe in life is to believe in God, because life is God in action. You may wish to exercise your faith in the direction pointed out by the following statement:

> *I rejoice in the magnificent way the life current responds to my growing faith in God.*

To believe in life is also to believe in Jesus Christ, the Savior of mankind, whose whole objective is to lift man's life experience and expression to the tone and quality of eternal life. The following statement outlines yet another way to stir up your faith in life and its infinite potential through you:

> *I give thanks for the powerful way the life current responds to my vigorous faith in Jesus Christ, His teaching, and His demonstration of eternal life.*

The Bible tells us that all who believe in Jesus Christ are given the power to become sons of God. The power to become a son or daughter of God is the power that dissolves the old sense of separation and limitation and lifts our whole being to new heights of performance.

It takes a great surge of the life current to lift man into the realization that he is truly a son of the Infinite, brother to Jesus Christ, and joint heir to the riches of the divine kingdom. The sons and daughters of the living God are so full of life that there is no room in them for disease, fear, guilt, resentment, condemnation, hatred, or any sense of separation from the Source of all. They are so charged with life that their whole being radiates love, oneness, forgiveness, joy, strength, peace, and wholeness to the entire world.

Life flows into specialized self-expression through the thinking process in man. Each one is free to choose how he will think; and the nature of his thoughts not only expresses life but conditions it by expanding or inhibiting its flow. The course of mental action outlined in the following words is life-expanding:

> *I rejoice in the life current that energizes my whole being as I think positively and constructively.*
> *I praise the life current that heals me as I think thoughts of health, vitality, and strength for myself and others.*
> *I rejoice in the life current that prospers me as I think generously, abundantly, lovingly, gratefully.*

As your thinking expands, your own increased awareness of life will inspire you to new and livelier patterns of thought, which will in turn increase the life flow in you. It is a lively circle of good and ever greater good. You are becoming a life thinker, and life itself expands and improves the whole operation of your mental processes.

It is in the feeling nature of man that life finds its richest, warmest, and most fulfilling expression. Feeling is the moving power that transforms the world in wonderful ways when it is in tune with divine love. As the life current quickens its operation in us, we become masters of feeling and emotion in a natural way. A lively person has healthy emotions. To help eliminate some old outworn, life-inhibiting habits, you may wish to take the following verbal statement of action into your mind and heart:

> *I rejoice in the wonderful way the life current renews me as I stop feeling sorry for myself, or thinking of myself as burdened, guilty, resentful, or limited in any way.*

Some elements of the foregoing life-inhibiting attitudes are present in all of us or we would not be on the human scene, and it is well to eliminate them (or to let life eliminate them) before we start the process of building in new patterns of feeling. Work with the ideas in a relaxed way, and you will soon begin to feel free. Then move confidently into the life action described in the next statement:

> *I praise the life current that rejuvenates me completely.*

Feeling is an inside job and a good feeling can be generated within regardless of outer conditions. Even a little practice will improve your ability to choose your own feelings without reference to outer conditions and increase the flow of life through you.

To feel strong, to feel healthy, to feel joyous and happy, to feel generous, to feel grateful, to feel confident, to feel successful, to feel forgiving, to feel one with God and your fellow man, to feel alive, alert, joyful, and enthusiastic, to feel free, all bring a rejuvenating surge of the life current to and through you that increases your ability to do a better job of living.

The master feeling is love, because God is love. According to the Bible, that textbook of life, we should give top priority to love of God, love of neighbor, and love of self. It takes a life-filled person to do this—no half-alive state of being can keep the love commandments. When we are alive enough, we cannot help being loving.

You may wish to use the following exercises, either in their present form or changed to suit your own taste:

> *I rejoice in the life current that fills my whole being. I love the Lord my God with all my heart, with all my soul, with all my mind, and with all my strength.*
>
> *I praise the life current that transforms my whole world as I not only love God but love my neighbor as myself.*

As you express love, you will discover the true nature of God, of your neighbor, and of yourself. You will feel the underlying unity of all creation, and your whole experience will change for the better. You will share in the feelings generated in the enlightened souls of all ages. Words like the following at least hint at this type of experience:

> *I rejoice in the miracles the life current works in me as I feel the underlying unity of all creation and recognize the Divine Presence within me and my neighbor.*

By this time you have the feel of the eternal life current operating through you, and it will be easy for you to adapt these ideas and exercises to your words, actions, and reactions. The life current will work miracles in and through you as you speak words of truth, love, and power; act generously, enthusiastically, lovingly; and react in positive and constructive ways in the practice of daily living.

You are experiencing a new birth, and you no longer are the victim of outer conditions and circumstances. You are becoming what Paul describes as a "life-giving spirit." An old you is passing out of existence and a new you is coming into being. You are in tune with the upward, progressive movement of life, and the Author of that life is pleased to have you on the eternal life team.

# 12

---

## LIFE IS FOREVER!

After many years in the ministry I am joyously convinced of two great truths. The first great truth is that life is eternal, everlasting, indestructible. Its forms, relationships, appearances, and disappearances are in a state of constant change—but life? It goes on forever! The second great truth is that the reality of each individual—the soul or spirit—which is life, is eternal, everlasting, indestructible. Forms, relationships, appearances and disappearances through which the soul or Spirit finds expression are in a state of constant change—but the individual soul? It goes on forever!

Life goes on forever, releasing old forms and generating new ones—and so do we! For we are life—exploring, experiencing and expressing our self potential. Our life did not begin with the experience we have labeled birth, and it does not end with the experience labeled death. With rapidly-clearing vision, strengthened by spiritual and scientific research and verification, we are in a position to take a new, freeing look at our earthly experience.

When we are born, we make our debut on the earthly stage through a door marked "entrance." The other side of that door bears the sign: "exit." When, for conscious and unconscious reasons, we leave this earthly space, we move through a door labeled "exit." The other side of that door bears the sign "entrance." What is often unthinkingly accepted as all of life—that sometimes turbulent, always challenging, truly inspiring experience of earth embodiment—is in reality only a tiny arc on the everlasting, upward spiral of eternal life. This realization, entertained in the mind and heart, at least as a possibility, will dissolve much of the stress and apprehension that contribute so powerfully to disease and unhappiness and no doubt shorten and detract from the life span here in this beautiful spaceship Earth.

To believe, even as a possibility, that we are eternal beings, exploring, experiencing and expressing our self potential through the ever changing energy systems of time and space will dramatically change our attitudes toward our Creator, our neighbor, our self, and the rest of creation. As one awakening human being to another I urge you to enter this healing experience with growing confidence, joy and enthusiasm. For convenience, here's a course of mental/emotional action outlined in words: "I happily entertain in mind and heart the very real possibility that I am an eternal being, exploring, experiencing and expressing my self potential in the energy systems of time and space."

As this seed idea takes root and expands in consciousness, a new order often takes place in our attitudes and priorities. We may decide that factors that have seemingly caused us stress, unhappiness and illness are just not that important to an eternal being, and, with a laugh or two we may give ourselves permission to drop old patterns, resentments and burdens and move to a healthier, more alive state. After all, since we are eternal, there is not much point in prolonging energy systems built on false premises, is there? Especially since we are undoubtedly going to have the opportunity to let ourself be healed of every disease somewhere along the everlasting spiral of life? Why not now?

It is amazing and inspiring to learn that researchers like Elizabeth Kubler-Ross, who start out to study death and dying suddenly realize that they are really probing into life

and living because there is no death, only change. The life
essence of the individual who supposedly dies goes on in the
continuum of energy systems that constitute the universe,
both visible and invisible, working out its salvation (healing)
in other energy systems and relationships designed to awaken,
heal and return each soul to ultimate wholeness.

Other researchers suggest that the tiniest particle of
"matter" never disappears without a trace—it moves into
other forms, relationships, energy systems or returns to the
ocean of pure energy from which it came originally. Nothing
is lost in the divine economy. The Creator is completely
capable of healing His image and likeness, man, and is
eternally doing so. No matter how fragmented, isolated, sick
or dying we may think and feel ourselves to be, the healing,
saving, restoring process is under way—we decide when we
surrender to it!

To Ev's great principle of self-realization through illness,
we can add the thought of self-realization through the change
called "death" if that becomes necessary. It becomes necessary apparently when the mental, emotional and physical
energy systems of self-expression become so clogged, inef-
ficient and overloaded by the debris, burdens, boredom and
stress of existing at a certain level that the soul decides to
"cash in its chips" and start over in other energy systems and
relationships. Enlightenment poses the question: "Why not
choose life instead of death?" and ultimately each soul
answers that question in its own unique way. There are mysteries here that are yet to be revealed—and each revelation
will bring a renewed surge of life.

St. Paul suggests that to die daily is an available down-to-
earth principle we can all apply profitably. To "die" daily to
resentment, fear, guilt, boredom, unhappiness and other
negations of life that clog and short-circuit our energy systems
—these "sins" whose wages are illness, isolation and death—
is certainly a healing, health-expanding, life-promoting therapy. To "die to" or forgive ourselves out of these toxic states
of mind and heart that literally shock our mental and bodily

energy systems to death is an act of love that helps to overcome the last enemy, death, in all its stages. As we die daily to the false beliefs and concepts that stifle our souls, we usually find that life takes over and promotes healing in mind, heart and body. As we practice the principle of greater self-realization through daily dying to negation of all kinds, we may soon feel so great we'll delay for a long time the laying aside of the "body" in the transition experience we have labeled death. And our daily life, too, will be richer and more meaningful. To practice the "little deaths" on a daily basis will eventually remove the necessity for the habitual death pattern all humanity has practiced so diligently and long.

Jesus revealed long ago that it is not flesh and blood or thought and feeling that give health, for it is the "Spirit that gives life." We live as a branch cut off from the tree of life, withering, sick and dying, until we are "born of the Spirit." Then a new dimension of our being starts to unfold and blossom as we realize, perhaps dimly at first, but with ever-growing clarity, that our real nature is Spirit, eternal, infinite and indestructible—the image of our Creator. We discover that the "hereafter" we have all been seeking consciously and unconsciously, with its promise of wholeness, eternal life, and bliss, is right *here after* we wake up to what's here in Spirit, soul and body.

It is our heartfelt prayer and deep desire that during your journey through the pages, words and ideas in this book, you have felt the movement of the eternal, life-giving Spirit in yourself. Healing for Everyone is healing in Everyone—the irresistible, irrepressible, irreversible, loving activity of God in us all.

# NOTES

## Chapter 1

1. Walt Whitman, *Leaves of Grass* (New York and Philadelphia: David McKay, 1900).

## Chapter 2

1. Donald H. Andrews, *The Symphony of Life* (Lees Summit, Mo.: Unity Books, 1966), p. 42.
2. Pierre Teilhard de Chardin, *The Phenomenon of Man* (New York: Harper Torch Books, 1961), p. 64.
3. Pitrim A. Sorokin, *The Ways and Power of Love* (Chicago: Gateway Edition, Henry Regnery Co., 1954), p. 6.
4. John Dryden, "A Song for St. Cecelia's Day," *Oxford Book of English Verse* (Oxford: Clarendon Press, 1939 edition), p. 479.
5. Concerning the work of Tintoretto, art critic B. Berenson points out that his paintings give a great sense of power and immense energy. Tintoretto had that great mastery of light and shadow, which enabled him to put into his pictures all the poetry there was in his soul. Bernhard Berenson, *The Venetian Painters of the Renaissance* (New York: G. P. Putnam's Sons, 1906), pp. 52–53.
6. Ibid.
7. Shafica Karagulla, *Breakthrough to Creativity* (Los Angeles: DeVorss and Co., 1967).
8. For further discussion of the symbolism of the caduceus see Manly P. Hall, *Man, Grand Symbol of the Mysteries* (Los Angeles: Philosopher's Press, 1932), p. 305.
9. Gal. 2:20.
10. *Bhaghavad Gita* (London: Temple Classics, 1905).
11. Matt. 17:2.
12. Donald H. Andrews: notes taken at a lecture in Los Angeles, 1970.
13. Ervin Seale: notes taken at a lecture in Los Angeles, 1970.
14. George Adams and Olive Whicher, *The Planet between the Sun*

*and Earth* (Worcestershire, England: Goethean Science Foundation, 1952), p. 1.
15. J. Allen Boone, *The Language of Silence* (New York: Harper and Row, 1970).
16. William Wordsworth, "Sonnets," *A Treasury of Great Poems* (New York: Simon and Schuster, 1942), p. 650.

*Special Note:* For those individuals wishing further information about the chakras or yoga, I can recommend the following: *Esoteric Healing* by Alice Bailey; *The Chakras* by C. W. Leadbetter; *Fundamentals of Yoga* by Rammurti Mishra, M.D.; *Man Made Clear for the Nuclear Age* by Roland Hunt; and *Scientific Yoga for the Man of Today* by Sri Surath.

## Chapter 3

1. Ruth Bircher, *Eating Your Way to Health*, trans. Claire Lowenfeld (London: Faber and Faber, 1961), p. 44.
2. Ibid.
3. Weston A. Price, D.D.S., *Nutrition and Physical Degeneration* (Santa Monica, Cal.: Price-Pottenger Foundation, 1971).
4. E. Cheraskin and W. M. Ringsdorf, *Predictive Medicine*, ch. 13, "Tolerance Testing" (Mountain View, Cal.: Pacific Press Publishing Association, 1973).
5. William Harvey, M.D., "Animal Generation," *Britannica Great Books*, vol. 28, p. 332.
6. The indications for the use of adrenal cortex extract and description of this conditions are contained in a booklet *Hypoadrenocorticism* by John W. Tintera, M.D., reprinted from the *New York State Journal of Medicine*, July 1, 1955, obtainable from The Adrenal Metabolic Research Society of the Hypoglycemia Foundation, Inc., P.O. Box 444, Scarsdale, N.Y., 10583.
7. Concerning the safety and value of adrenal cortex extract, I refer the reader to *Dispensatory of the United States of America*, Edition 25:

> Action and uses—For use in the maintenance of patients with chronic adrenal insufficiency. . . . The dose may be repeated as often as necessary. . . . Extracts of adrenal cortex contain several substances that influence electrolyte, water or carbohydrate me-

tabolism in various degrees. Injections of suitable extracts of adrenal cortex that contain little or no epinephrine may restore even the moribund to apparently vigorous health for as long as the injections are continued.

8. Doctors Tom Spies, E. Cheraskin, George Watson, Roger Williams, Carlton Fredericks, and others have been "voices crying in the wilderness" trying to right this situation. Fortunately, several new professional societies have come into existence in the last few years that are emphasizing this area, such as the International Academy of Metabology, the International College of Applied Nutrition, and the Academy of Orthomolecular Psychiatry, all of which are multidisciplinary, encouraging membership among physicians, dentists, veterinarians, Ph.D's in biochemistry, and so on.
9. Hair analyses are available for physicians through Ethical Data, Inc., P.O. Box 263, West Chicago, Ill., 60185.
10. David Hawkins and Linus Pauling, *Orthomolecular Psychiatry* (San Francisco: W. H. Freeman and Co.), p. 202.
11. Dr. Roger Williams, *Nutrition against Disease* (New York: G. P. Putnam's Sons, 1971), p. 158.
12. Dr. Francis Pottenger, Jr., M.D., in *American Journal of Orthodontics and Oral Surgery*, vol. 32, no. 8, pp. 467-85.
13. *Report on Food and Nutrition*, National Academy of Sciences, National Research Council, on suggested vitamin standards:

|  | *Adults* | *Children and Pregnant Women* |
|---|---|---|
| Vitamin A | 4,000 units | 9,000 units |
| Vitamin D | 400 units | 1,200 units |
| Vitamin B$_1$ | 1 mg. | 3 mg. |
| Vitamin B$_2$ | 1.2 mg. | 2.5 mg. |
| Niacin | 10 mg. | 27 mg. |
| Vitamin C | 30 mg. | 60 mg. |
| Calcium | 750 mg. | 2,250 mg. |
| Phosphorus | 750 mg. | 2,250 mg. |
| Iodine | 0./ mg. | 0.2 mg. |
| Iron | 10 mg. | 18 mg. |

14. The valuable work of the Drs. Shute in regard to vitamin E is monumental, and their evidence is overwhelming. From reading the international abstracts they have been publishing on the therapeutic effects of vitamin E, it would appear that these effects are recognized around the world except in the United States. I can only say that those who oppose its use certainly have not considered the evidence. Note for instance the reference: Drs. Shute, *The Summary* (London: Shute Foundation for Medical Research).

## Chapter 4

1. John Dryden, "Epistle to John Dryden of Chesterton."
2. Thomas Cureton, *Physical Fitness and Dynamic Health* (New York: Dial Press, 1965). Note accompanying Standard Test of Physical Fitness.
3. "Royal Canadian Air Force Exercise Plans for Physical Fitness," *This Week* Magazine, 1962.
4. Dr. Kenneth Cooper, *Aerobics* (Philadelphia and New York: Lippincott, 1968).
5. Linnie M. Wolfe, *Son of the Wilderness: The Life of John Muir* (New York: Knopf, 1951).

## Chapter 5

1. Edgar Cayce, *A Commentary on the Book of the Revelation* (Virginia Beach, Va.: Association for Research and Enlightenment, Inc., 1961), p. 34.
2. Hans Selye, M.D., *The Stress of Life* (New York: McGraw-Hill, 1956).
3. The tests most frequently used include the PBI, T3, and T4, the serum thyroxin, the BMR and the achilleometer test, and the cholesterol test.
4. Murray Israel, M.D., "Continuous Thyroid Hormone Therapy of Euthyroid Man, A 30-Year Experience," address given, May 16, 1966; American College of Endocrinology—Vascular Research Foundation, 265 Locust Avenue, Roslyn Heights, L.I., N.Y.
5. This hyperactivity is regularly associated with adrenal cortical insufficiency.

6. In the Babinski test, a firm stroke is made across the bottom of the foot just below the toes (this is done only after the child is past the age of six months). The great toe should bend downward. If, instead, it rises, this is a good evidence of a brain lesion.

7. This test includes a pack of cards on which are printed True and False statements that are indicators of the ability to perceive reality and ascertain mood changes. The score in this case was consistent with a schizophrenic state.

8. George Thommen, *Biorhythm, Is This Your Day?* (New York: Award Books, 1964).

9. Philip Norman, M.D., "Fundamentals of Nutrition for Physicians and Dentists," *Oral Surgery* 33, pp. 780–85.

# Chapter 6

1. Henry R. Harrower, *Practical Endocrinology* (Milwaukee, Wis.: Lee Foundation for Nutritional Research, 1932).

2. Pitrim Sorokin, *The Ways and Power of Love* (Chicago: Gateway Edition, Henry Regnery Co., 1954).

3. Samuel Hahnemann, M.D., *The Organon of Medicine*, Sixth Edition, translated with preface by Wm. Boericke, M.D., and Introduction by James Krauss, M.D. (Calcutta: Roysingh and Co., 1962).

4. Alexis Carrel, M.D., *The Voyage to Lourdes* (New York: Harper and Bros., 1941).

5. Edson J. Andrews, "Moon Talk: The Cyclic Periodicity of Postoperative Hemorrhage," *Journal of Florida Medical Association,* May 1960, p. 1362.

6. A biopsy is the removal of a piece of diseased tissue for microscopic study in order to determine the nature of the disease; it is particularly important in determining the presence of cancer.

7. Alexis Carrel, *The Voyage to Lourdes*; and Ruth Cranston, *The Miracle of Lourdes* (New York: McGraw Hill, 1955).

8. E. Grey Dimond, "Educating the Future Physician," *Saturday Review/World*, October 9, 1973, p. 52.

9. Physicians, dentists, or veterinarians wishing to take a postgraduate course in Homeopathic Medicine should contact the American Foundation for Homeopathy, Suite 506, 6231 Leesburg Pike, Falls Church, Va. 22044. This course is given in August each sum-

mer at Millersville State College under the direction of Allan D.
Sutherland, M.D., and lasts two weeks.
10. Samuel Hahnemann, M.D., *The Chronic Diseases, Their Specific Nature and Treatment*, transl. by Chas. J. Hempel, M.D. (New York: Wm. Radde, 1845).
11. James T. Kent, M.D., *Lectures in Homeopathic Philosophy* (New York: Altai Press, 1968).
12. Robert L. Meiers, M.D., and Allan Cott, M.D.
13. An autogenous vaccine is prepared by making a bacteriological culture from the secretions of the troubled organ, in this case, the nose and throat. From this a vaccine is made that is administered to the patient in a series of injections to increase immunity to these troublesome organisms.

## Chapter 7

1. Cadbury, Henry J., *George Fox's Book of Miracles,* pp. 33, Cambridge University Press '48
2. Stechschulte, D. and Dunn, M.; *Starvation and Heart Failure,* J. of Kansas Medical Society, Nov. '65 pp. 500
   Suzuki et al.; *Fasting Therapy for Psychosomatic Diseases with special reference to its indications and therapeutic mechanism;* Tohuku J. Experimental Medicine, 118 Suppl. 245, 1976
   Duncan, Garfield—In fasting 1300 patients, Allan Cott reports his success with the treatment of hypertension, impaired pulmonary function, chronic heart disease and psoriasis
3. Cott, Allan; *Fasting; the Ultimate Diet,* Bantam Books '75
4. Shelton, Herbert; *The Hygenic System, Fasting and Sunbathing* Vol. III Dr. Shelton's Health School, San Antonio, Tex. 1934 revised 1963
5. Knutson, K.E. and Selinus, R.; *Fasting in Ethiopia; An Anthropological and Nutritional Study;* Am. J. Clinical Nutrition 23 (7) July '70.
6. Gandhi, M.K.; *Gandhi's Autobiography, the Story of My Experiments with Truth;* Public Affairs Press; Washington, D.C. '48

7. Coca, Arthur F., *The Pulse Test;* Arco Publ. Co. N.Y. Randolph, Philpott and Mandell; various papers delivered to groups interested in Medical Ecology. Also see Dickey, Lawrence; *Medical Ecology;* Thoms, Springfield '76
8. Bircher, Ruth, Ralph, Alfred and von Brasch; *Eating Your Way to Health,* A Penguin Handbook; Baltimore '72
9. Luce, Gay Gaer; *Body Time,* Pantheon Books '71 National Institute of Mental Health, Chevy Chase, Md., '70; *Biological Rhythms in Psychiatry and Medicine* '70 Tompkins and Bird; *The Secret Life of Plants;* Harper and Row Publ. '72
10. Sakr, Ahmad; *Fasting in Islam;* Am. Diabetic Ass'n. Vol. 67, July '75
11. Boyd, Doug: *Rolling Thunder;* Random House, N.Y. '74
12. Theosophical Research Center, London: *Some Unrecognized Factors in Medicine;* Theosophical Press, Wheaton, Ill. '39
13. Assagioli, Roberto: *Psychosynthesis;* Hobbs, Dorman Co. N.Y. '65
14. Levi: *The Aquarian Gospel of Jesus the Christ;* Leo Dowling, publisher, Los Angeles, 1908
15. Potassium supplement: Sodium bicarbonate    2 parts
                      Potassium chloride or citrate  1 part
                      Citric acid    2 parts
16. PH indicator papers - obtainable through Micro Essential Lab. Brooklyn, N.Y. specify range 6-8
17. Spencer: Lancet '68
    Mount: Lancet July 6, 1944
    Sakr, Ahmad (see note #10)
18. Bieler Broth: Equal amounts of green beans, celery and zucchini are placed in a saucepan with a small amount of parsley. Water is added. Cook on low heat for ten minutes until vegetables are just tender. This is blended till of a creamy consistency and then served.
19. Wine, D.B., Crumpton, E: *Group Psychotherapy with 27 Starving Men,* Psychiatry Digest 29 (7): 17-20, July '68
20. Muesli: Note 8 above

## Chapter 9

1. Karlfried Graf von Dürckheim, *Hara* (London: George Allen and Unwin Ltd., 1962).
2. Olle Hagnell, New York Academy of Sciences *Annals* 125 (January 21, 1966), p. 846.
3. Dr. Artur Jores, International Meeting, Médicine de la Personne, 1966, Woudschoten, Holland.
4. Dr. Paul Tournier, *The Whole Person in a Broken World* (New York: Harper and Row, 1965).
5. Maxwell Maltz, *Psychocybernetics* (Englewood Cliffs, N.J.: Prentice-Hall, 1960).
6. This center was visited in the summer of 1973 by the Meadowlark staff tour group.

    Motion Picture Director's Award winner Ray Garner has made an hour-long television film entitled *Healing the Whole Man*, which deals with Dr. Max Bircher's unique center and includes an interview with him, along with seven other European physicians who are involved in similar work. Others mentioned in this book and taking part in the film include Dr. Paul Tournier, shown at his home in Geneva, and Dr. Karlfried Dürckheim, at his center for experiencing self-realization through Zen and allied techniques, which is located in Germany's Black Forest. The film can be rented from Meadowlark. Write to Friendly Hills Fellowship, Meadowlark, 26126 Fairview Avenue, Hemet, Calif. 92343.
7. The identity of the author must be kept secret.
8. Roberto Assagioli, M.D., *Psychosynthesis: A Manual of Principles* (New York: Hobbs, Dorman and Co., 1965).
9. Nicholas Herman (Brother Lawrence), *Practice of the Presence of God* (New York: Morehouse-Barlow).
10. Ernest Wood, *Concentration and Approach to Meditation* (Wheaton, Ill.: Theosophical Publishing House, 1967).
11. Walt Whitman, "Song of the Open Road," *Leaves of Grass*.
12. Linnie M. Wolfe, *Son of the Wilderness*.
13. Robert Henri, *The Art Spirit* (Philadelphia: J. B. Lippincott, 1940), p. 47.
14. From Arthur M. Abell, *Talks with Great Composers* (New York: Philosophical Library, 1955), p. 6.
15. Gustaf Stromberg, *The Soul of the Universe* (New York and Philadelphia: David McKay, 1940), p. 235.

16. Pierre Teilhard de Chardin, *The Hymn of the Universe* (New York: Harper and Row, 1961), p. 65.
17. Sri Ramakrishna Math, *Sayings of Sri Ramakrishna* (Mylapore, Madras, India, 1943), p. 59.
18. Alfred Lord Tennyson, "The Ancient Sage," *The Poetic and Dramatic Works* (Boston: Houghton Mifflin, 1899).
19. Thomas Kelly, *A Testament of Devotion* (New York: Harper and Row, 1941), p. 35.
20. George Fox, *The Book of Miracles*, with note and introduction by Henry Cadbury (Toronto: Macmillan, 1949).
21. Alexis Carrel, *The Voyage to Lourdes.*
22. Dr. Smiley Blanton, *Love or Perish* (New York: Fawcett World Library, 1969).
23. Walt Whitman, "Song of the Open Road," *Leaves of Grass.*

## Chapter 11

1. J. Sig Paulson, "The Three D's of Health." This section first appeared in an article in *New Thought Quarterly*, Spring issue 1973.
2. J. Sig Paulson, "A Life Treatment." This section first appeared as an article in the August 1970 *Daily Word* published by Unity.

# INDEX